The second book of Kings, from chapter VIII and the books of Chronicles, Ezra and Nehemiah Volume 12

Maclaren, Alexander, 1826-1910

Nabu Public Domain Reprints:

You are holding a reproduction of an original work published before 1923 that is in the public domain in the United States of America, and possibly other countries. You may freely copy and distribute this work as no entity (individual or corporate) has a copyright on the body of the work. This book may contain prior copyright references, and library stamps (as most of these works were scanned from library copies). These have been scanned and retained as part of the historical artifact.

This book may have occasional imperfections such as missing or blurred pages, poor pictures, errant marks, etc. that were either part of the original artifact, or were introduced by the scanning process. We believe this work is culturally important, and despite the imperfections, have elected to bring it back into print as part of our continuing commitment to the preservation of printed works worldwide. We appreciate your understanding of the imperfections in the preservation process, and hope you enjoy this valuable book.

EXPOSITIONS OF HOLY SCRIPTURE

Expositions of Holy Scripture

A Commentary on the Entire Bible,
to be Completed in Thirty Volumes

ALEXANDER MACLAREN, D.D., LIT.D.

To be published in series of six large octavo volumes, magnificently bound in red buckram cloth, printed in special type of unique and beautiful face, and on specially imported English featherweight paper.

Dr. ALEXANDER MACLAREN'S incomparable position as the prince of expositors has for more than a generation been recognized throughout the English-speaking world. He holds an unchallenged position, and it it is believed that this series, embodying as it does the treasure store of DR. MACLAREN'S life-work, will be found of priceless value by preachers, teachers, and readers of the bible generally.

What Ministers say of Dr. Maclaren

THEODORE L. CUYLER, D.D.: "Alexander Maclaren is the King of Preachers."

W. ROBERTSON NICOLL, D.D., LL.D.: "He is the Prince of Expositors."

DONALD SAGE MACKAY, D.D.: "The present idea of gathering the cream of Dr. Maclaren's expository genius from Genesis to Revelation is a fitting climax to his splendid contributions to scripture exposition."

MARCUS DODS, D.D.: "Dr. Maclaren is one of those exceptional men who can afford to print all they utter. Spiritual wisdom, sound and lucid exposition, apt and picturesque illustrations."

What the Press says of Dr. Maclaren

"These volumes are a treasury of thought for preachers, Sunday-school teachers and all who study the scriptures for a practical purpose."—*The Outlook*, New York.

"Unless we are very much mistaken 'Expositions of Holy Scripture' will have a permanent place in the library, of every thoughtful minister and layman."—*The British Weekly*, London, England.

"Taken all in all 'Expositions of Holy Scripture' equal if not exceed in value for ministers any similar body of production —ancient or modern."—*The Observer*, New York.

SOLD ONLY IN SERIES OF SIX VOLUMES
$7.50 net

FIRST SERIES, SIX VOLUMES

GENESIS   ISAIAH   JEREMIAH   ST. MATTHEW (3 vols.)

SECOND SERIES, SIX VOLUMES

EXODUS, LEVITICUS AND NUMBERS   DEUTERONOMY, JOSHUA
JUDGES AND RUTH   1ST AND 2D SAMUEL   1ST AND 2D KINGS
ST. MARK (2 vols.)   ACTS (1st vol.)

THIRD SERIES, SIX VOLUMES:

ACTS, VOL. 2   ST. JOHN, VOLS. 1, 2, 3
SECOND BOOK OF KINGS, from Chap. 7.   CHRONICLES, EZRA
NEHEMIAH   ESTHER   JOB   PROVERBS   ECCLESIASTES

THE
SECOND BOOK OF KINGS

FROM CHAP. VIII., AND THE BOOKS OF

CHRONICLES, EZRA, AND NEHEMIAH

BY

ALEXANDER MACLAREN

D.D., Litt.D.

NEW YORK

A. C. ARMSTRONG AND SON

3 & 5 WEST EIGHTEENTH STREET

LONDON: HODDER AND STOUGHTON

MCMVIII

CONTENTS

THE SECOND BOOK OF KINGS

	PAGE
THE STORY OF HAZAEL (2 Kings viii. 9-15)	1
IMPURE ZEAL (2 Kings x. 18-31)	6
JEHOIADA AND JOASH (2 Kings xi. 1-16)	13
METHODICAL LIBERALITY (2 Kings xii. 4-15)	19
THE SPIRIT OF POWER (2 Kings xiii. 16)	24
A KINGDOM'S EPITAPH (2 Kings xvii. 6-18)	33
DIVIDED WORSHIP (2 Kings xvii. 33)	40
HEZEKIAH, A PATTERN OF DEVOUT LIFE (2 Kings xviii. 5, 6)	47
'HE UTTERED HIS VOICE, THE EARTH MELTED' (2 Kings xix. 20-22; 28-37)	54
THE REDISCOVERED LAW AND ITS EFFECTS (2 Kings xxii. 8-20)	60
THE END (2 Kings xxv. 1-12)	66

CONTENTS

THE FIRST BOOK OF CHRONICLES

	PAGE
THE KING'S POTTERS (1 Chron. iv. 23)	74
DAVID'S CHORISTERS (1 Chron. vi. 32, R.V. margin)	79
DRILL AND ENTHUSIASM (1 Chron. xii. 33)	87
DAVID'S PROHIBITED DESIRE AND PERMITTED SERVICE (1 Chron. xxii. 6-16)	96
DAVID'S CHARGE TO SOLOMON (1 Chron. xxviii. 1-10)	101
THE WAVES OF TIME (1 Chron. xxix. 30)	106

THE SECOND BOOK OF CHRONICLES

THE DUTY OF EVERY DAY (2 Chron. viii. 12-13, R.V.)	114
CONTRASTED SERVICES (2 Chron. xii. 8)	121
THE SECRET OF VICTORY (2 Chron. xiii. 18)	129
ASA'S REFORMATION, AND CONSEQUENT PEACE AND VICTORY (2 Chron. xiv. 2-8)	136
ASA'S PRAYER (2 Chron. xiv. 11)	139
THE SEARCH THAT ALWAYS FINDS (2 Chron. xv. 15)	147
JEHOSHAPHAT'S REFORM (2 Chron. xvii. 1-10)	155
AMASIAH (2 Chron. xvii. 16)	161
'A MIRROR FOR MAGISTRATES' (2 Chron. xix. 1-11)	165

CONTENTS

	PAGE
A Strange Battle (2 Chron. xx. 12)	170
Holding Fast and Held Fast (2 Chron. xx. 20)	176
Joash (2 Chron. xxiv. 2, 17)	184
Glad Givers and Faithful Workers (2 Chron. xxiv. 4-14)	191
Prudence and Faith (2 Chron. xxv. 9)	199
Jotham (2 Chron. xxvii. 6)	207
Costly and Fatal Help (2 Chron. xxviii. 23)	215
A Godly Reformation (2 Chron. xxix. 1-11)	225
Sacrifice Renewed (2 Chron. xxix. 18-31)	232
A Loving Call to Reunion (2 Chron. xxx. 1-13)	238
A Strange Reward for Faithfulness (2 Chron. xxxii. 1)	243
Manasseh's Sin and Repentance (2 Chron. xxxiii. 9-16)	251
Josiah (2 Chron. xxxiv. 1-13)	257
Josiah and the Newly Found Law (2 Chron. xxxiv. 14-28)	262
The Fall of Judah (2 Chron. xxxvi. 11-21)	269

EZRA

The Eve of the Restoration (Ezra i. 1-11)	275
Altar and Temple (Ezra iii. 1-13)	282
Building in Troublous Times (Ezra iv. 1-5)	291

CONTENTS

	PAGE
THE NEW TEMPLE AND ITS WORSHIP (Ezra vi. 14-22)	294
GOD THE JOY-BRINGER (Ezra vi. 22)	301
HEROIC FAITH (Ezra viii. 22, 23, 31, 32)	309
THE CHARGE OF THE PILGRIM PRIESTS (Ezra viii. 29)	317

THE BOOK OF NEHEMIAH

A REFORMER'S SCHOOLING (Neh. i. 1-11)	326
THE CHURCH AND SOCIAL EVILS (Neh. i. 4)	334
'OVER AGAINST HIS HOUSE' (Neh. iii. 28)	343
DISCOURAGEMENTS AND COURAGE (Neh. iv. 9-21)	354
AN ANCIENT NONCONFORMIST (Neh. v. 15)	361
READING THE LAW WITH TEARS AND JOY (Neh. viii. 1-12)	371
THE JOY OF THE LORD (Neh. viii. 10)	379
SABBATH OBSERVANCE (Neh. xiii. 15-22)	391

THE SECOND BOOK OF KINGS

THE STORY OF HAZAEL

'So Hazael went to meet him, and took a present with him, even of every good thing of Damascus, forty camels' burden, and came and stood before him, and said, Thy son Ben-hadad king of Syria hath sent me to thee, saying, Shall I recover of this disease? 10. And Elisha said unto him, Go, say unto him, Thou mayest certainly recover: howbeit the Lord hath shewed me that he shall surely die. 11. And he settled his countenance stedfastly, until he was ashamed: and the man of God wept. 12. And Hazael said, Why weepeth my lord? And he answered, Because I know the evil that thou wilt do unto the children of Israel: their strong holds wilt thou set on fire, and their young men wilt thou slay with the sword, and wilt dash their children, and rip up their women with child. 13. And Hazael said, But what, is thy servant a dog, that he should do this great thing? And Elisha answered, The Lord hath shewed me that thou shalt be king over Syria. 14. So he departed from Elisha, and came to his master; who said to him, What said Elisha to thee? and he answered, He told me that thou shouldest surely recover. 15. And it came to pass on the morrow, that he took a thick cloth, and dipped it in water, and spread it on his face, so that he died: and Hazael reigned in his stead.'—2 KINGS viii. 9-15.

THIS is a strange, wild story. That Damascene monarchy burst into sudden power, warlike and commercial—for the two things went together in those days. As is usually the case, Hazael the successful soldier becomes ambitious. His sword seems to be the real sceptre, and he will have the dominion. Many years before this Elijah had anointed him to be king over Syria. That had wrought upon him and stirred ambition in him. Elijah's other appointments, coeval with his own, had already taken effect, Jehu was king of Israel, Elisha was prophet, and he only had not attained the dignity to which he had been designated.

He comes now with his message from the king of Damascus to Elisha. No doubt he had been often contrasting his own vigour with the decrepit, nominal king, and many a time had thought of the anointing, and had nursed ambitious hopes, which gradually turned to dark resolves.

He hoped, no doubt, that Ben-hadad was mortally sick, and it must have been a cruel, crushing disappointment when he heard that there was nothing deadly in the illness. Another hope was gone from him. The throne seemed further off than ever. I suppose that, at that instant, there sprang in his heart the resolve that he would kill Ben-hadad. The recoil of disappointment spurred Hazael to the resolution which he then and there took. It had been gathering form, no doubt, through some years, but now it became definite and settled. While his face glowed with the new determination, and his lips clenched themselves in the firmness of his purpose, the even voice of the prophet went on, 'howbeit he shall certainly die,' and the eye of the man of God searched him till he turned away ashamed because aware that his inmost heart was read.

Then there followed the prophet's weeping, and the solemn announcement of what Hazael would do when he had climbed to the throne. He shrank in real horror from the thought of such enormity of sin. 'Is thy servant a dog that he should do such a thing?' Elisha sternly answers: 'The Lord hath shewed me that thou shalt be king over Syria.' The certainty is that in his character occasion will develop evil. The certainty is that a course begun by such crime will be of a piece, and consistent with itself.

This conversation with Elisha seems to have accelerated Hazael's purpose, as if the prediction were to his mind a justification of his means of fulfilling it.

How like Macbeth he is!—the successful soldier,

stirred by supernatural monitions of a greatness which he should achieve, and at last a murderer.

This narrative opens to us some of the solemn, dark places of human life, of men's hearts, of God's ways. Let us look at some of the lessons which lie here.

I. Man's responsibility for the sin which God foresees.

It seems as if the prophet's words had much to do in exciting the ambitious desires which led to the crime. Hazael's purpose of executing the deed is clearly known to the prophet. His ascending the throne is part of the divine purpose. He could find excuses for his guilt, and fling the responsibility for firing his ambition on the divine messenger. It may be asked—What sort of God is this who works on the mind of a man by exciting promises, and having done so, and having it fixed in His purposes that the man is to do the crime, yet treats it when done as guilt?

But now, whatever you may say, or whatever excuses Hazael might have found for himself, here is just in its most naked form that which is true about all sin. God foresees it all. God puts men into circumstances where they will fall, God presents to them things which they will make temptations. God takes the consequences of their wrongdoing and works them into His great scheme. That is undeniable on one side, and on the other it is as undeniable that God's foreseeing leaves men free. God's putting men into circumstances where they fall is not His tempting them. God's non-prevention of sin is not permission to sin. God's overruling the consequences of sin is not His condoning of sin as part of the scheme of His providence.

Man is free. Man is responsible. God hates sin. God foresees and permits sin.

It is all a terrible mystery, but the facts are as undeniable as the mystery of their co-existence is inscrutable.

II. The slumbering possibilities of sin.

Hazael indignantly protests against the thought that he should do such a thing. There is conscience left in him yet. His example suggests how little any of us know what it is in us to be or to do. We are all of us a mystery to ourselves. Slumbering powers lie in us. We are like quiescent volcanoes.

So much in us lies dormant, needing occasion for its development, like seeds that may sleep for centuries. That is true in regard to both the good and the bad in us. Life reveals us to ourselves. We learn to know ourselves by our actions, better than by mental self-inspection.

All sin is one in essence, and may pass into diverse forms according to circumstances. Of course characters differ, but the root of sin is in us all. We are largely good because not tempted, as a house may well stand firm when there are no floods. By the nature of the case, thorough self-knowledge is impossible.

Sin has the power of blinding us to its presence. It comes in a cloud as the old gods were fabled to do. The lungs get accustomed to a vitiated atmosphere, and scarcely are conscious of oppression till they cease to play.

All this should teach us—

Lessons of wary walking and humility. We are good because we have not been tried.

Lessons of charity and brotherly kindness. Every thief in the hulks, every prostitute on the streets, is our brother and sister, and they prove their fraternity by their sin. 'Whatever man has done man may do.' *Nihil humanum alienum a me puto.* 'Let him that is without sin cast the first stone.'

III. The fatal necessity by which sin repeats itself in aggravated forms.

See how Hazael is drifted into his worst crimes. His first one leads on by fell necessity to others. A man who has done no sin is conceivable, but a man who has done only one is impossible. Did you ever see a dam bursting or breaking down? Through a little crack comes one drop: will it stop there—the gap or the trickle? No! The drop has widened the crack, it has softened the earth around, it has cleared away some impediments. So another and another follow ever more rapidly, until the water pours out in a flood and the retaining embankment is swept away.

No sin 'is dead, being alone.' The demon brings seven other devils worse than himself. The reason for that aggravation is plain.

There is, first, habit.

There is, second, growing inclination.

There is, third, weakened restraint.

There is, fourth, a craving for excitement to still conscience.

There is, fifth, the necessity of the man's position.

There is, sixth, the strange love of consistency which tones all life down or up to one tint, as near as may be. There comes at last despair.

But not merely does every sin tend to repeat itself and to draw others after it. It tends to repeat itself in aggravated forms. There is growth, the law of increase as well as of perpetuity. The seed produces 'some sixty and some an hundredfold.'

And so the slaughtered soldiers and desolated homesteads of Israel were the sequel of the cloth on Benhadad's face. The secret of much enormous crime is the kind of relief from conscience which is found in committing a yet greater sin. The Furies drive with whips of scorpions, and the poor wretch goes plunging and kicking deeper and deeper in the mire, further and further from the path. So you can never say: 'I will only do this one wrong thing.'

We see here how powerless against sin are all restraints. The prophecy did not prevent Hazael from his sins. The clear sense that they were sins did not prevent him. The horror-struck shudder of conscience did not prevent him. It was soon gagged.

Hear, then, the conclusion of the whole matter. Christ reveals us to ourselves. Christ breaks the chain of sin, makes a new beginning, cuts off the entail, reverses the irreversible, erases the indelible, cancels the irrevocable, forgives all the faultful past, and by the power of His love in the soul, works a mightier miracle than changing the Ethiopian's skin; teaches them that are accustomed to evil to do well, and though sins be as scarlet, makes them white as snow. He gives us a cleansed past and a bright future, and out of all our sins and wasted years makes pardoned sinners and glorified, perfected saints.

IMPURE ZEAL

'And Jehu gathered all the people together, and said unto them, Ahab served Baal a little; but Jehu shall serve him much. 19. Now therefore call unto me all the prophets of Baal, all his servants, and all his priests; let none be wanting: for I have a great sacrifice to do to Baal; whosoever shall be wanting, he shall not live. But Jehu did it in subtilty, to the intent that he might destroy the worshippers of Baal. 20. And Jehu said, Proclaim a solemn assembly for Baal. And they proclaimed it. 21. And Jehu sent through all Israel: and all the worshippers of Baal came, so that there was not a man left that came not. And they came into the house of Baal; and the house of Baal was full from one end to another. 22. And he said unto him that was over the vestry, Bring forth vestments for all the worshippers of Baal. And he brought them forth vestments. 23. And Jehu went, and Jehonadab the son of Rechab, into the house of Baal, and said unto the worshippers of Baal, Search, and look that there be here with you none of the servants of the Lord, but the worshippers of Baal only. 24. And when they went in to offer sacrifices and burnt offerings, Jehu appointed fourscore men without, and said, If any of the men whom I have brought into your hands escape, he that letteth him go, his life shall be for the life of him. 25. And it came to pass, as soon as he had made an end of offering the burnt offering, that Jehu said to the guard and to the captains, Go in, and slay them; let none come forth. And they smote them with the edge of the sword; and the guard and the captains cast them out, and went to the city of the house of Baal. 26. And they brought forth the images out of the house of Baal, and burned them. 27. And they brake down the image of Baal, and brake down the house of Baal, and made it a draught house unto this day. 28. Thus Jehu destroyed Baal out of Israel. 29. Howbeit from the sins of Jeroboam the son of Nebat, who made Israel to sin, Jehu departed not from after them, to wit, the golden calves that were in Beth-el, and that were in Dan. 30. And the Lord said unto Jehu, Because thou hast done well in executing that which is right in Mine eyes, and hast done unto the house of Ahab according to all that was in Mine heart, thy children of the fourth generation shall sit on the throne of Israel. 31. But Jehu took no heed to walk in the law of the Lord God of Israel with all his heart: for he departed not from the sins of Jeroboam, which made Israel to sin.'—2 KINGS x. 18-31.

THE details of this story of bloodshed need little elucidation. Jehu had 'driven furiously' to some purpose. Secrecy and swiftness joined to unhesitating severity had crushed the dynasty of Ahab, which fell unlamented and unsupported, as if lightning-struck. The nobler elements had gathered to Jehu, as represented by the Rechabite, Jehonadab, evidently a Jehovah worshipper, and closely associated with the fierce soldier in this chapter. Jehu first secured his position, and then smote the Baal worship as heavily and conclusively as he had done the royal family. He struck once, and struck no more; for the single blow pulverised.

The audacious pretext of an intention to outdo the fallen dynasty in Baal worship must have sounded strange to those who knew how his massacre of Ahab's house had been represented by him as fulfilling Jehovah's purpose, but it was not too gross to be believed. So we can fancy the joyous revival of hope with which from every corner of the land the Baal priests, prophets, and worshippers, recovered from their fright, came flocking to the great temple in Samaria, till it was like a cup filled with wine from brim to brim. The worship cannot have numbered many adherents if one temple could hold the bulk of them. Probably it had never been more than a court fashion, and, now that Jezebel was dead, had lost ground. A token of royal favour was given to each of the crowd, in the gift of a vestment from the royal wardrobe. Then Jehu himself, accompanied by the ascetic Jehonadab, entered the court of the temple, a strangely assorted pair, and a couple of very 'distinguished' converts. The Baal priests would thrill with gratified pride when these two came to worship. The usual precautions against the intrusion of non-worshippers were taken at Jehu's command, but with a sinister meaning, undreamed of by the eager searchers. That was a sifting for destruction, not for preservation. So they all passed into the inner court to offer sacrifice.

The story gives a double picture in verse 24. Within are the jubilant worshippers; without, the grim company of their executioners, waiting the signal to draw their swords and burst in on the unarmed mob. Jehu carried his deception so far that he himself offered the burnt offering, with Jehonadab standing by, and then withdrew, followed, no doubt, by grateful acclamations. A step or two brought him to the 'eighty men without.' Two stern words, 'Go, smite them,' are enough. They storm in, and 'the songs of the temple' are turned to 'howlings in that day.' The defenceless, surprised crowd, huddled together in the dimly lighted shrine, were massacred to a man. The innermost sanctuary was then wrecked, corpses and statues thrown pell-mell into the outer courts or beyond the precincts, fires lit to burn the abominations, and busy hands, always more ready for pillage and destruction than for good work, pulled down the temple, the ruins of which were turned to base uses. The writer, picturing the wild scene, sums up with a touch of exultation: 'Thus Jehu destroyed Baal out of Israel'—where note the emphatic prominence of the three names of the king, the god, and the nation. That is the vindication of the terrible deed.

Now the main interest of this passage lies in its disclosure of the strangely mingled character of Jehu, and in the fact that his bloody severity was approved by God, and rewarded by the continuance of his dynasty for a longer time than any other on the throne of Israel.

Jehu was influenced by 'zeal for the Lord,' however much smoke mingled with the flame. He acted under the conviction that he was God's instrument, and at each new deed of blood asserted his fulfilment of prophecy. His profession to Jehonadab (ver. 16) was not hypocrisy nor ostentation. The Rechabite sheikh was evidently a man of mark, and apparently one of the leaders of those who had not 'bowed the knee to Baal'; and Jehu's disclosure of his animating motive was meant to secure the alliance of that party through one of its chiefs. No doubt many elements of selfishness and many stains mingled with Jehu's zeal. It was much on the same level as the fanaticism of the immediate successors of Mohammed; but, low as it was, look at its power. Jehu swept like a whirlwind, or like leaping fire among stubble, from Ramoth to Jezreel, from Jezreel to Samaria, and nothing stood before his fierce onset. Promptitude, decision, secrecy, —the qualities which carry enterprises to success—

marked his character; partly, no doubt, from natural temperament, for God chooses right instruments, but from temperament heightened and invigorated by the conviction of being the instrument whom God had chosen. We may learn how even a very imperfect form of this conviction gives irresistible force to a man, annihilates fear, draws the teeth of danger, and gathers up all one's faculties to a point which can pierce any opposition. We may all recognise that God has sent us on His errands; and if we cherish that conviction, we shall put away from us slothfulness and fear, and out of weakness shall be made strong.

But Jehu sets forth the possible imperfections of 'zeal for the Lord.' We may defer for a moment the consideration of the morality of his slaughter of the royal house and the Baal worshippers, and point to the taint of selfishness and to the leaven of deceit in his enthusiasm. We have not to analyse it. That is God's work. But clearly the object which he had in view was not merely fulfilment of prophecy, but securing the throne; and there was more passion, as well as selfish policy, in his massacres, than befitted a minister of the divine justice, who should let no anger disturb the solemnity of his terrible task. Such dangers ever attend the path of the great men who feel themselves to be sent by God. In our humbler lives they dog our steps, and religious fervour needs ever to keep careful watch on itself, lest it should degenerate unconsciously into self-will, and should allow the muddy stream of earth-born passion to darken its crystal waters.

Many a great name in the annals of the Church has fallen before that temptation. We all need to remember that 'the wrath of man worketh not the righteousness of God,' and to take heed lest we should be guided by our own stormy impatience of contradiction, and by a determination to have our own way, while we think ourselves the humble instruments of a divine purpose. There was a 'Zelotes' in the Apostolate; but the coarse, sanguinary 'zeal' of his party must have needed much purifying before it learned what manner of spirit the zeal of a true disciple was of.

Another point of interest is the divine emphatic approval of Jehu's bloody acts (ver. 30). The massacre of the Baal worshippers is not included in the acts which God declares to have been 'according to all that was in Mine heart,' and it may be argued that it was not part of Jehu's commission. Certainly the accompanying deceit was not 'right in God's eyes,' but the slaughter in Baal's temple was the natural sequel of the civil revolution, and is most probably included in the deeds approved.

Perhaps Elisha brought Jehu the message in verse 30. If so, what a contrast between the two instruments of God's purposes! At all events, Jehovah's approval was distinctly given. What then? There need be no hesitation in recognising the progressive character of Scripture morality, as well as the growth of the revelation of the divine character, of which the morality of each epoch is the reflection. The full revelation of the God of love had to be preceded by the clear revelation of the God of righteousness; and whilst the Old Testament does make known the love of God in many a gracious act and word, it especially teaches His righteous condemnation of sin, without which His love were mere facile indulgence and impunity. The slaughter of that wicked house of Ahab and of the Baal priests was the act of divine justice, and the question is simply whether that justice was entitled to slay them. To that question believers in a divine providence can give but one answer. The destruction of Baal worship and the annihilation of its stronghold in Ahab's family were sufficient reasons, as even we can see, for such a deed. To bring in Jehu into the problem is unnecessary. He was the sword, but God's was the hand that struck. It is not for men to arraign the Lord of life and death for His methods and times of sending death to evil-doers. Granted that the 'long-suffering' which is 'not willing that any should perish' speaks more powerfully to our hearts than the justice which smites with death, the later and more blessed revelation is possible and precious only on the foundation of the former. Nor will a loose-braced generation like ours, which affects to be horrified at the thought of the 'wrath of God,' and recoils from the contemplation of His judgments, ever reach the innermost secrets of the tenderness of His love.

From the merely human point of view, we may say that revolutions are not made with rose-water, and that, at all crises in a nation's history, when some ancient evil is to be thrown off, and some powerful system is to be crushed, there will be violence, at which easy-going people, who have never passed through like times, will hold up their hands in horror and with cheap censure. No doubt we have a higher law than Jehu knew, and Christ has put His own gentle commandment of love in the place of what was 'said to them of old time.' But let us, while we obey it for ourselves, and abjure violence and blood, judge the men of old 'according to that which they had, and not according to that which they had not.' Jehu's bloody deeds are not held up for admiration. His obedience is what is praised and rewarded. Well for us if we obey our better law as faithfully!

The last point in the story is the imperfection of the obedience of Jehu. He contented himself with rooting out Baal, but left the calves. That shows the impurity of his 'zeal,' which flamed only against what it was for his advantage to destroy, and left the more popular and older idolatry undisturbed. Obedience has to be 'all in all, or not at all.' We may not 'compound for sins we are inclined to, by' zeal against those 'we have no mind to.' Our consciences are apt to have insensitive spots in them, like witch-marks. We often think it enough to remove the grosser evils, and leave the less, but white ants will eat up a carcass faster than a lion. Putting away Baal is of little use if we keep the calves at Dan and Beth-el. Nothing but walking in the law of the Lord 'with all the heart' will secure our walking safely. 'Unite my heart to fear Thy name' needs to be our daily prayer. 'One foot on sea and one on shore' is not the attitude in which steadfastness or progress is possible.

JEHOIADA AND JOASH

'And when Athaliah the mother of Ahaziah saw that her son was dead, she arose and destroyed all the seed royal. 2. But Jehosheba, the daughter of king Joram, sister of Ahaziah, took Joash the son of Ahaziah, and stole him from among the king's sons which were slain; and they hid him, even him and his nurse, in the bedchamber from Athaliah, so that he was not slain. 3. And he was with her hid in the house of the Lord six years. And Athaliah did reign over the land. 4. And the seventh year Jehoiada sent and fetched the rulers over hundreds, with the captains and the guard, and brought them to him into the house of the Lord, and made a covenant with them, and took an oath of them in the house of the Lord, and shewed them the king's son. 5. And he commanded them, saying, This is the thing that ye shall do; A third part of you that enter in on the sabbath shall even be keepers of the watch of the king's house; 6. And a third part shall be at the gate of Sur; and a third part at the gate behind the guard: so shall ye keep the watch of the house, that it be not broken down. 7. And two parts of all you that go forth on the sabbath, even they shall keep the watch of the house of the Lord about the king. 8. And ye shall compass the king round about, every man with his weapons in his hand: and he that cometh within the ranges, let him be slain: and be ye with the king as he goeth out and as he cometh in. 9. And the captains over the hundreds did according to all things that Jehoiada the priest commanded: and they took every man his men that were to come in on the sabbath, with them that should go out on the sabbath, and came to Jehoiada the priest. 10. And to the captains over hundreds did the priest give king David's spears and shields, that were in the temple of the Lord. 11. And the guard stood, every man with his weapons in his hand, round about the king, from the right corner of the temple to the left corner of the temple, along by the altar and the temple. 12. And he brought forth the king's son, and put the crown upon him, and gave him the testimony; and they made him king, and anointed him; and they clapped their hands, and said, God save the king. 13. And when Athaliah heard the noise of the guard and of the people, she came to the people into the temple of the Lord. 14. And when she looked, behold, the king stood by a pillar, as the manner was, and the princes and the trumpeters by the king, and all the people of the land rejoiced, and blew with trumpets: and Athaliah rent her clothes, and cried, Treason, Treason. 15. But Jehoiada the priest commanded the captains of the hundreds, the officers of the host, and said unto them, Have her forth without the ranges: and him that followeth her kill with the sword. For the priest had said, Let her not be slain in the house of the Lord. 16. And they laid hands on her; and she went by the way by the which the horses came into the king's house: and there was she slain.'—2 KINGS xi. 1-16.

THE king of Judah has been killed, his alliance with the king of Israel having involved him in the latter's fate. Jehu had also murdered 'the brethren of Ahaziah,' forty-two in number. Next, Athaliah, the mother of Ahaziah and a daughter of Ahab, killed all the males of the royal family, and planted herself on the throne. She had Jezebel's force of character, unscrupulousness and disregard of human life. She was a tigress of a woman, and, no doubt, her six years' usurpation was stained with blood and with the nameless abominations of Baal worship. Never had the kingdom of Judah been at a lower ebb. One infant was all that was left of David's descendants. The whole promises of God seemed to depend for fulfilment on one little, feeble life. The tree had been cut down, and there was but this one sucker pushing forth a tiny shoot from 'the root of Jesse.'

We have in the passage, first, the six years of hiding in the temple. It is a pathetic picture, that of the infant rescued by his brave aunt from the blood-bath, and stowed away in the storeroom where the mats and cushions which served for beds were kept when not in use, watched over by two loving and courageous women, and taught infantile lessons by the husband of his aunt, Jehoiada the high priest. Many must have been aware of his existence, and there must have been loyal guarding of the secret, or Athaliah's sword would have been reddened with the baby's blood. Like the child Samuel, he had the Temple for his home, and his first impressions would be of daily sacrifices and white-robed priests. It was a better school for him than if he had been in the palace close by. The opening flower would have been soon besmirched there, but in the holy calm of the Temple courts it unfolded unstained. A Christian home should breathe the same atmosphere as surrounded Joash, and it, too, should be a temple, where holy peace rules, and where the first impressions printed on plastic little minds are of God and His service.

We have next the disclosure and coronation of the boy king. The narrative here has to be supplemented from that in 2 Chron. xxiii., which does not contradict that in this passage, as is often said, but completes it. It informs us that before the final scene in the Temple, Jehoiada had in Jerusalem assembled a large force of Levites and of the 'heads of the fathers' houses' from all the kingdom. That statement implies that the revolution was mainly religious in its motive, and was national in its extent. Obviously Jehoiada would have been courting destruction for Joash and himself, unless he had made sure of a strong backing before he hoisted the standard of the house of David. There must, therefore, have been long preparation and much stir; and all the while the foreign woman was sitting in the palace, close by the Temple, and not a whisper reached her. Evidently she had no party in Judah, and held her own only by her indomitable will and by the help of foreign troops. Anybody who remembers how the Austrians in Italy were shunned, will understand how Athaliah heard nothing of the plot that was rapidly developing a stone's throw from her isolated throne. Strange delusion, to covet such a seat, yet no stranger than many another mistaking of serpents for fish, into which we fall!

Jehoiada's caution was as great as his daring. He does not appear to have given the Levites and elders any inkling of his purpose till he had them safe in the Temple, and then he opened his mind, swore them to stand by him, and 'showed them the king's son.' What a scene that would be—the seven-year-old child there among all these strange men, the joyful surprise flashing in their eyes, the exultation of the faithful women that had watched him so lovingly, the stern facing of the dangers ahead. Most of the assembly must have thought that none of David's house remained, and that thought would have had much to do with their submitting to Athaliah's usurpation. Now that they saw the true heir, they could not hesitate to risk their lives to set him on his throne. Show a man his true king, and many a tyranny submitted to before becomes at once intolerable. The boy Joash makes Athaliah look very ugly.

Jehoiada's plans are somewhat difficult to understand, owing to our ignorance of the details as to the usual arrangements of the guards of the palace, but the general drift of them is plain enough. The main thing was to secure the person of the king, and, for that purpose, the two companies of priests who were relieved on the Sabbath were for once kept on duty, and their numbers augmented by the company that would, in the ordinary course, have relieved them. This augmented force was so disposed as, first, to secure the Temple from attack; and, second, to 'compass the king'—in his chamber, that is. We learn from 2 Chronicles that it consisted of priests and Levites, and some would see in that statement a tampering with the account in this passage, in the interests of a later conception of the sanctity of the Temple and of the priestly order. Our narrative is said to make the foreign mercenaries of the palace guard the persons referred to; but surely that cannot be maintained in the face of the plain statement of verse 7, that they kept the watch of the Temple, for that was the office of the priests. Besides, how should foreign soldiers have needed to be armed from the Temple armoury? And is it probable on the face of it that the palace guard, who were Athaliah's men, and therefore antagonistic to Joash, and Baal worshippers, should have been gained over to his side, or should have been the guards of the house of Jehovah? If, however, we understand that these guards were Levites, all is plain, and the arming of them with 'the spears and shields that had been king David's' becomes intelligible, and would rouse them to enthusiasm and daring.

Not till all these dispositions for the boy king's safety, and for preventing an assault on the Temple, had been carried out, did the prudent Jehoiada venture to bring Joash out from his place of concealment. Note that in verse 12 he is not called 'the king,' as in the previous verses, but, as in verse 4, 'the king's son.' He was king by right, but not technically, till he had been presented to, and accepted by, the representatives of the people, had had 'the testimony' placed in his hands, and been anointed by the high-priest. So 'they *made* him king.' The three parts of the ceremony were all significant. The delivering of 'the testimony' (the Book of the Law—Deut. xvii. 18, 19) taught him that he was no despot to rule by his own pleasure and for his own glory, but the viceroy of the true King of Judah, and himself subject to law. The people's making him king taught him and them that a true royalty rules over willing subjects, and both guarded the rights of the nation and set limits to the power of the ruler. The priest's anointing witnessed to the divine appointment of the monarch and the divine endowment with fitness for his office. Would that these truths were more recognised and felt by all rulers! What a different thing the page of history would be!

The vigilance of the tigress had been eluded, and Athaliah had a rude awakening. But she had her mother's courage, and as soon as she heard in the palace the shouts, she dashed to the Temple, alone as she was, and fronted the crowd. The sight might have made the boldest quail. Who was that child standing in the royal place? Where had he come from? How had he been hidden all these years? What was all this frenzy of rejoicing, this blare of trumpets, these ranks of grim men with weapons in their hands? The stunning truth fell on her; but, though she felt that all was lost, not a whit did she blench, but fronted them all as proudly as ever. One cannot but admire the dauntless woman, 'magnificent in sin.' But her cry of 'Treason! treason!' brought none to her side. As she stood solitary there, she must have felt that her day was over, and that nothing remained but to die like a queen. Proudly as ever, she passed down the ranks and not a face looked pity on her, nor a voice blessed her. She was reaping what she had sown, and she who had killed without compunction the innocents who stood between her and her ambitions, was pitilessly slain, and all the land rejoiced at her death.

So ended the all but bloodless revolution which crushed Baal worship in Judah. It had been begun by Elijah and Elisha, but it was completed by a high priest. It was religious even more than political. It was a national movement, though Jehoiada's courage and wisdom engineered it to its triumph. It teaches us how God watches over His purposes and their instruments when they seem nearest to failure, for one poor infant was all that was left of the seed of David; and how, therefore, we are never to despair, even in the darkest hour, of the fulfilment of His promises. It teaches us how much one brave, good man and woman can do to change the whole face of things, and how often there needs but one man to direct and voice the thoughts and acts of the silent multitude, and to light a fire that consumes evil.

METHODICAL LIBERALITY

'And Jehoash said to the priests, All the money of the dedicated things that is brought into the house of the Lord, even the money of every one that passeth the account, the money that every man is set at, and all the money that cometh into any man's heart to bring into the house of the Lord, 5. Let the priests take it to them, every man of his acquaintance; and let them repair the breaches of the house, wheresoever any breach shall be found. 6. But it was so, that in the three and twentieth year of king Jehoash the priests had not repaired the breaches of the house. 7. Then king Jehoash called for Jehoiada the priest, and the other priests, and said unto them, Why repair ye not the breaches of the house? Now therefore receive no more money of your acquaintance, but deliver it for the breaches of the house. 8. And the priests consented to receive no more money of the people, neither to repair the breaches of the house. 9. But Jehoiada the priest took a chest, and bored a hole in the lid of it, and set it beside the altar, on the right side as one cometh into the house of the Lord: and the priests that kept the door put therein all the money that was brought into the house of the Lord. 10. And it was so, when they saw that there was much money in the chest, that the king's scribe and the high priest came up, and they put up in bags, and told the money that was found in the house of the Lord. 11. And they gave the money, being told, into the hands of them that did the work, that had the oversight of the house of the Lord: and they laid it out to the carpenters and builders that wrought upon the house of the Lord, 12. And to masons, and hewers of stone, and to buy timber and hewed stone to repair the breaches of the house of the Lord, and for all that was laid out for the house to repair it. 13. Howbeit there were not made for the house of the Lord bowls of silver, snuffers, basons, trumpets, any vessels of gold, or vessels of silver, of the money that was brought into the house of the Lord: 14. But they gave that to the workmen, and repaired therewith the house of the Lord. 15. Moreover they reckoned not with the men, into whose hand they delivered the money to be bestowed on workmen: for they dealt faithfully.'— 2 KINGS xii. 4-15.

'THE sons of Athaliah, that wicked woman, had broken up the house of God,' says Chronicles. The dilapidation had not been complete, but had been extensive, as may be gathered from the large expenditure recorded in this passage for repairs, and the enumeration of the artisans employed. No doubt Joash was guided by Jehoiada in setting about the restoration, but the fact that he gives the orders, while the high priest is not mentioned, throws light on the relative position of the two authorities, and on the king's office as guardian of the Temple and official 'head of the church.' The story comes in refreshingly and strangely among the bloody pages in which it is embedded, and it suggests some lessons as to the virtue of plain common sense and business principles applied to religious affairs. If 'the outward business of the house of God' were always guided with as much practical reasonableness as Joash brought to bear on it, there would be fewer failures or sarcastic critics.

We note, first, the true source of money for religious purposes. There was a fixed amount for which 'each man is rated,' and that made the minimum, but there was also that which 'cometh into any man's heart to bring,' and that was infinitely more precious than the exacted tax. The former was appropriate to the Old Testament, of which the animating principle was law and the voice: 'Thou shalt' or 'Thou shalt not.' The latter alone fits the New Testament, of which the animating principle is love and the voice: 'Though I have all boldness in Christ to enjoin thee ... yet for love's sake I rather beseech.' What disasters and what stifling of the spirit of Christian liberality have marred the Church for many centuries, and in many lands, because the great anachronism has prevailed of binding its growing limbs in Jewish swaddling bands, and degrading Christian giving into an assessment! And how shrunken the stream that is squeezed out by such a process, compared with the abundant gush of the fountain of love opened in a grateful, trusting heart!

Next, we have the negligent, if not dishonest, officials. We do not know how long Joash tried the experiment of letting the priests receive the money and superintend the repairs; but probably the restoration project was begun early in his reign, and if so, he gave the experiment of trusting all to the officials, a fair, patient trial, till the twenty-third year of his reign. Years gone and nothing done, or at least nothing completed! We do not need to accuse them of intentional embezzlement, but certainly they were guilty of carelessly letting the money slip through their fingers, and a good deal of it stick to their hands. It is always the temptation of the clergy to think of their own support as a first charge on the church, nor is it quite unheard of that the ministry should be less enthusiastic in religious objects than the 'laity,' and should work the enthusiasm of the latter for their own advantage. Human nature is the same in Jerusalem in Joash's time, and to-day in Manchester, or New York, or Philadelphia, and all men who live by the gifts of Christian people have need to watch themselves, lest they, like Ezekiel's false shepherds, feed themselves and not the flock, and seek the wool and the fat and not the good of the sheep.

Next we have the application of businesslike methods to religious work. It was clearly time to take the whole matter out of the priests' hands, and Joash is not afraid to assume a high tone with the culprits, and even with Jehoiada as their official head. He was in some sense responsible for his subordinates, and probably, though his own hands were clean, he may have been too lax in looking after the disposal of the funds. Note that while Joash rebuked the priests, and determined the new arrangements, it was Jehoiada who carried them out and provided the chest for receiving the contributions. The king wills, the high priest executes, the rank and file of the priests, however against the grain, consent. The arrangement for collecting the contributions 'saved the faces' of the priests to some extent, for the gifts were handed to them, and by them put into the chest. But, of course, that was done at once, in the donor's presence. If changes involving loss of position are to work smoothly, it is wise to let the deposed officials down as easily as may be.

Similar common sense is shown in the second step, the arrangement for ascertaining the amounts given. The king's secretary and the high-priest (or a representative) jointly opened the chest, counted and bagged up the money. They checked each other, and prevented suspicion on either side. No man who regards his own reputation will consent to handle public money without some one to stand over him and see what he does with it. One would be wise always to suspect people who appeal for help 'for the Lord's work' and are too 'spiritual' to have such worldly things as committees or auditors of their books. Accurate accounts are as essential to Christian work as spirituality or enthusiasm. The next stage was to hand over the money to the 'contractors,' as we should call them; and there similar precautions were taken against possible peculation on the part of the two officials who had received the money, for it was apparently 'weighed out into the hands' of the overseers, who would thus be able to check what they received by what the secretary and the high-priest had taken from the chest, and would be responsible for the expenditure of the amount which the two officials knew that they had received.

But all this system of checks seems to break down at the very point where it should have worked most searchingly, for 'they reckoned not with the men, into whose hand they delivered the money' to pay the workmen, 'for they dealt faithfully.' That last clause looks like a hit at the priests who had not dealt so, and contrasts the methods of plain business men of no pretensions, with those of men whose very calling should have guaranteed their trustworthiness. The contrast has been repeated in times and places nearer home. But another suggestion may also be made about this singular lapse into what looks like unwise confidence. These overseers had proved their faithfulness and earned the right to be trusted entirely, and the way to get the best out of a man, if he has any reliableness in him, is to trust him utterly, and to show him that you do. 'It is a shame to tell Arnold a lie; he always believes us,' said the Rugby boys about their great head-master. There is a time for using all precautions, and a time for using none. Businesslike methods do not consist in spying at the heels of one's agents, but in picking the right men, and, having proved them, giving them a free hand. And is not that what the great Lord and Employer does with His servants, and is it not part of the reason why Jesus gets more out of us than any one else can do, that He trusts us more?

One more point may be noticed; namely, the order of precedence in which the necessary works were done. Not a coin went to provide the utensils for sacrifice till the Temple was completely repaired. After they had 'set up the house of God in its state,' as Chronicles tells us, they took the balance of the funds to the king and Jehoiada, and spent that on 'vessels for the house.' A clear insight to discern what most needs to be done, and a firm resolve to 'do the duty that lies nearest thee,' and to let everything else, however necessary, wait till it is done, is a great part of Christian prudence, and goes far to make works or lives truly prosperous. 'First things first'!—it is a maxim that carries us far and as right as far.

THE SPIRIT OF POWER

'And Elisha said to the king of Israel, Put thine hand upon the bow. And he put his hand upon it: and Elisha put his hands upon the king's hands.'—2 KINGS xiii. 16.

THIS is part of one of the strangest narratives in the Old Testament. Elisha is on his deathbed, 'sick of the sickness' wherewith he 'should die.' A very different scene, that close sick-chamber, from the open plain beyond Jordan from which Elijah had gone up; a very different way of passing from life by wasting sickness than by fiery chariot! But God is as near His servant in the one place as in the other, and the slow wasting away is as much His messenger as the sudden apocalypse of the horsemen of fire. The king of Israel comes to the old prophet, and very significantly repeats over him his own exclamation over Elijah, 'My father! My father! the chariot of Israel and the horsemen thereof.' Elisha takes no notice of the grief and reverence expressed by the exclamation, but goes straight to his work, and what follows is remarkable indeed.

Here is a prophet dying; and his last words are not edifying moral and religious reflections, nor does he seem to be much concerned to leave with the king his final protest against Israel's sin, but his thoughts are all of warfare, and his last effort is to stir up the sluggish young monarch to some of his own enthusiasm in the conflict with the enemy. It does not sound like an edifying deathbed. People might have said, 'Ah! secular and political affairs should be all out of a man's mind when he comes to his last moments.' But Elisha thought that to stick to his life's work till the last breath was out of him, and to devote the last breath to stimulating successors who might catch up the torch that dropped from his failing hands, was no unworthy end of a prophet's life.

So there followed what perhaps is not very familiar to some of us, that strange scene in which the dying man is far fuller of energy and vigour than the young king, and takes the upper hand of him, giving him a series of curt, authoritative commands, each of which he punctiliously obeys. 'Take bow and arrow,' and he took them. Then the prophet lays his wasted hand for a moment on the strong, young hand, and having thus, either in symbol or reality—never mind which—communicated power, he says to him, 'Fling open the casement towards the quarter where the enemy's territory lies,' and he flings it open. 'Now, shoot,' and he shoots. Then the old man gathers himself up on his bed, and with a triumphant shout exclaims, 'The Lord's arrow of victory! . . . Thou shalt smite the Syrians till they be consumed.'

That is not all. There is a second stage. The promise is given; the possibility is opened before the king, and now all depends on the question whether he will rise to the height of the occasion. So the prophet says to him, 'Take the sheaf of arrows in your hand'; and he takes them. And then he says, 'Now smite upon the ground.' It is a test. If he had been roused and stirred by what had gone before; if he had any earnestness of belief in the power that was communicated, and any eagerness of desire to realise the promises that had been given of complete victory, what would he have done? What would Elisha have done if *he* had had the quiver in his hand? This king smites three perfunctory taps on the floor, and having done what will satisfy the old man's whim, and what in decency he had to do, he stops, as if weary of the whole performance. So the prophet bursts out in indignation on his dying bed—'Thou shouldst have smitten five or six times; then hadst thou conquered utterly. Now thou shalt conquer but thrice.' A strange story; very far away from our atmosphere and latitude! Yet are there not obviously in it great principles which may be disentangled from their singular setting, and fully applied to us? I think so. Let us try and draw them from it.

I. Here we have the power communicated.

Now the story seems to indicate that it was only for a moment that the prophet's hands were laid on the king's hands, because, after they had been so laid, he is bidden to go to the window and fling it open, and the bedridden man could not go there with him; then he is bidden to draw the bow, and another hand upon his would have been a hindrance rather than a help. So it was but a momentary touch, a communication of power in reality or in symbol that the muscular young hand needed, and the wasted old one could give. And is that not a parable for us? We, too, if we are Christian men and women, have a gospel of which the very kernel is that there is to us a communication of power, and the very name of that divine Spirit whom it is Christ's greatest work to send flashing and flaming through the world, is the 'Spirit of Power.' And so the old promise that ye shall be clothed with strength from on high is the standing prerogative of the Christian Church. There is not merely some partial communication, as when hand touched hand, but every organ is vitalised and quickened; as in the case of the other miracle of this prophet, when he stretched himself on the dead child eye to eye, and mouth to mouth, and hand to hand; and each part received the vitalising influence. We have, if we are Christian people, a Spirit given to us, and are 'strengthened with might by the Spirit in the inner man.'

That gift, that strength comes to us by contact, not with Elisha, but with Elisha's Lord and Master. Christ's touch, when He was on earth, brought sight to the blind, healing to the sick, vigour to the limbs of the lame, life to the dead. And you and I can have that touch, far more truly, and far more mightily operative upon us than they had, who only felt the contact of His finger, and only derived corporeal blessing. For we can draw near to Him, and in union with Him by faith and love and obedience, can have His Spirit in close contact with our spirits, and strengthening us for all service, and for every task. Brethren! that touch which gives strength is a real thing. It is no mere piece of mystical exaggeration when we speak of our spirits being in actual contact with Christ's Spirit. Many of us have no clear conception, and still less a firm realisation, of that closer than corporeal contact, more real than bodily presence, and more intimate than any possible physical union, which is the great gift of God in Jesus Christ, and brings to us, if we will, life and strength according to our need. I would that the popular Christianity of this day had a far larger infusion of the sound, mystical element that lies in the New Testament Christianity, and did not talk so exclusively about a Christ that is for us as to have all but lost sight of the second stage of our relation to Christ, and lost a faith in a Christ that is in us. Brethren! He can lay His hand upon your spirit's hand. He can flash light into your spirit's eye from His eye. He can put breath and eloquence into your spirit's lips from His lips, and His heart beating against yours can transfuse—if I may so say—into you His own life-blood, which cleanses from all sin, and fits for all conflict.

Then, further, let me remind you that this power, which is bestowed on condition of contact, is given before duties are commanded. This king, in our acted parable, first had the touch of Elisha's fingers, and then received the command from Elisha's lips, 'Shoot!' So Jesus Christ gives before He commands, and commands nothing which He has not fitted us to perform. He is not 'an austere man, reaping where He did not sow, and gathering where He did not straw'; but He comes first to us saying, 'I give thee Myself,' and then

He looks us in the eyes and says, 'Wilt thou not give Me thyself?' He bestows the strength first, and He commands the consequent duty afterwards.

Further, this strength communicated is realised in the effort to obey Christ's great commands. Joash felt nothing when the prophet's hand was laid upon his but, perhaps, some tingling. But when he got the bow in his hand and drew the arrow to its head, the infused power stiffened his muscles and strengthened him to pull; and though he could not distinguish between his own natural corporeal ability and that which had been thus imparted to him, the two co-operated in the one act, and it was when he drew his bow that he felt his strength. 'Stretch forth thine hand,' said Christ to the lame man. But the very infirmity to be dealt with was his inability to stretch it forth. At the command he tried, and, to his wonder, the stiffened sinews relaxed, and the joint that had been immovable had free play, and he stretched out his hand, and it was restored whole as the other. So He gives what He commands, and in obeying the command we realise and are conscious of the power. Elisha and Joash but act an illustration of the great word of Paul: 'Work out your own salvation ... for it is God that worketh in you.'

II. And now, secondly, look at the perfected victory that is possible.

When the arrows, by God's strength operating through Joash's arm, had been shot, the prophet says, 'The arrow of the Lord's victory! ... thou shalt smite ... till thou have consumed.' Yes, of course; if the arrow is the Lord's arrow, and the strength is His strength, then the only issue corresponding to the power is perfect victory. I would that Christian people realised more than they do practically in their lives that while men's ideals and aims may be all unaccomplished, or but partially approximated to, since God is God, His nature is perfection, and nothing that He does can fall beneath His ideal and purpose in doing it. All that comes from Him must correspond to Him from whom it comes. He never leaves off till He has completed, nor can any one say about any of His work, 'He began to build, and was not able to finish.' So, Christian people! I would that we should rise to the height of our prerogatives, and realise the fact that perfect victory is possible, regard being had to the power which 'teaches our hands to war and our fingers to fight.' A great deal of not altogether profitable jangling goes on at present in reference to the question of whether absolute sinlessness is possible for a Christian man on earth. Whatever view we take upon that question, it ought not to hide from us the fact which should loom very much more largely in our daily operative belief than it does with most of us, that in so far as the power which is given to us is concerned, perfect victory is within our grasp, and is the only worthy and correspondent result to the perfect power which worketh in us. So there is no reason, as from any defect of the divine gift to the weakest of us, why our Christian lives should have ups and downs, why there should be interruptions in our devotion, fallings short in our consecration, contradictions in our conduct, slidings backward in our progress. There is no reason why, in our Christian year, there should be summer and winter; but according to the symbolical saying of one of the old prophets, 'The ploughman may overtake the reaper, and he that treadeth out the grapes him that soweth the seed.' In so far as our Christian life is concerned, the perfection of the power that is granted to us involves the possibility of perfection in the recipient.

And the same thing is true in reference to a Christian man's work in the world. God's Church has ample resources to overcome the evil of the world. The fire is tremendous, but the Christian Church has possession of the floods that can extinguish the fire. If we utilised all that we have, we might 'smite till we had consumed,' and turned the world into the Church of God. That is the ideal, the possibility, when we look at the Christian man as possessor of the communicated power of God. And then we turn to the reality, to our own consciences, to the state of our religious communities everywhere, and we see what seems to be blank contradiction of the possibility. Where is the explanation?

III. That brings me to my last point, the partial victory that is actually won.

'Thou shouldst have smitten five or six times; then hadst thou smitten the Syrians till they were consumed. But now thou shalt conquer but thrice.' All God's promises and prophecies are conditional. There is no such thing as an unconditional promise of victory or of defeat; there is always an 'if.' There is always man's freedom as a factor. It is strange. I suppose no thinking, metaphysical or theological, ever has solved or ever will, that great paradox of the power of a finite will to lift itself up in the face of, and antagonism to, an Infinite Will backed by infinite power, and to thwart its purposes. 'How often *would I* have gathered ... and ye *would not.*' Here is all the power for a perfect victory, and yet the man that has it has to be contented with a very partial one.

It is a solemn thought that the Church's unbelief can

limit and hinder Christ's work in the world, and we have here another illustration of that truth. You will find now and then in the newspapers, stories—they may be true or false—about caterpillars stopping a train. There is an old legend of that fabulous creature the remora, a tiny thing that fastened itself to the keel of a ship, and arrested it in mid-ocean. That is what we do with God and His purposes, and with His power granted to us.

A low expectation limits the power. This king did not believe, did not expect, that he would conquer utterly, and so he did not. You believe that you can do a thing, and in nine cases out of ten that goes nine-tenths of the way towards doing it. If we cast ourselves into our fight expecting victory, the expectation will realise itself in nine cases out of ten. And the man who in faith refuses to say 'that beast of a word —impossible!' will find that 'all things are possible to him that believeth.' 'Expect great things of God,' and you will feel His power tingling to your very finger-tips, and will be able to draw the arrow to its head, and send it whizzing home to its mark.

Small desires block the power. Where there is an iron-bound coast running in one straight line, the whole ocean may dash itself on the cliffs at the base, but it enters not into the land; but where the shore opens itself out into some deep gulf far inland, and broad across at the entrance, then the glad water rushes in and fills it all. Make room for God in your lives by your desires and you will get Him in the fullness of His power.

The use of our power increases our power. Joash had an unused quiver full of arrows, and he only smote thrice. 'To him that hath shall be given, and from him that hath not shall be taken.' The reason why many of us professing Christians have so little of the strength of God in our lives is because we have made so little use of the strength that we have. Stow away your seed-corn in a granary and do not let the air into it, and weevils and rats will consume it. Sow it broadcast on the fields with liberal hand, and it will spring up, 'some thirty, some sixty, some an hundredfold.' Use increases strength in all regions, and unused organs atrophy and wither.

So, dear friends! if we will keep ourselves in contact with Christ, and tremulously sensitive to His touch, if we will expect power according to our tasks and our needs, if we will desire more of His grace, and if we will honestly and manfully use the strength that we have, then He will 'teach our hands to war and our fingers to fight,' and will give us strength, 'so that a bow of brass is bent by' our arms, and we shall be 'more than conquerors through Him that loved us.'

A KINGDOM'S EPITAPH

'In the ninth year of Hoshea the king of Assyria took Samaria, and carried Israel away into Assyria, and placed them in Halah and in Habor by the river of Gozan, and in the cities of the Medes. 7. For so it was, that the children of Israel had sinned against the Lord their God, which had brought them up out of the land of Egypt, from under the hand of Pharaoh king of Egypt, and had feared other gods, 8. And walked in the statutes of the heathen, whom the Lord cast out from before the children of Israel, and of the kings of Israel, which they had made. 9. And the children of Israel did secretly those things that were not right against the Lord their God, and they built them high places in all their cities, from the tower of the watchmen to the fenced city. 10. And they set them up images and groves in every high hill, and under every green tree: 11. And there they burnt incense in all the high places, as did the heathen whom the Lord carried away before them; and wrought wicked things to provoke the Lord to anger: 12. For they served idols, whereof the Lord had said unto them, Ye shall not do this thing. 13. Yet the Lord testified against Israel, and against Judah, by all the prophets and by all the seers, saying, Turn ye from your evil ways, and keep My commandments and My statutes, according to all the law which I commanded your fathers, and which I sent to you by My servants the prophets. 14. Notwithstanding they would not hear, but hardened their necks, like to the neck of their fathers, that did not believe in the Lord their God. 15. And they rejected His statutes, and His covenant that He made with their fathers, and His testimonies which He testified against them; and they followed vanity, and became vain, and went after the heathen that were round about them, concerning whom the Lord had charged them, that they should not do like them. 16. And they left all the commandments of the Lord their God, and made them molten images, even two calves, and made a grove, and worshipped all the host of heaven, and served Baal. 17. And they caused their sons and their daughters to pass through the fire, and used divination and enchantments, and sold themselves to do evil in the sight of the Lord, to provoke Him to anger. 18. Therefore the Lord was very angry with Israel, and removed them out of His sight: there was none left but the tribe of Judah only.'—2 KINGS xvii. 6-18.

THE brevity of the account of the fall of Samaria in verse 6 contrasts with the long enumeration of the sins which caused it, in the rest of this passage. Modern critics assume that verses 7-23 are 'an interpolation by the Deuteronomic writer,' apparently for no reason but because they trace Israel's fall to its cause in idolatry. But surely the bare notice in verse 6, immediately followed by verse 24, cannot have been all that the original historian had to say about so tragic an end of so large a part of the people of God. The whole purpose of the Old Testament history is not to chronicle events, but to declare God's dealings, and the fall of a kingdom was of little moment, except as revealing the righteousness of God.

The main part of this passage, then, is the exposition of the causes of the national ruin. It is a *post mortem* inquiry into the diseases that killed a kingdom. At first sight, these verses seem a mere heaping together, not without some repetition, of one or two charges; but, more closely looked at, they disclose a very striking progress of thought. In the centre stands verse 13, telling of the mission of the prophets. Before it, verses 7-12, narrate Israel's sin, which culminates in provoking the Lord to anger (ver. 11). After it, the sins are reiterated with noticeable increase of emphasis, and again culminate in provoking the Lord to anger (ver. 17). So we have two degrees of guilt—one before and one after the prophets' messages; and two kindlings of God's anger—one which led to the sending of the prophets, and one which led to the destruction of Israel. The lessons that flow from this obvious progress of thought are plain.

I. The less culpable apostasy before the prophets' warnings. The first words of verse 7, rendered as in the Revised Version, give the purpose of all that follows; namely, to declare the causes of the calamity just told. Note that the first characteristic of Israel's sin was ungrateful departure from God. There is a world of pathos and meaning in that 'their God,' which is enhanced by the allusion to the Egyptian deliverance. All sins are attempts to break the chain which binds us to God—a chain woven of a thousand linked benefits. All practically deny His possession of us, and ours of Him, and display the short memory which ingratitude has. All have that other feature hinted at here—the contrast, so absurd if it were not so sad, between the worth and power of the God who is left and the other gods who are preferred. The essential meanness and folly of Israel are repeated by every heart departing from the living God.

The double origin of the idolatry is next set forth. It was in part imported and in part home-made. We have little conception of the strength of faith and courage which were needed to keep the Jews from becoming idolaters, surrounded as they were by such. But the same are needed to-day to keep us from learning the ways of the world and getting a snare to our souls. Now, as ever, walking with God means walking in the opposite direction from the crowd, and that requires some firm nerve. The home-made idolatry is gibbeted as being according to 'the statutes of the kings.' What right had they to prescribe their subjects' religion? The influence of influential people, especially if exerted against the service of God, is hard to resist; but it is no excuse for sin that it is fashionable.

The blindness of Israel to the consequences of their sin is hinted in the reference to the fate of the nations whom they imitated. They had been cast out; would not their copyists learn the lesson? We, too, have examples enough of what godless lives come to, if we had the sense to profit by them. The God who cast out the vile Canaanites and all the rest of the wicked crew before the sons of the desert has not changed, and will treat Israel as He did them, if Israel come down to their level. Outward privileges make idolatry or any sin more sinful, and its punishment more severe.

Another characteristic of Israel's sin is its being done 'secretly.' Of the various meanings proposed for that word (ver. 9) the best seems to be that it refers to the attempt to combine the worship of God and of idols, of which the calf worship is an instance. Elijah had long ago taunted the people with trying 'to hobble on both knees,' or on 'two opinions' at once; and here the charge is of covering idolatry with a cloak of Jehovah worship. A varnish of religion is convenient and cheap, and often effectual in deceiving ourselves as well as others; but 'as a man thinketh in his heart, so is he,' whatever his cloak may be; and the thing which we count most precious and long most for is our god, whatever our professions of orthodox religion.

The idolatry is then described, in rapid touches, as universal. Wherever there was a solitary watchman's tower among the pastures there was a high place, and they were reared in every city. Images and Asherim deformed every hill-top and stood under every spreading tree. Everywhere incense loaded the heavy air with its foul fragrance. The old scenes of unnamable abomination, which had been so terribly avenged, seemed to have come back, and to cry aloud for another purging by fire and sword.

The terrible upshot of all was 'to provoke the Lord to anger.' The New Testament is as emphatic as the Old in asserting that there is the capacity of anger in the God whose name is love, and that sin calls it forth. The special characteristic of sin, by which it thus attracts that lightning, is that it is disobedience. As in the first sin, so in all others, God has said, 'Ye shall not do this thing'; and we say, 'Do it we will.' What can the end of that be but the anger of the Lord? 'Because of these things cometh the wrath of God upon the children of disobedience.'

II. Verse 13 gives the pleading of Jehovah. The mission of the prophets was God's reply to Israel's rebellion, and was equally the sign of His anger and of His love. The more sin abounds, the more does God multiply means to draw back to Himself. The deafer the ears, the louder the beseeching voice of His grieved and yet pitying love. His anger clothes itself in more stringent appeals and clearer revelations of Himself before it takes its slaughtering weapons in hand. The darker the background of sin, the brighter the beams of His light show against it. Man's sin is made the occasion for a more glorious display of God's character and heart. It is on the storm-cloud that the sun paints the rainbow. Each successive stage in man's departure from God evoked a corresponding increase in the divine effort to attract him back, till 'last of all He sent unto them His Son.' In nature, attraction diminishes as distance increases; in the realms of grace, it grows with distance. The one desire of God's heart is that sinners would return from their evil ways, and He presses on them the solemn thought of the abundant intimations of His will which have been given from of old, and are pealed again into all ears by living voices. His law for us is not merely an old story spoken centuries ago, but is vocal in our consciences to-day, and fresh as when Sinai flamed and thundered above the camp, and the trumpet thrilled each heart.

III. The heavier sin that followed the divine pleading. That divine voice leaves no man as it finds him. If it does not sway him to obedience, it deepens his guilt, and makes him more obstinate. Like some perverse ox in the yoke, he stiffens his neck, and stands the very picture of brute obduracy. There is an awful alternative involved in our hearing of God's message, which never returns to Him void, but ever does something to the hearer, either softening or hardening, either scaling the eyes or adding another film on them, either being the 'savour of life unto life or of death unto death.' The mission of the prophets changed forgetfulness of God's 'statutes' into 'rejection' of them, and made idolatry self-conscious rebellion. Alas, that men should make what is meant to be a bond to unite them to God into a wedge to part them farther from Him! But how constantly that is the effect of the gospel, and for the same reason as in Israel—that they 'did not believe in the Lord their God'!

The miserable result on the sinners' own natures is described with pregnant brevity in verse 15. 'They followed vanity, and became vain.' The worshipper became like the thing worshipped, as is always the case. The idol is vanity, utter emptiness and nonentity; and whoever worships nothingness will become in his own inmost life as empty and vain as it is. That is the retribution attendant on all trust in, and longing after, the trifles of earth, that we come down to the level of what we set our hearts upon. We see the effects of that principle in the moral degradation of idolaters. Gods lustful, cruel, capricious, make men like themselves. We see it working upwards in Christianity, in which God becomes man that men may become like God, and of which the whole law is put into one precept, which is sure to be kept, in the measure of the reality of a man's religion. 'Be ye therefore imitators of God, as beloved children.'

In verses 16 and 17 the details of the idolatry follow the general statement, as in verses 9 to 12, but with additions and with increased severity of tone. We hear now of calves and star worship, and Baal, and burning children to Moloch, and divination and enchantment. The catalogue is enlarged, and there is added to it the terrible declaration that Israel had 'sold themselves to do evil in the sight of the Lord.' The same thing was said by Elijah to Ahab—a noble instance of courage. The sinner who steels himself against the divine remonstrance, does not merely go on in his old sins, but adds new ones. Begin with the calves, and fancy that you are worshipping Jehovah, and you will end with Baal and Moloch. Refuse to hear God's pleadings, and you will sell your freedom, and become the lowest and only real kind of slave—the bondsman of evil. When that point of entire abandonment to sin, which Paul calls being 'sold under sin,' is reached, as it may be reached, at all events by a nation, and corruption has struck too deep to be cast out, once again the anger of the Lord is provoked; but this time it comes in a different guise. The armies of the Assyrians, not the prophets, are its messengers now. Israel had made itself like the nations whom God had used it to destroy, and now it shall be destroyed as they were.

To be swept out of His sight is the fate of obstinate rejection of His commandments and pleadings. Israel made itself the slave of evil, and was made the captive of Assyria. Self-willed freedom, which does as it likes, and heeds not God, ends in bondage, and is itself bondage. God's anger against sin speaks pleadingly to us all, saying, 'Do not this abominable thing that I hate.' Well for us if we hearken to His voice when 'His anger is kindled but a little.' If we do not yield to Him, and cast away our idols, we shall become vain as they. Our evil will be more fatal, and our obstinacy more criminal, because He called, and we refused. 'Who may abide the day of His coming? and who shall stand when He appeareth?' These captives, dragging their weary limbs, with despair in their hearts, across the desert to a land of bondage, were but shadows, in the visible region of things, of the far more doleful and dreary fate that sooner or later must fall on those who would none of God's counsel, and despised all His reproof, but cling to their idol till they and it are destroyed together.

DIVIDED WORSHIP

'These nations feared the Lord, and served their own gods.'—2 KINGS xvii. 33.

THE kingdom of Israel had come to its fated end. Its king and people had been carried away captives in accordance with the cruel policy of the great Eastern despotisms, which had so much to do with weakening them by their very conquests. The land had lain desolate and uncultivated for many years, savage beasts had increased in the untilled solitudes, even as weeds and nettles grew in the gardens and vineyards of Samaria. At last the king of Assyria resolved to people the country; and for this purpose he sent a mixed multitude from the different nationalities of his empire to the land of Israel. They were men of five nationalities, most of them recently conquered. Israel had been deported to different parts of the Assyrian empire; men from different parts of the empire were deported to the land of Israel. Such cruel uprootings seemed to be wisdom, but were really a policy that kept alive disaffection. It was the same mistake (and bore the same fruits) as Austria pursued in sending Hungarian regiments to keep down Venice, and Venetian-born soldiers to overawe Hungary.

These new settlers brought with them their national peculiarities, and among the rest, their gods. They knew nothing about the Jehovah whom they supposed to be the local deity of Israel; and when they were troubled by the wild beasts which had, of course, rapidly increased in the land, they attributed it to their neglect of His worship, and sent an embassy to the king of Assyria telling that as they 'know not the manners of the God of the land,' He has sent lions among them.

This is an instructive example of the heathen way of thinking. They have their local deities. Each land, each valley, each mountain top, has its own. They are ready to worship them all, for they have no real worship for any. Their reason for worship is to escape from harm, to pay the tribute to which the god has a right on his own territory, lest he should make it the worse for them if they neglect it. 'The mild tolerance of heathendom' simply means the utter absence of religion and an altogether inadequate notion of deity.

So the settlers have sent to them one of these schismatic priests who had belonged to the extinct sanctuary at Beth-el, and he, apparently, not having any truer notions of God or of worship than they had, nothing loth, teaches them the rites of the Israelite worship, which was not like that of Judah, as is distinctly stated in the context. This worship of Jehovah was, however, blended by them with their own national idolatry. How contemptuously the historian enumerates the hard names of their gods and the rabble rout of them which each nation made! 'The men of Babylon *made* Succoth-benoth' (probably a deity, though the name may mean booths for purposes of prostitution) and the others '*made* Nergal and Ashima and Nibhaz and Tartak.' What names, and what a pantheon! 'They feared the Lord and served their own gods.'

This was the beginning of the Samaritan people, whom we find through the rest of Scripture even down to the Acts of the Apostles, retaining some trace of their heathen origin. Simon Magus bewitched them in his sorceries. They began as heathen, though in lapse of years they came to be pure monotheists, even more rigid than the Jews themselves, and to-day, if you went to Nablûs, you would find the small remnant of their descendants adhering to Moses and the law, guarding their sacred copy of the Pentateuch with unintelligent awe, and eating the Paschal Lamb with wild rites. They have changed the object of their worship, but one fears that it is little more real and deep than in old days, 2500 years ago, when their forefathers 'feared the Lord and served their own gods.'

Now I venture to take this verse as indicative of a tendency which belongs to a great many more people than the confused mass of settlers that were shot down on the hills of Israel by the king of Assyria. It is really a description of a great deal of what goes by the name of religion amongst us.

I. The Religion of Fear.

These people would never have thought about God if it had not been for the lions. When they did think of Him it was only to tremble before Him. The reason for their trembling was that they did not know the etiquette of His worship; that they thought of Him as having rights over them because they had come into His territory, which He would exact, or punish them for omitting. In a word, their notion of God was that of a jealous, capricious tyrant, whose ways were inscrutable to them, in whose territory they found themselves without their will, and who needed to be propitiated if they would live in peace.

And this is the thought which is most operative in many minds, though it is veiled in more seemly phrases, and which darkens and injures all those on whom it lays hold. Need I spend time in showing you how, point by point, this picture is a picture of many among us? How many of you think of God when you are ill, and forget Him when you are well? How many of you pour out a prayer when you are in trouble, and forget all about Him and it when you are prosperous? How many of you see God in your calamities and not in your joys? Why do people call sudden deaths and the like the 'visitation of God'? How many of us are like Italian sailors who burn candles and shriek out to the Madonna when the storm catches them, and get drunk in the first wine-shop which they come to when they land! Is not many a man's thought of God, 'I knew Thee that Thou wert an austere Man, and I was afraid'?

The popular religion is largely a religion of fear.

There is a fear which is right and noble. That is reverend, humble adoration at the sight or thought of God's great perfections. Angels veil their faces with their wings. Such awe has no thought of personal consequences—is inseparable from all true knowledge of God; for all greatness of character is perfected by love. Of such fear we are not now speaking.

Terror of God is deep in men's hearts.

Fear is the apprehension of personal evil from some person or thing. Now I believe that terror has its place in the human economy, and in religion, as the sense of pain has. There is something in man's relations to God to cause it.

The Bible sets forth 'the terror of the Lord,' that men may tremble before Him. Moses said, 'I exceedingly fear and quake.' But that terror is only right when it proceeds from a sense of God's holiness and a consciousness of my own sinfulness. It is not right when it is a mere dread of a hard tyrant. That terror is only right when it leads to a joyful acceptance of God's revelation of His love in Christ.

Fear was never meant to be permanent, it is only the alarum-bell which rings to wake up the soul that sleeps on when in mortal peril. And it should pass into penitence, faith, joy in Jesus. 'We have access with confidence by the faith of Him.' The brightness is great and awful, but go nearer, as you can in Jesus, and lo! there is love in the brightness. You see it all tender and sweet. A heart and a hand are there, and from the midst of it the Father's voice speaks, and says, 'My son, give Me thine heart.'

The religion of fear is worthless. It produces no holiness, it does nothing for a man, it does not bind him to God. He is none the stronger for it. It paralyses so far as it does anything.

It is spasmodic and intermittent. It is impossible to keep it up, so it comes in fits and starts. When the morning comes men laugh at their terrors. It leads to wild endeavours to forget God—atheism—to insensibility. He who begins by fearing when there was no need, ends by not fearing when he ought.

II. The Religion of Form.

The Samaritans' whole worship was outward worship. They did the things which the Beth-el priest taught them to do, and that was all.

And this again is a type, very common in our day. Religion must have forms. The forms often help to bring us the spirit. But we are always in danger of trusting to them too much.

How many of us have our Christianity only in outward seeming? The only thing that unites men to God is love.

So your external connection with God's worship is of no use at all unless you have that.

Church and chapel-goers are alike exposed to the danger of erecting the forms of worship to a place in which they cannot be put without marring the spirit of worship. Whether our worship be more or less symbolic, whether we have a more or less elaborate ritual, whether we think more or less of sacraments, whether we put hearing a sermon as more or less prominent, or even if we follow the formless forms of the Friends, we are all tempted to substitute our forms for the spirit which alone is worship.

III. The Religion of Compromise or Worldliness.

They had God and they had gods. They liked the latter best. They gave God formal worship, but they gave the others more active service.

Such a kind of religion is a type of much that we see around us; the attempt to be Christians and worldlings, the indecision under which many men labour all their lives, being drawn one way by their consciences, another by their inclinations.

You cannot unite the two. God requires all. He fills the heart, and claims supreme control over all the nature. There cannot be two supreme in the soul. It cannot be God and self. It must be God or self. You may look now one way and now another, but the way the heart goes is the thing. Mr. Facing-both-ways does not really face both ways. He only turns quickly round from one to the other.

Such divided religion is impossible in the nature of God—of the soul—of religion.

To attempt it, then, is really to decide against God.

It is weak and unmanly to be thus vague and decided by circumstances. You would have been a Mohammedan if you had been born in Turkey.

You ought to decide for God.

He claims, He deserves, He will reward and bless, your whole soul.

'Choose you this day whom ye will serve. If the Lord be God, follow Him.' If Baal or Succoth-benoth, then follow him. 'You cannot serve God and Mammon.' 'He that is not for us is against us.' Be one thing or the other.

HEZEKIAH, A PATTERN OF DEVOUT LIFE

'Hezekiah trusted in the Lord God of Israel. . . . 6. He clave to the Lord, and departed not from following Him, but kept His commandments.'—2 KINGS xviii. 5, 6.

DEVOUT people in all ages and stations are very much like each other. The elements of godliness are always the same. This king of Israel, something like two thousand six hundred years ago, and the humblest Christian to-day have the family likeness on their faces. These words, which are an outline sketch of the king's character, are really a sketch of the religious life at all times and in all places. He realised it; why may not we? He achieved it amid much ignorance; why should not we amid our blaze of knowledge? He accomplished it amid the temptations of a monarchy; why should not we in our humbler spheres?

There are four things set forth here as constituting a religious life. We begin at the bottom with the foundation of everything. 'He trusted in the Lord God of Israel.' The Old Testament is just as emphatic in declaring that there is no religion without trust, and that trust is the very nerve and life-blood of religion, as is the New. Only that in the one half of the book our translators have chosen to use the word 'trust,' and in the other half of the book they have chosen to use, for the very same act, the word 'faith.' They have thus somewhat obscured the absolute identity which exists in the teaching of the Old and of the New Testament as regards the bond which unites men to God. That union always was, and always will be, begun in the simple attitude and exercise of trust, and everything else will come out of that, and without that nothing else will come.

So this king had a certain measure of knowledge about the character of God, and that measure of knowledge led him to lean all his weight upon the Lord. You and I know a great deal more about God and His ways and purposes than Hezekiah did, but we can make no better use of it than he did—translate our knowledge into faith, and rely with simple, absolute confidence on Him whose name we know in Christ more **fully** and blessedly than was possible to Hezekiah.

And need I remind you of how, in this life of which the outline is here given and the inmost secret is here disclosed, there were significant and magnificent instances of the power of humble trust to bring to an else helpless man all the blessings that he needs, and to put a crystal wall round about him that will preserve him from every evil, howsoever threatening it may seem?

'It has come addressed to me, but it is meant for Thee. Vindicate Thine own cause by delivering Thine own servant.' And so, 'when the morning dawned, they were all dead men,' and faith rejoiced in a perfect deliverance. And you and I may get the same answer, in the midst of all our trials, difficulties, toils, and conflicts, if only we will go the same way to get it, and let our faith work, as Hezekiah's worked, and take everything that troubles us to our Father in the heavens, and be quite sure that He is the God 'who daily bears our burdens.' Let us begin with the simple act of confidence in Him. That is the foundation, and on that we may build everything besides.

Let us see what this man further built upon it. The second story, if I may so say, of the temple-fortress of his life, upon the foundation of faith, was, 'He clave to the Lord.'

That is to say, the act of confidence must be followed and perfected by tenacious adherence with all the tendrils of a man's nature to the God in whom he says that he trusts. The metaphor is a very forcible one, so familiar in Scripture as that we are apt to overlook its emphasis. Let me recall one or two of the instances in which it is employed about other matters which throw light on its force here.

First of all, remember that sweet picture of the widow woman from Moab and the two daughters-in-law, one sent back, not reluctantly, to her home; and the other persisting in keeping by Naomi's side, in spite of difficulties and remonstrances. With kisses of real love Orpah went back, but she did go back, to her people and her gods, but 'Ruth clave unto her.' So should we cling to God, as Ruth flung her arms round Naomi, and twined her else lonely and desolate heart about her dear and only friend, for whose sweet sake she became a willing exile from kindred and country. Is that how we cleave to the Lord?

More sacred still are the lessons that are suggested by the fact that this is the word employed to describe the blessed and holy union of man and woman in pure wedded life, and I suppose some allusion to that use of the expression underlies its constant application to the relation of the believing soul to Jehovah. For by trust the soul is wedded to Him, and so 'joined to the Lord' as to be 'one spirit.'

Or if we do not care to go so deep as that, let us take the metaphor that lies in the word itself, without reference to its Scriptural applications. As the limpet holds on to its rock, as the ivy clings to the wall, as a shipwrecked sailor grasps the spar which keeps his head above water, so a Christian man ought to hold on to God, with all his energy, and with all parts of his nature. The metaphor implies tenacity; closeness of adhesion, in heart and will, in thought, in desire, and in all the parts of our receptive humanity, all of which can touch God and be touched by Him, and all of which are blessed only in the measure in which, yielding to Him, they are filled and steadied and glorified.

And there is implied, too, not only tenacity of adherence, but tenacity in the face of obstacles. There must be resistance to all the forces which would detach, if there is to be union with God in the midst of life in the world. Or, to recur for a moment to the figure that I employed a moment ago, as the sailor clings to a spar, though the waves dash round him, and his fingers get stiffened with cold and cramped with keeping the one position, and can scarcely hold on, but he knows that it is life to cling and death to loosen, and so tightens his grasp; thus have we to lay hold of God, and in spite of all obstacles, to keep hold of Him. Our grasp tends to slacken, and is feeble at the best, even if there were nothing outside of us to make it difficult for us to get a good grip. But there are howling winds and battering waves blowing and beating on us, and making it hard to keep our hold.

Do not let us yield to these, but in spite of them all let our hearts tighten round Him, for it is only in His sweet, eternal, perfect love that they can be at rest. And let our thoughts keep close to Him in spite of all distractions, for it is only in the measure in which His light fills our minds and His truth occupies our thoughts that our thinking spirits will be at rest. And let our desires, as the tentacles of some shell-fish fasten upon the rock, and feel out towards the ocean that is coming to it, let our desires go all out towards Him until they touch that after which they feel, and curl round it in repose and in blessedness.

The whole secret of a joyful, strong, noble Christian life lies here—that on the foundation of faith we should rear tenacious adherence to Him in spite of all obstacles. So it was a most encyclopædic, though laconic, exhortation that that 'good man' sent down from Jerusalem to encourage the first heathen converts gave, when instead of all other instruction or advice, or inculcation of less important, and yet real, Christian duties, Barnabas exhorted them all 'that with purpose of heart'—the full devotion of their inmost natures—'they should cleave to the Lord.'

Then the third stage, or the third story, in this building is that, cleaving to the Lord, 'he departed not from following Him.' The metaphor of cleaving implies proximity and union; the metaphor of following implies distance which is being diminished. These two are incongruous, and the very incongruity helps to give point to the representation. The same two ideas of union and yet of pursuit are brought still more closely together in other parts of Scripture. For instance, there is a remarkable saying in one of the Psalms, translated in our Bible—'My soul followeth hard after Thee. Thy right hand upholdeth me,' where the expression 'followeth hard after' is a lame attempt at translating the perhaps impossible-to-be-translated fullness of the original, which reads 'My soul cleaveth after Thee.' It is an incongruous combination of ideas, by its very incongruity and paradoxical form suggesting a profound truth—viz. that in all the conscious union and tenacious adherence to God which makes the Christian life, there is ever, also, a sense of distance which kindles aspiration and leads to the effort after continual progress. However close we may be to God, it is always possible to press closer. However full may be the union, it may always be made fuller; and the cleaving spirit will always be longing for a closer contact and a more blessed sense of being in touch with God.

So, as we climb, new heights reveal themselves, and the further we advance in the Christian life the more are we conscious of the infinite depths that yet remain to be traversed. Hence arises one great element of the blessedness of being a Christian—namely, that we need not fear ever coming to the end of the growth in holiness and the increase of joy and power that are possible to us. So that weariness, and the sense of having reached the limits that are possible on a given path, which sooner or later fall upon men that live for anything but God, can never be ours if we live for Him. But the oldest and most experienced will have the same forward-looking glances of hope and forward-directed steps of strenuous effort as the youngest beginner on the path; and a Paul will be able to say when he is 'Paul the aged,' and 'the time of his departure is at hand,' that he 'forgets the things that are behind, and reaches forth unto the things that are before, while he presses towards the mark.' Let us be thankful for the endless progress which is possible to the Christian, and let us see to it that we are never paralysed into supposing that 'to-morrow must be *as* this day,' but trust the infinite resources of our God, and be sure that we growingly make our own the growing gifts which He bestows.

And so, lastly, the fourth element in this analysis of a devout life is 'He kept the commandments of the

Lord.' That is the outcome of them all. Faith, adhesion, aspiration, and progress, all vindicate their value and reality in the simple, homely way of practical obedience.

Let us learn two things. One as to the worthlessness of all these others, if they do not issue in this. Not that these inward emotions are ever to be despised, but that, if they are genuine in our hearts, they cannot but manifest themselves in our lives. And so, dear Christian friends! do you not build upon your faith, on your adherence to God, on your aspirations after Him, unless you can bring into court, as witnesses for these, daily and hourly, your efforts after the conformity of your will to His, in the great things and in the small. Then, and only then, may we be sure that our confidence is not a delusion, and that it is to Him that we cleave when our feet tread in the paths of goodness.

And on the other hand, let us learn that all attempts to be obedient to a divine will which do not begin with trust and cleaving to Him are vain. There is no other way to get that conformity of will except by that union of spirit. All other attempts are beginning at the wrong end. You do not begin building your houses with the chimney-pots, but many a man who seeks to obey without trusting does precisely commit that fault. Let us be sure that the foundations are in, and then let us be sure that we do not stop half-way up, lest all that pass by should mock and say, 'This man began to build and was not able to finish.'

How many professing Christians' lives are half-finished and unroofed houses, because they have not 'added to their faith'—that is, to their 'cleaving to the Lord'—endless aspiration and continual progress, and to their aspiration and their progress the peaceable fruit of practical righteousness! If these things be in us and abound, they mark us as devout men after God's pattern. And if we want to be devout men after God's pattern, we must follow God's sequence, which begins with trust and ends with obedience.

'HE UTTERED HIS VOICE, THE EARTH MELTED'

'Then Isaiah the son of Amoz sent to Hezekiah, saying, Thus saith the Lord God of Israel, That which thou hast prayed to Me against Sennacherib king of Assyria I have heard. 21. This is the word that the Lord hath spoken concerning him; The virgin, the daughter of Zion, hath despised thee, and laughed thee to scorn; the daughter of Jerusalem hath shaken her head at thee. 22. Whom hast thou reproached and blasphemed? and against whom hast thou exalted thy voice, and lifted up thine eyes on high? even against the Holy One of Israel.... 28. Because thy rage against Me and thy tumult is come up into Mine ears, therefore I will put My hook in thy nose, and My bridle in thy lips, and I will turn thee back by the way by which thou camest. 29. And this shall be a sign unto thee, Ye shall eat this year such things as grow of themselves, and in the second year that which springeth of the same; and in the third year sow ye, and reap, and plant vineyards, and eat the fruits thereof. 30. And the remnant that is escaped of the house of Judah shall yet again take root downward, and bear fruit upward. 31. For out of Jerusalem shall go forth a remnant, and they that escape out of mount Zion: the zeal of the Lord of hosts shall do this. 32. Therefore thus saith the Lord concerning the king of Assyria, He shall not come into this city, nor shoot an arrow there, nor come before it with shield, nor cast a bank against it. 33. By the way that he came, by the same shall he return, and shall not come into this city, saith the Lord. 34. For I will defend this city, to save it, for Mine own sake, and for My servant David's sake. 35. And it came to pass that night, that the angel of the Lord went out, and smote in the camp of the Assyrians an hundred fourscore and five thousand: and when they arose early in the morning, behold, they were all dead corpses. 36. So Sennacherib king of Assyria departed, and went and returned, and dwelt at Nineveh. 37. And it came to pass, as he was worshipping in the house of Nisroch his god, that Adrammelech and Sharezer his sons smote him with the sword; and they escaped into the land of Armenia: and Esarhaddon his son reigned in his stead.'—2 KINGS xix. 20-22; 28-37.

AT an earlier stage of the Assyrian invasion Hezekiah had sent to Isaiah, asking him to pray to his God for deliverance, and had received an explicit assurance that the invasion would be foiled. When the second stage was reached, and Hezekiah was personally summoned to surrender, by a letter which scoffed at Isaiah's promise, he himself prayed before the Lord. Isaiah does not seem to have been present, and may not have known of the prayer. At all events, the answer was given to him to give to the king; and it is noteworthy that, as in the former case, he does not himself come, but sends to Hezekiah. He did come when he had to bring a message of death, and again when he had to rebuke (chap. xx.), but now he only sends. As the chosen speaker of Jehovah's will, he was mightier than kings, and must not imperil the dignity of the message by the behaviour of the messenger. In a sentence, Hezekiah's prayer is answered, and then the prophet, in Jehovah's name, bursts into a wonderful song of triumph over the defeated invader. 'I have heard.' That is enough. Hezekiah's prayer has, as it were, fired the fuse or pulled the trigger, and the explosion follows, and the shot is sped. 'Whereas thou hast prayed,... I have heard,' is ever true, and God's hearing is God's acting in answer. The methods of His response vary, the fact that He responds to the cry of despair driven to faith by extremity of need does not vary.

But it is noteworthy that, with that brief, sufficient assurance, Hezekiah, as it were, is put aside, and instead of three fighters in the field, the king, with God to back him, and on the other side Sennacherib, two only, appear. It is a duel between Jehovah and the arrogant heathen who had despised Him. Jerusalem appears for a moment, in a magnificent piece of poetical scorn, as despising and making gestures of contempt at the baffled would-be conqueror, as Miriam and her maidens did by the Red Sea. The city is 'virgin,' as many a fortress in other lands has been named, because uncaptured. But she, too, passes out of sight, and Jehovah and Sennacherib stand opposed on the field. God speaks now not 'concerning,' but to, him, and indicts him for insane pride, which was really a denial of dependence on God, and passionate antagonism to Him, as manifested not only in his war against Jehovah's people, but also in the tone of his insolent defiances of Hezekiah, in which he scoffed at the vain trust which the latter was placing in his God, and paralleled Jehovah with the gods of the nations whom he had already conquered (Isaiah xix. 12).

The designation of God, characteristic of Isaiah, as 'the Holy One of Israel,' expresses at once His elevation above, and separation from, all mundane, creatural limitations, and His special relation to His people, and both thoughts intensify Sennacherib's sin. The Highest, before whose transcendent height all human elevations sink to a uniform level, has so joined Israel to Himself that to touch it is to strike at Him, and to vaunt one's self against it is to be arrogant towards God. That mighty name has received wider extension now, but the wider sweep does not bring diminished depth, and lowly souls who take that name for their strong tower can still run into it and be safe from 'the oppressor's wrong, the proud man's contumely,' and the strongest foes.

There is tremendous scorn in the threat with which the divine address to Sennacherib ends. The dreaded world-conqueror is no more in God's eyes than a wild beast, which He can ring and lead as He will, and not even as formidable as that, but like a horse or a mule, that can easily be bridled and directed. What majestic assertion lies in these figures and in '*My* hook' and '*My* bridle!' How many conquerors and mighty men since then have been so mastered, and their schemes balked! Sennacherib had to return by 'the way that he came,' and to tramp back, foiled and disappointed, over all the weary miles which he had trodden before with such insolent confidence of victory. A modern parallel is Napoleon's retreat from Moscow. But the same experience really befalls all who order life regardless of God. Their schemes may seem to succeed, but in deepest truth they fail, and the schemers never reach their goal.

In verse 29 the prophet turns away abruptly and almost contemptuously from Sennacherib to speak comfortably to Jerusalem, addressing Hezekiah first, but turning immediately to the people. The substance of his words to them is, first, the assurance that the Assyrian invasion had limits of time set to it by God; and, second, that beyond it lay prosperous times, when the prophetic visions of a flourishing Israel should be realised in fact. For two seed-times only field work was to be impossible on account of the Assyrian occupation, but it was to foam itself away, like a winter torrent, before a third season for sowing came round.

But how could this sequence of events, which required time for its unfolding, be 'a sign'? We must somewhat modify our notions of a sign to understand the prophet. The Scripture usage does not only designate by that name a present event or thing which guarantees the truth of a prophecy, but it sometimes means an event, or sequence of events, in the future, which, when they have come to pass in accordance with the divine prediction of them, will shed back light on other divine words or acts, and demonstrate that they were of God. Thus Moses was given as a sign of his mission the worshipping in Mount Sinai, which was to take place only after the Exodus. So with Isaiah's sign here. When the harvest of the third year was gathered in, then

Israel would know that the prophet had spoken from God when he had sung Sennacherib's defeat. For the present, Hezekiah and Judah had to live by faith; but when the deliverance was complete, and they were enjoying the fruits of their labours and of God's salvation, then they could look back on the weary years, and recognise more clearly than while these were slowly passing how God had been in all the trouble, and had been carrying on His purposes of mercy through it all. And there will be a 'sign' for us in like manner when we look back from eternity on the transitory conflicts of earthly life, and are satisfied with the harvest which He has caused to spring from our poor sowings to the Spirit.

The definite promise of deliverance in verses 32-34 is addressed to Judah, and emphasises the completeness of the frustration of the invader's efforts. There is a climax in the enumeration of the things that he will not be allowed to do—he will not make his entry into the city, nor even shoot an arrow there, nor even make preparation for a siege. His whole design will be overturned, and as had already been said (ver. 28), he will retrace his steps a baffled man.

Note the strong antithesis: 'He shall not come into this city, ... for I will defend this city.' Zion is impregnable because Jehovah defends it. Sennacherib can do nothing, for he is fighting against God. And if we 'are come unto the city of the living God,' we can take the same promise for the strength of our lives. God saves Zion 'for His own sake,' for His name is concerned in its security, both because He has taken it for His own and because He has pledged His word to guard it. It would be a blot on His faithfulness, a slur on His power, if it should be conquered while it remains true to Him, its King. His honour is involved in protecting us if we enter into the strong city of which the builder and maker is God. And 'for David's sake,' too, He defends Zion, because He had sworn to David to dwell there. But Zion's security becomes an illusion if Zion breaks away from God. If it becomes as Sodom, it shares Sodom's fate.

It is remarkable that neither in the song of triumph nor in the prophecy of deliverance is there allusion to the destruction of the Assyrian army. How the exultant taunts of the one and the definite promises of the other were to be fulfilled was not declared till the event declared it. But faithful expectation had not long to wait, for 'that night' the blow fell, and no second was needed. We are not told where the Assyrian army was, but clearly it was not before Jerusalem. Nor do we learn what was the instrument of destruction wielded by the 'angel of the Lord,' if there was any. The catastrophe may have been brought about by a pestilence, but however effected, it was 'the act of God,' the fulfilment of His promise, the making bare of His arm. 'By terrible things in righteousness' did He answer the prayer of Hezekiah, and give to all humble souls who are oppressed and cry to Him a pledge that 'as they have heard, so' will they 'see, in the city of' their 'God.' How much more impressive is the stern, naked brevity of the Scriptural account than a more emotional expansion of it, like, for instance, Byron's well-known, and in their way powerful lines, would have been! To the writer of this book it seemed the most natural thing in the world that the foes of Zion should be annihilated by one blow of the divine hand. His business is to tell the facts; he leaves commentary and wonder and triumph or terror to others.

There is but one touch of patriotic exultation apparent in the half-sarcastic and half-rejoicing accumulation of synonyms descriptive of Sennacherib's retreat. He 'departed, and went and returned.' It is like the picture in Psalm xlviii., which probably refers to the same events: 'They saw it, and so they marvelled; they were troubled, and hasted away.'

About twenty years elapsed between Sennacherib's retreat and his assassination. During all that time he 'dwelt at Nineveh,' so far as Judah was concerned. He had had enough of attacking it and its God. But the notice of his death is introduced here, not only to complete the narrative, but to point a lesson, which is suggested by the fact that he was murdered 'as he was worshipping in the house of Nisroch his god.' Hezekiah had gone into the house of *his* God with Sennacherib's letter, and the dead corpses of an army showed what Jehovah could do for His servant; Sennacherib was praying in the temple of *his* god, and his corpse lay stretched before his idol, an object lesson of the impotence of Nisroch and all his like to hear or help their worshippers.

THE REDISCOVERED LAW AND ITS EFFECTS

'And Hilkiah the high priest said unto Shaphan the scribe, I have found the book of the law in the house of the Lord: and Hilkiah gave the book to Shaphan, and he read it. 9. And Shaphan the scribe came to the king, and brought the king word again, and said, Thy servants have gathered the money that was found in the house, and have delivered it into the hand of them that do the work, that have the oversight of the house of the Lord. 10. And Shaphan the scribe shewed the king, saying, Hilkiah the priest hath delivered me a book: and Shaphan read it before the king. 11. And it came to pass, when the king had heard the words of the book of the law, that he rent his clothes. 12. And the king commanded Hilkiah the priest, and Ahikam the son of Shaphan, and Achbor the son of Michaiah, and Shaphan the scribe, and Asahiah a servant of the king's, saying, 13. Go ye, enquire of the Lord for me, and for the people, and for all Judah, concerning the words of this book that is found: for great is the wrath of the Lord that is kindled against us, because our fathers have not hearkened unto the words of this

THE REDISCOVERED LAW

book, to do according unto all that which is written concerning us. 14. So Hilkiah the priest, and Ahikam, and Achbor, and Shaphan, and Asahiah, went unto Huldah the prophetess, the wife of Shallum the son of Tikvah, the son of Harhas, keeper of the wardrobe; (now she dwelt in Jerusalem in the college;) and they communed with her. 15. And she said unto them, Thus saith the Lord God of Israel, Tell the man that sent you to me, 16. Thus saith the Lord, Behold, I will bring evil upon this place, and upon the inhabitants thereof, even all the words of the book which the king of Judah hath read: 17. Because they have forsaken Me, and have burnt incense unto other gods, that they might provoke Me to anger with all the works of their hands; therefore My wrath shall be kindled against this place, and shall not be quenched. 18. But to the king of Judah, which sent you to enquire of the Lord, thus shall ye say to him, Thus saith the Lord God of Israel, As touching the words which thou hast heard; 19. Because thine heart was tender, and thou hast humbled thyself before the Lord, when thou heardest what I speak against this place, and against the inhabitants thereof, that they should become a desolation and a curse, and hast rent thy clothes, and wept before Me; I also have heard thee, saith the Lord. 20. Behold, therefore, I will gather thee unto thy fathers, and thou shalt be gathered into thy grave in peace; and thine eyes shall not see all the evil which I will bring upon this place. And they brought the king word again.'—2 KINGS xxii. 8-20.

WE get but a glimpse into a wild time of revolution and counter-revolution in the brief notice that the 'servants of Amon,' Josiah's father, conspired and murdered him in his palace, but were themselves killed by a popular rising, in which the 'people of the land made Josiah his son king in his stead,' and so no doubt balked the conspirators' plans. Poor boy! he was only eight years old when he made his first acquaintance with rebellion and bloodshed. There must have been some wise heads and strong arms and loyal hearts round him, but their names have perished. The name of David was still a spell in Judah, and guarded his childish descendant's royal rights. In the eighteenth year of his reign, the twenty-sixth of his age, he felt himself firm enough in the saddle to begin a work of religious reformation, and the first reward of his zeal was the finding of the book of the law. Josiah, like the rest of us, gained fuller knowledge of God's will in the act of trying to do it so far as he knew it. 'Light is sown for the upright.'

I. We have, first, the discovery of the law. The important and complicated critical questions raised by the narrative cannot be discussed here, nor do they affect the broad lines of teaching in the incident. Nothing is more truthful-like than the statement that, in course of the repairs of the Temple, the book should be found,—probably in the holiest place, to which the high priest would have exclusive access. How it came to have been lost is a more puzzling question; but if we recall that seventy-five years had passed since Hezekiah, and that these were almost entirely years of apostasy and of tumult, we shall not wonder that it was so. Unvalued things easily slip out of sight, and if the preservation of Scripture depended on the estimation which some of us have of it, it would have been lost long ago. But the fact of the loss suggests the wonder of the preservation. It would appear that this copy was the only one existing,—at all events, the only one known. It alone transmitted the law to later days, like some slender thread of water that finds its way through the sand and brings the river down to broad plains beyond. Think of the millions of copies now, and the one dusty, forgotten roll tossing unregarded in the dilapidated Temple, and be thankful for the Providence that has watched over the transmission. Let us take care, too, that the whole Scripture is not as much lost to us, though we have half a dozen Bibles each, as the roll was to Josiah and his men.

Hilkiah's announcement to Shaphan has a ring of wonder and of awe in it. It sounds as if he had not known that such a book was anywhere in the Temple. And it is noteworthy that not he, but Shaphan, is said to have read it. Perhaps he could not,—though, if he did not, how did he know what the book was? At all events, he and Shaphan seem to have felt the importance of the find, and to have consulted what was to be done. Observe how the latter goes cautiously to work, and at first only says that he has received 'a book.' He gives it no name, but leaves it to tell its own story,—which it was then, and is still, well able to do. Scripture is its own best credentials and witnesses whence it comes. Again Shaphan is the reader, as it was natural that a 'scribe' should be, and again the possibility is that Josiah could not read.

II. One can easily picture the scene while the reader's voice went steadily through the commandments, threatenings, and promises,—the deepening eagerness of the king, the gradual shaping out before his conscience of God's ideal for him and his people, and the gradual waking of the sense of sin in him, like a dormant serpent beginning to stir in the first spring sunshine.

The effect of God's law on the sinful heart is vividly pictured in Josiah's emotion. 'By the law is the knowledge of sin.' To many of us that law, in spite of our outward knowledge of it, is as completely absent from our consciousness as it had been from the most ignorant of Josiah's subjects; and if for once its searchlight were thrown into the hidden corners of our hearts and lives, it would show up in dreadful clearness the skulking foes that are stealing to assail us, and the foul things that have made good their lodgment in our hearts and lives. It always makes an epoch in a life when it is really brought to the standard of God's law; and it is well for us if, like Josiah, we rend our clothes, or rather 'our heart, and not our garments,' and take home the conviction, 'I have sinned against the Lord.'

The dread of punishment sprang up in the young king's heart, and though that emotion is not the highest motive for seeking the Lord, it is not an unworthy one, and is meant to lead on to nobler ones than itself. There is too much unwillingness, in many modern conceptions of Christ's gospel, to recognise the place which the apprehension of personal evil consequences from sin has in the initial stages of the process by which we are 'translated from the kingdom of darkness into that of God's dear Son.'

III. The message to Huldah is remarkable. The persons sent with it show its importance. The high priest, the royal secretary, and one of the king's personal attendants, who was, no doubt, in his confidence, and two other influential men, one of whom, Ahikam, is known as Jeremiah's staunch friend, would make some stir in 'the second quarter,' on their way to the modest house of the keeper of the wardrobe. The weight and number of the deputation did honour to the prophetess, as well as showed the king's anxiety as to the matter in hand. Jeremiah and Zephaniah were both living at this time, and we do not know why Huldah was preferred. Perhaps she was more accessible. But conjecture is idle. Enough that she was recognised as having, and declared herself to have, direct authoritative communications from God.

For what did Josiah need to inquire of the Lord 'concerning the words of this book'? They were plain enough. Did he hope to have their sternness somewhat mollified by the words of a prophetess who might be more amenable to entreaties or personal considerations than the unalterable page was? Evidently he recognised Huldah as speaking with divine authority, and he might have known that two depositories of God's voice could not contradict each other. But possibly his embassy simply reflected his extreme perturbation and alarm, and like many another man when God's law startles him into consciousness of sin, he betook himself to one who was supposed to be in God's counsels, half hoping for a mitigated sentence, and half uncertain of what he really wished. He confusedly groped for some support or guide. But, confused as he was, his message to the prophetess implied repentance, eager desire to know what to do, and humble docility. If dread of evil consequences leads us to such a temper, we shall hear, as Josiah did, answers of peace as authoritative and divine as were the threatenings that brought us to our senses and our knees.

IV. The answer which Josiah received falls into two parts, the former of which confirms the threatenings of evil to Jerusalem, while the latter casts a gleam athwart the thundercloud, and promises Josiah escape from the national calamities. Observe the difference in the designation given him in the two parts. When the threatenings are confirmed, his individuality is, as it were, sunk; for that part of the message applies to any and every member of the nation, and therefore he is simply called 'the man that sent you.' Any other man would have received the same answer. But when his own fate is to be disclosed, then he is 'the king of Judah, who sent you,' and is described by the official position which set him apart from his subjects.

Huldah has but to confirm the dread predictions of evil which the roll had contained. What else can a faithful messenger of God do than reiterate its threatenings? Vainly do men seek to induce the living prophet to soften down God's own warnings. Foolishly do they think that the messenger or the messenger's Sender has any 'pleasure in the death of the wicked'; and as foolishly do they take the message to be unkind, for surely to warn that destruction waits the evildoer is gracious. The signal-man who waves the red flag to stop the train rushing to ruin is a friend. Huldah was serving Judah best by plain reiteration of the 'words of the book.'

But the second half of her message told that in wrath God remembered mercy. And that is for ever true. His thunderbolts do not strike indiscriminately, even when they smite a nation. Judah's corruption had gone too far for recovery, and the carcase called for the gathering together of the vultures, but Josiah's penitence was not in vain. 'I have heard thee' is always said to the true penitent, and even if he is involved in widespread retribution, its strokes become different to him. Josiah was assured that the evil should not come in his days. But Huldah's promise seems contradicted by the circumstances of his death. It was a strange kind of being gathered to his grave in peace when he fell on the fatal field of Megiddo, and 'his servants carried him in a chariot dead, . . . and buried him in his own sepulchre' (2 Kings xxiii. 30). But the promise is fulfilled in its real meaning by the fact that the threatenings which he was inquiring about did not fall on Judah in his time, and so far as these were concerned, he *did* come to his grave in peace.

THE END

'And it came to pass in the ninth year of his reign, in the tenth month, in the tenth day of the month, that Nebuchadnezzar king of Babylon came, he, and all his host, against Jerusalem, and pitched against it; and they built forts against it round about. 2. And the city was besieged unto the eleventh year of king Zedekiah. 3. And on the ninth day of the fourth month the famine prevailed in the city, and there was no bread for the people of the land. 4. And the city was broken up, and all the men of war fled by night by the way of the gate, between two walls, which is by the king's garden; (now the Chaldees were against the city round about;) and the king went the way toward the plain. 5. And the army of the Chaldees pursued after the king, and overtook him in the plains of Jericho: and

THE END

'all his army were scattered from him. 6. So they took the king, and brought him up to the king of Babylon to Riblah; and they gave judgment upon him. 7. And they slew the sons of Zedekiah before his eyes, and put out the eyes of Zedekiah, and bound him with fetters of brass, and carried him to Babylon. 8. And in the fifth month, on the seventh day of the month, which is the nineteenth year of king Nebuchadnezzar king of Babylon, came Nebuzar-adan, captain of the guard, a servant of the king of Babylon, unto Jerusalem: 9. And he burnt the house of the Lord, and the king's house, and all the houses of Jerusalem, and every great man's house burnt he with fire. 10. And all the army of the Chaldees, that were with the captain of the guard, brake down the walls of Jerusalem round about. 11. Now the rest of the people that were left in the city, and the fugitives that fell away to the king of Babylon, with the remnant of the multitude, did Nebuzar-adan, the captain of the guard, carry away. 12. But the captain of the guard left of the poor of the land to be vine-dressers and husbandmen.'—2 KINGS xxv. 1-12.

EIGHTEEN months of long-drawn-out misery and daily increasing famine preceded the fall of the doomed city. The siege was a blockade. No assaults by the enemy, nor sorties by the inhabitants, are narrated, but the former grimly and watchfully drew their net closer, and the latter sat still in their despair. The passionless tone of the narrative here is very remarkable. Not a word escapes the writer to show his feelings, though he is telling his country's fall. We must turn to Lamentations for sighs and groans. There we have the emotions of devout hearts; here we have the calm record of God's judgment. It is all one long sentence, for in the Hebrew each verse begins with 'and,' clause heaped on clause, as if each were a footstep of the destroying angel in his slow, irresistible march.

The narrative falls into two principal parts—the fate of the king and that of the city. It is unnecessary to dwell on the details. The confusion of counsels, the party strife, the fierce hatred of God's prophet, the agony of famine, are all suppressed here, but painted with terrible vividness in the Book of Jeremiah. At last the fatal day came. On the north side a breach was made in the wall, and through it the fierce besiegers poured—the 'princes of the king of Babylon,' with their idolatrous and barbarous names, 'came in, and sat in the middle gate.' It was night. The sudden appearance of the conquerors in the heart of the city shot panic into the feeble king and his 'men of war' who had never struck one blow for deliverance; and they hurried under cover of darkness, and hidden between two walls, down the ravine to the king's garden, once the scene of pleasure, but waste now, and thence, as best they could, round or over Olivet to the road to Jericho. The king's flight by night had been foretold by Ezekiel far away in captivity (Ezek. xii. 12); and the same prophet received on that very day a divine message announcing the fall of the city, and bidding him 'write thee the name of the day, even of this selfsame day,' as that on which the king of Babylon 'drew close unto Jerusalem' (Ezek. xxiv. 1 *et seq.*).

Down the rocky road went the flying host, with 'their shaftless, broken bows,' closely followed by the avenging foe with 'red pursuing spear.' Where Israel had first set foot on its inheritance, the last king of David's line was captured and his monarchy shattered. The scene of the first victory, when Jericho fell before unarmed men trusting in God, was the scene of the last defeat. The spot where the covenant was renewed, and the reproach of Israel rolled away, was the spot where the broken covenant was finally avenged and abrogated. The end came back to the beginning, and the cradle was the coffin.

Away up to Riblah, in the far north, under the shadow of Lebanon, the captive was dragged to meet the conqueror. The name of each is a profession of belief. The one means 'Jehovah is righteousness'; the other, 'Nebo, protect the crown.' The idol seemed to have overcome, but the defeat of the unbelieving confessor of the true God at the hands of the idolater is really the victory of the righteousness which the name celebrated and the bearer of the name insulted. His murdered sons were the last sight which he saw before he was blinded, according to the ferocious practice of the East. It was ingenuity of cruelty to let him see for so long, and then to give him that as the last thing seen, and therefore often remembered. Note how the enigma of Ezekiel's prophecy (Ezek. xii. 13) and its apparent contradiction of Jeremiah's (Jer. xxxii. 4; xxxiv. 3) are reconciled, and learn how easily the fact, when it comes, clears the riddles of prophecy, and how easily, probably, the whole facts, if we knew them, would clear the difficulties of Scripture history. The blinded king was harmless, but according to Jewish tradition, was set to work in a mill (though that is probably only an application of Samson's story), and according to Jeremiah (Jer. lii. 11), was kept in prison till his death. So ended the monarchy of Judah.

The fate of the city was not settled for a month, during which, no doubt, there was much consultation at Riblah whether to garrison or destroy it. The king of Babylon did not go in person, but despatched a force commanded by a high officer, to burn palace, Temple, the more important houses (the poorer people would probably be lodged in huts not worth burning), and to raze the fortifications. In accordance with the practice of the great Eastern despotisms, deportation followed victory—a clever though cruel device for securing conquests. But some were left behind; for the land, if deserted, would have fallen out of cultivation, and been profitless to Babylon. The bulk of the people of Jerusalem, the fugitives who had joined the invaders during the siege, and the mass of the general population, were carried off, in such a long string of misery as we may still see on the monuments, and a handful left behind, too poor to plot, and stirred to diligence by necessity. So ended the possession by Israel of its promised inheritance.

Now this fall of Jerusalem is like an object-lesson to teach everlasting truth as to the retributive providence of God. What does it say?

It declares plainly what brings down God's judgments. The terms on which Israel prospered and held its land were obedience to God's law. We cannot directly apply the principles of God's government of it to modern nations. The present analogue of Israel is the Church, not the nation. But when all deductions have been made, it is still true that a nation's religious attitude is a most potent factor in its prosperous development. It is not accidental that, on the whole, stagnant Europe and America are Roman Catholic, and the progressive parts Protestant. Nor was it causes independent of religion that scattered a decaying Christianity in the lands of the Eastern Church before the onslaught of wild Arabs, who, at all events, did believe in Allah. So there are abundant lessons for politics and sociology ir the story of Jerusalem's fall.

But these lessons have direct application to the individual and to the Christian Church. All departure from God is ruin. We slay ourselves by forsaking Him, and every sinner is a suicide. We live under a moral government, and in a system of things so knit together as that even here every transgression receives its just recompense—if not visibly and palpably in outward circumstances, yet really and punctually in effects on mind and heart, which are more solemn and awful. 'Behold the righteous shall be recompensed in the earth: much more the wicked and the sinner.' Sin and sorrow are root and fruit.

Especially does that crash of Jerusalem's fall thunder the lesson to all churches that their life and prosperity are inseparably connected with faithful obedience and turning away from all worldliness, which is idolatry. They stand in the place that was made empty by Israel's later fall. Our very privileges call us to beware. 'Because of unbelief they were broken off, and thou standest by faith.' That great seven-branched candlestick was removed out of its place, and all that is left of it is its sculptured image among the spoils on the triumphal arch to its captor. Other lesser candlesticks have been removed from their places, and Turkish oppression brings night where Sardis and Laodicea once gave a feeble light. The warning is needed to-day; for worldliness is rampant in the Church. 'If God spared not the natural branches, take heed lest He also spare not thee.' The fall of Jerusalem is not merely a tragic story from the past. It is a revelation, for the present, of the everlasting truth, that the professing people of God deserve and receive the sorest chastisement, if they turn again to folly.

Further, we learn the method of present retribution. Nebuchadnezzar knew nothing of the purposes which he fulfilled. 'He meaneth not so, neither doth his heart think so.' He was but the 'axe' with which God hewed. Therefore, though he was God's tool, he was also responsible, and would be punished even for performing God's 'whole work upon Jerusalem,' because of 'the glory of his high looks.' The retribution of disobedience, so far as that retribution is outward, needs no 'miracle.' The ordinary operations of Providence amply suffice to bring it. If God wills to sting, He will 'hiss for the fly,' and it will come. The ferocity and ambition of a grim and bloody despot, impelled by vainglory and lust of cruel conquest, do God's work, and yet the doing is sin. The world is full of God's instruments, and He sends punishments by the ordinary play of motives and circumstances, which we best understand when we see behind all His mighty hand and sovereign will. The short-sighted view of history says 'Nebuchadnezzar captured Jerusalem B.C. so and so,' and then discourses about the tendencies of which Babylonia was exponent and creature. The deeper view says, God smote the disobedient city, as He had said, and Nebuchadnezzar was 'the rod of His anger.'

Again, we learn the Divine reluctance to smite. More than four hundred years had passed since Solomon began idolatry, and steadily, through all that time, a stream of prophecy of varying force and width had flowed, while smaller disasters had confirmed the prophets' voices. 'Rising up early and sending' his servants, God had been in earnest in seeking to save Israel from itself. Men said then, 'Where is the promise of His coming?' and mocked His warnings and would none of His reproof; but at last the hour struck and the crash came. 'As a dream when one awaketh; so, O Lord! when Thou awakest, Thou shalt despise their image.' His judgment seems to slumber, but its eyes are open, and it remains inactive, that His long-suffering may have free scope. As long as His gaze can discern the possibility of repentance, He will not strike; and when that is hopeless, He will not delay. The explanation of the marvellous tolerance of evil which sometimes tries faith and always evokes wonder, lies in the great words, which might well be written over the chair of every teacher of history: 'The Lord is not slack concerning His promise, as some men count slackness; but is long-suffering to us-ward.' Alas, that that divine patience should ever be twisted into the ground of indurated disobedience! 'Because sentence against an evil work is not executed speedily, therefore the heart of the sons of men is fully set in them to do evil.'

God's reluctance to punish is no reason for doubting that He will. Judgment is His 'strange work,' less congenial, if we may so paraphrase that strong word of the prophet's, than pure mercy, but it will be done nevertheless. The tears over Jerusalem that witnessed Christ's sorrow did not blind the eyes like a flame of fire, nor stay the outstretched hand of the Judge, when the time of her final fall came. The longer the delay, the worse the ruin. The more protracted the respite and the fuller it has been of entreaties to return, the more terrible the punishment. 'Behold, therefore, the goodness and severity of God: towards them which fell, severity; but toward thee, goodness, if thou continue in His goodness: otherwise thou also shalt be cut off.'

THE FIRST BOOK OF CHRONICLES

THE KING'S POTTERS

'There they dwelt with the king for his work.'—1 CHRON. iv. 23.

IN these dry lists of names which abound in Chronicles, we now and then come across points of interest, oases in the desert, which need but to be pondered sympathetically to yield interesting suggestions. Here for example, buried in a dreary genealogical table, is a little touch which repays meditating on. Among the members of the tribe of Judah were a hereditary caste of potters who lived in 'Netaim and Gederah,' if we adhere to the Revised Version's text, or 'among plantations and hedges' if we prefer the margin. But they are also described as dwelling 'with the king.' That can only mean on the royal estates, for the king himself resided in Jerusalem. He, however, held large domains in the territory of Judah, on some of which these ceramic artists were settled down and followed their calling. They were kept on the royal estates and kept in comfort, not needing to till, but fed and cared for, that they might be free to mould, out of common clay, forms of beauty and 'vessels meet for the master's use.' Surely we may read into the brief statement of the text a meaning of which the writer of it never dreamt, and see in the description of these forgotten artisans, a symbol of our Christian relations to our Lord and of our life's work.

I. We, too, dwell with the King.

The Davidic king was in Jerusalem, and the potters were 'among plantations and hedges,' yet in a real sense they 'dwelt with the king,' though some of them might never have seen his face or trod the streets of the sacred city. Perhaps now and then he came to visit them on his outlying domains, but they were always parts of his household. And have we, Christ's servants, not His gracious parting word: 'I am with you always'? True, we are not beside Him in the great city, but He is beside us in His outlying domains, and we may be with Him in His glory, if while we still outwardly live among the 'plantations and hedges' of this life, we dwell in spirit, by faith and aspiration, with our risen and ascended Lord. If we so 'dwell with the King,' He will dwell with us, and fill our humble abode with the radiance of His presence, 'making that place of His feet glorious.' That He should be with us is supreme condescension, that we should be with Him is the perfection of exaltation. How low He stoops, how high we can rise! The vigour of our Christian life largely depends on our keeping vivid the consciousness of our communion with Jesus and the sense of His real presence with us. How life's burdens would be lightened if we faced them all in the strength of the felt nearness of our Lord! How impossible it would be that we should ever feel the dreary sense of solitude, if we felt that unseen, but most real, Presence wrapping us round! It is only when our faith in it has fallen asleep that any earthly good allures, or any earthly evil frightens us. To be sure, in our thrilling consciousness, that we dwell with Jesus is an impenetrable cuirass that blunts the points of all arrows and keeps the breast that wears it unwounded in the fray. The world has no voices which can make themselves heard above that low sovereign whisper: 'I am with you always, even to the end of the world'—and after the end has come, then we shall be with Him.

But we find in this notice a hint that leads us in yet another direction. They 'dwelt with the king' in the sense that they were housed and cared for on his lands. And in like manner, the true conception of the Christian life is that each of us is 'a sojourner with Thee,' set down on Christ's domains, and looked after by Him in regard to provision for outward wants. We have nothing in property, but all is His and held by His gift and to be used for Him. The slave owns nothing. The patch of ground which he cultivates for his food and what grows on it, are his master's. These workmen were not slaves, but they were not owners either. And we hold nothing as our own, if we are true to the terms on which it is given us to hold.

So if we rightly appreciate our position as dwelling on the King's lands, our delusion of possession will vanish, and we shall feel more keenly the pressure of responsibility while we feel less keenly the grip of anxiety. We are for the time being entrusted with a tiny piece of the royal estates. Let us not strut about as if we were owners, nor be for ever afraid that we shall not have enough for our needs. One sometimes comes on a model village close to the gates of some ducal palace, and notes how the lordly owner's honour prompts its being kept up to a high standard of comfort and beauty. We may be sure that the potters were well lodged and looked after, and that care for their personal wants was shifted from their shoulders to the king's. So should ours be. He will not leave His servants to starve. They should not dishonour Him and disturb themselves by worries and cares that would be reasonable only if they had no Provider. He has said, 'All things are given to Me of My Father,' and He gives us all that God has given Him.

II. We dwell with the King for His work.

The king's potters had not to till the land nor do any work but to mould clay into vessels for use and beauty. For that purpose they had their huts and bits of ground assigned them. So with us, Christ has a purpose in His provision for us. We are set down on His domains, and we enjoy His presence and providing in order that, set free from carking cares and low ends, we may, with free and joyous hearts, yield ourselves to His joyful service. The law of our life should be that we please not ourselves, nor consult our own will in choosing our tasks, nor seek our own profit or gratification in doing them, but ever ask of Him: 'Lord, what wilt Thou have me to do?' and when the answer comes, as come it will to all who ask with real desire to learn and with real inclination to do His will, that we 'make haste and delay not, but make haste to keep His commandments.' The spirit which should animate our active lives is plainly enough taught us in that little word, they 'dwelt with the king for his work.'

Nor are we to forget that, in a very profound sense, dwelling with the King must go before doing His work. Unless we are living continually under the operation of the stimulus of communion with Jesus, we shall have neither quickness of ear to know what He wishes us to do, nor any resolute concentration of ourselves on our Christ-appointed tasks. The spring of all noble living is communion with noble ideals, and fellowship with Jesus sets men agoing, as nothing else will, in practical lives of obedience to Jesus. Time given to silent, retired meditation on that sweet, sacred bond that knits the believing soul to the redeeming Lord is not lost with reference to active work for Jesus. The meditative and the practical life are not antagonistic, but complementary. Mary and Martha are sisters, though sometimes they differ, and foolish people try to set them against each other.

But we must beware of a common misconception of what the King's work is. The royal potters did not make only things of beauty, but very common vessels designed for common and ignoble uses. There were vessels of dishonour dried in their kilns as well as vessels 'meet for the master's use.' There is a usual and lamentable narrowing of the term 'Christian work,' to certain conventional forms of service, which has done and is doing an immense amount of harm. The King's work is far wider in scope than teaching in Sunday-schools, or visiting the sick, or any similar acts that are usually labelled with the name. It covers all the common duties of life. A shallow religion tickets some selected items with the name; a robuster, truer conception extends the designation to everything. It is not only when we are definitely trying to bring others into touch with Jesus that we are doing Him service, but we may be equally serving Him in everything. The difference between the king's work and the poor potters' own lay not so much in the nature as in the motive of it, and whatever we do for Christ's sake and with a view to His will is work that He owns, while a regard to self in our motive or in our end decisively strikes any service tainted by it out of the category.

We are to hallow all our deeds by drawing the

motive for them from the King and by laying the fruits of them at His feet. Thus, and only thus, will the most 'secular' actions be sanctified and the narrowest life be widened to contain a present Christ.

There are subsidiary motives which may legitimately blend with the supreme one. The potters would be stimulated to work hard and with their utmost skill when they thought of how well they were paid in house and store for their work. We have ample reasons for dedicating our whole selves to Jesus when we think of His gift of Himself to us, of His wages beforehand, of His joyful presence with His eye ever on us, marking our purity of motive and our diligence.

There is a final thought that may well stimulate us to put all our skill and effort into our work. The potters' work went to Jerusalem. It was for the king. What can be too good for him? He will see it, therefore let us put our best into it. And we shall see it too, when we too enter 'the city of the great King.' Jars that perhaps were wrought by these very workmen of whom we have been speaking turn up to-day in the excavations in Palestine. So much has perished and they remain, speaking symbols of the solemn truth that nothing human ever dies. Our 'works do follow us.' Let us so live that these may be 'found unto praise and honour and glory' at the appearing of 'the King.'

DAVID'S CHORISTERS

'They stood in their office, according to their order.'
1 CHRON. vi. 32 (R.V. margin).

THIS brief note is buried in the catalogue of the singers appointed by David for 'the service of song in the house of the Lord.' The waves of their choral praise have long ages since ceased to eddy round the 'tabernacle of the tent of meeting,' and all that is left of their melodious companies is a dry list of names, in spite of which the dead owners of them are nameless. But the chronicler's description of them may carry some lessons for us, for is not the Church of Christ a choir, chosen to 'shew forth the praises of Him who has called us out of darkness into His marvellous light'? We take a permissible liberty with this fragment, when we use it to point lessons that may help that great band of choristers who are charged with the office of making the name of Jesus ring through the world. Now, in making such a use of the text, we may linger on each important word in it and find each fruitful in suggestions which we shall be the better for expanding in our own meditations.

We pause on the first word, which is rendered in the Authorised and Revised Versions 'waited,' and in the margin of the latter 'stood.' The former rendering brings into prominence the mental attitude with which the singers held themselves ready to take their turns in the service, the latter points rather to their bodily attitude as they fulfilled their office. We get a picture of the ranked files gathered round their three leaders, Heman, Asaph, and Ethan. These three names are familiar to us from the Psalter, but how all the ranks behind them have fallen dim to us, and how their song has floated into inaudible distance! They 'stood,' a melodious multitude, girt and attent on their song, or waiting their turn to fill the else silent air with the high praises of Jehovah, and glad when it came to their turn to open their lips in full-throated melody.

Now may we not catch the spirit of that long

vanished chorus, and find in the two possible renderings of this word a twofold example, the faithful following of which would put new vigour into our service? We are called to a loftier office, and have heavenly harmonies entrusted to us to be made vocal by our lips, compared with which theirs were poor. 'They waited on' their office, and shall not we, in a higher fashion, wait on our ministry, and suffer no inferior claims to block our way or hamper our preparedness to discharge it? To let ourselves be entangled with 'the affairs of this life,' or to 'drowse in idle cell,' sleepily letting summonses that should wake us to work sound unheeded and almost unheard, is flagrant despite done to our high vocation as Christians. 'They also serve who only stand and wait,' but not if in their waiting their eyes are straying everywhere but to their Master's pointing hand or directing eye. The world is full of voices calling Christ's folk to help; but what a host of so-called Christians fail to hear these piteous and despairing cries, because the noise of their own whims, fancies, and self-centred desires keeps buzzing in their ears. A constant accompaniment of deafness is constant noises in the head; and the Christians who are hardest of hearing when Christ calls are generally afflicted with noises which are probably the cause, and not merely an accompaniment, of their deafness. For indeed it demands no little detachment of spirit from self and sense, from the world and its clamant suitors, if a Christian soul is to be ready to mark the first signal of the great Conductor's baton, and to answer the lightest whisper, intrusting it with a task for Him, with its self-consecrating 'Here am I. Send me.'

It used to be said that they who watched for providences never wanted providences to watch for; it is equally true that they who are on the watch for opportunities for service never fail to find them, and that ears pricked to 'hear what God the Lord shall speak,' summoning to work for Him, will not listen in vain. Paul saw in a vision 'a *man* of Macedonia' begging for his help, and 'straightway' he concluded that '*God* had called' him to preach in Europe. Happy are these Christian workers who hear God's voice speaking through men's needs, and recognise a divine imperative in human cries!

May we not see in the attitude of David's choristers as they sang, hints for our own discharge of the tasks of our Christian service? There was a curse of old on him who did the work of the Lord 'negligently,' and its weight falls still on workers and work. For who can measure the harm done to the Christian life of the negligent worker, and who can expect any blessing to come either to him or to others from such half-hearted seeming service? The devil's kingdom is not to be cast down nor Christ's to be builded up by workers who put less than their whole selves, the entire weight of their bodies, into their toil. A pavior on the street brings down his rammer at every stroke with an accompanying exclamation expressing effort, and there is no place in Christ's service for dainty people who will not sweat at their task, and are in mortal fear of over-work. Strenuousness, the gathering together of all our powers, are implied in the attitude of Heman and his band as they 'stood' in their office. Idle revellers might loll on their rose-strewn couches as they 'sing idle songs to the sound of the viol and devise for themselves instruments of music, like David,' but the austerer choir of the Temple despised ease, and stood ready for service and in the best bodily posture for song.

The second important word of the text brings other thoughts no less valuable and rich in practical counsel. The singers in the Temple stood in their 'office,' which was song. Their special work was praise. And that is the highest task of the Church. As a matter of fact, every period of quickened earnestness in the Church's life has been a period marked by a great outburst of Christian song. All intense emotion seeks expression in poetry, and music is the natural speech of a vivid faith. Luther chanted the Marseillaise of the Reformation, 'A safe stronghold our God is still,' and many another sweet strain blended strangely with the fiery and sometimes savage words from his lips. The Scottish Reformation, grim in some of its features as it was, had yet its 'Gude and Godly Ballads.' At the birth of Methodism, as round the cradle at Bethlehem, hovered as it were angel voices singing, 'Glory to God in the highest.' A flock of singing birds let loose attends every revival of Christian life.

The Church's praise is the noblest expression of the Church's life. Its hymns go deeper than its creeds, touch hearts more to the quick, minister to the faith which they enshrine, and often draw others to see the preciousness of the Christ whom they celebrate. How little we should have known of Old Testament religion, notwithstanding law and prophets, if the Psalter had perished!

And it is true, in a very deep sense, that we shall do more for Christ and men by voicing our own deep thankfulness for His great gifts and speaking simply our valuation of, and our thankfulness for, what we draw from Him than by any other form of so-called Christian work. We can offend none by saying: 'We have found the Messias,' and are adoringly glad that we have. The most effectual way of moving other souls to participate in our joy is to let our joy speak. 'If you wish me to weep,' your own tears must not be held back, and if you wish others to know the preciousness of Christ, you must ring out His name with fervour of emotion and the triumphant confidence. We are the 'secretaries of God's praise,' as George Herbert has it, for we have possession of His greatest gift, and have learned to know Him in loftier fashion than Heman's choristers dreamed of, having seen 'the glory of God in the face of Jesus Christ,' and tasted the sweetness of redeeming love. The Apocalyptic seer sets forth a great truth when he tells us that he first heard a new song from the lips of the representatives of the Church, who could sing, 'Thou wast slain and didst redeem us to God with Thy blood,' and then heard their adoration echoed from ' many angels round about the throne,' and finally heard the song reverberated from every created thing in heaven and earth, in the sea and all deep places. A praising Church has experiences of its own which angels cannot share, and it sets in motion the great sea of praise whose surges break in music and roll from every side of the universe in melodious thunder to the great white throne. Without our song even angel voices would lack somewhat.

> ' God said, " A praise is in Mine ear;
> There is no doubt in it, no fear:
> Clearer loves sound other ways:
> I miss My little human praise."'

The song of the redeemed has in it a minor strain that gives a sweetness far more poignant than belongs to those who cannot say: 'Out of the depths I cried unto Thee.' 'The sweetest songs are those which tell of saddest thought,' and recount experiences of conquered sin and life springing from death.

But it is also true that no kind of Christian service will be effectual, if it lacks the element of grateful praise as its motive and mainspring. Perhaps there would be fewer complaints of toiling all night and wearily hauling in empty nets, if the nets were oftener let down not only 'at Thy word,' but with glad remembrance of the fishermen's debt to Jesus, and in the spirit of praise. When all our work is a sacrifice of praise, it is pleasing to God and profitable to ourselves and to others. If we would oftener bethink ourselves, and herald every deed with a silent dedication of it and of ourselves to Him who died for us, we should less often have to complain that we have sowed much and brought back little. A pinch of incense cast into the common domestic fire makes its flame sacrificial and fragrant.

The last important word of the text is also fertile in hints for us. The singers stood in their office 'according to their order.' That last expression may either refer to rotation of service or to distribution of parts in the chorus. They did not sing in unison, grand as the effect of such a song from a multitude sometimes is, but they had their several parts. The harmonious complexity of a great chorus is the ideal for the Church. Paul puts the same thought in a sterner metaphor when he tells the Colossian Christians that he joys 'beholding your order and the steadfastness of your faith in Christ,' where he is evidently thinking of the Roman legion with its rigid discipline and its solid, irresistible, ranked weight. Division of function and consequent concordant action of different parts is the lesson taught by both metaphors, and by the many modern examples of the immense results gained in machinery that almost simulates vital action, and by organisations for great purposes in which men combine. The Church should be the highest example of such combination, for it is the shrine of the noblest life, even the life of its indwelling Lord. Every member of it should have and know his place. Every Christian should know his part in the great chorus, for he has a part, even if it is only that of tinkling the triangle in the orchestra or beating a drum. That division of function and concordance of action apply to all forms of the Church's action, and are enforced most chiefly by the great Apostolic metaphor of the body and its members. Paul did not delight in 'uniformity.' Inferiors calling themselves his successors have often aimed at enforcing it, but nature has been too strong for them, and the hedge will grow its own way in spite of pedants' shears. 'If the whole body were an eye, where the hearing?' The monotony of a church in which uniformity was the ideal would be intolerable. The chorus has its parts, and the soprano cannot say to the bass, 'I have no need of you,' nor the bass to the tenor, 'I have no need of thee.'

So let us see that we find our own place, and see that we fill it, singing our own part lustily, and not being either confused or made dumb because another has other notes to sing than are written on our score. Let us recognise unity made more melodious by diversity, the importance of the humblest, and 'having gifts differing according to the grace given unto us let us wait on our ministry,' and stand in our office according to our order.

DRILL AND ENTHUSIASM

'[Men that] could keep rank, they were not of double heart.'—1 CHRON. xii. 33.

THESE words come from the muster-roll of the hastily raised army that brought David up to Hebron and made him King. The catalogue abounds in brief characterisations of the qualities of each tribe's contingent. For example, Issachar had 'understanding of the times.' Our text is spoken of the warriors of Zebulon, who had left their hills and their flocks in the far north, and poured down from their seats by the blue waters of Tiberias to gather round their king. They were not only like their brethren expert in war and fully equipped, but they had some measure of discipline too, a rare thing in the days when there were no standing armies. They 'could keep rank,' could march together, had been drilled to some unanimity of step and action, could work and fight together, were an army, not a crowd, and not only so, but also 'they were not of double heart.' Each man, and the whole body, had a brave single resolve; they had one spirit animating the whole, and that was to make David king, an enthusiastic loyalty which made them brave, and a discipline which kept the courage from running to waste.

I take, then, this text as bringing before us two very important characteristics which ought to be found in every Christian church, and without which no real prosperity and growth is possible. These two may be put very briefly: organisation and enthusiastic devotion. These are both important, but in very different degrees. Organisation without valour is in a worse plight than valour without organisation. The one is fundamental, the other secondary. The one is the true cause, so far as men are concerned, of victory, the other is but the instrument by which the cause works. There have been many victories won by undisciplined valour, but disciplined cowardice and apathy come to no good.

These two have been separated and made antagonistic, and churches are to be found which glory in the one, and others in the other. Some have gone in for order, and are like butterflies in a cabinet all ticketed and displayed in place, but a pin is run through their bodies and they are dead; and others have prided themselves on unfettered freedom, and been not an army, but a mob. The true relation, of course, is that life should shape and inform organisation, and organisation should preserve, manifest and obey life. There must be body to hold spirit, there must be spirit to keep body from rotting.

I. Organisation.

This is not the strong point of Nonconformist churches. We pride ourselves on our individualism, and that is all very well. We believe in direct access of each soul to Christ, that men must come to Him one by one, that religion is purely a personal matter, and the firmness with which we hold this tends to make us weak in combined action. It cannot be truthfully denied that both in the relations of our churches to one another, and in the internal organisation of these, we are and have been too loosely compacted, and have forgotten that two is more than one *plus* one, so that we are only helping to redress the balance a little when we insist upon the importance of organisation in our churches.

And first of all—remember the principles in subordination to which our organisation must be framed.

What are we united by? Common love and faith to Christ, or rather Christ Himself. 'One is your Master, even Christ, and all ye are brethren.' So there must be nothing in our organisation which is inconsistent with Christ's supreme place among us, and with our individual obedience to Him. There are to be no 'lords over God's heritage' in the Church of Christ. There are churches in which the temptation to be such affects the official chiefly, and there are others, with a different polity, in which it is chiefly a Diotrephes, who loves to have pre-eminence. Character, zeal, social station, even wealth will always confer a certain influence, and their possessors will be tempted to set up their own will or opinions as dominant in the Church. Such men are sinning against the very bond of Christian union. Organisation which is bought by investing one man with authority, is too dearly purchased at the cost of individual development on the individual's own lines. A row of clipped yew-trees is not an inspiring sight.

And yet again what are we organised for? Not merely for our own growth or spiritual advantage, but also, and more especially, for spreading faith in Christ and advancing His glory. All our organisation, then, is but an arrangement for doing our work, and if it hinders that, it is cumbrous and must be cut away or modified, at all hazards. Ecclesiastical martinets are still to be found, to whom drill is all-important, and who see no use in irregular valour, but they are a diminishing number, and they may be recommended to ponder the old wise saying: 'Where no oxen are, the crib is clean, but much increase is by the strength of the ox.' If the one aim is a 'clean crib,' the best way to secure that is to keep it empty; but if a harvest is the aim, there must be cultivation, and one must accept the consequences of having a strong team to plough. The end of drill is fighting. The parade-ground and its exercising is in order that a corps may be hurled against the enemy, or may stand unmoved, like a solid breakwater against a charge which it flings off in idle spray, and the end of the Church's organisation is that it may move *en masse*, without waste, against the enemy.

But a further guiding principle to shape Christian organisation is that of the Church as the body of Christ. That requires that there shall be work for every member. Christ has endowed His members with varying gifts, powers, opportunities, and has set them in diverse circumstances, that each may give his own contribution to the general stock of work. Our theory is that each man has his own proper gift from God, 'one after this manner, and another after that.' But what is our practice? Take any congregation of Christian people in any of our churches, and especially in the Free Churches of which I know most, and is there anything like this wide diversity of forms of service, to which each contributes? A handful of people do all the work, and the remainder are idlers. The same small section are in evidence always, and the rest are nowhere. There are but a few bits of coloured glass in a kaleidoscope, they take different patterns when the tube is turned, but they are always the same bits of glass.

There needs to be a far greater variety of forms of work for our people and more workers in the field. There are too few wheels for the quantity of water in the river, and, partly for that reason, the amount of water that runs waste over the sluice is deplorable. There is a danger in having too many spindles for the power available, but the danger in modern church organisation is exactly the other way.

Every one should have his own work. In all living creatures, differentiation of organs increases as the creature rises in the scale of being, from the simple sac which does everything up to the human body with a distinct function for every finger. It should not be possible for a lazy Christian to plead truly as his vindication that 'no man had hired' him. It should be the Church's business to find work for the unemployed.

The example in our text should enforce the necessity of united work. David's levies could keep rank. They did not let each man go at his own rate and by his own road, but kept together, shoulder to shoulder, with equal stride. They were content to co-operate and be each a part of a greater whole. That keeping rank is a difficult problem in all societies, where individual judgments, weaknesses, wills, and crotchets are at work, but it is apt to be especially difficult in Christian communities, where one may expect to find individual characteristics intensified, a luxuriant growth of personal peculiarities, an intense grip of partial aspects of the great truths and a corresponding dislike of other aspects of these, and of those whose favourite truths they are. One would do nothing to clip that growth, but still Christians who have not learned to subordinate themselves in and for united work are of little use to God or man. What does such united work require? Mainly the bridling of self, the curbing of one's own will, not insisting on forcing one's opinions on one's brother, not being careful of having one's place secured and one's honour asserted. Without such virtues no association of men could survive for a year. If the world managed its societies as the Church manages its unity, they would collapse quickly. Indeed it is a strong presumption in favour of Christianity that the Churches have not killed it long ago. Vanity, pride, self-importance, masterfulness, pettishness get full play among us. Diotrephes has many descendants to-day. A cotton mill, even if it were a co-operative one, could not work long without going into bankruptcy, if there were no more power of working together than some Christian congregations have. A watch would be a poor timekeeper, where every wheel tried to set the pace and be a mainspring, or sulked because the hands moved on the face in sight of all men, while it had to move round and fit into its brother wheel in the dark.

Subordination is required as well as co-operation. For if there be harmonious co-operation in varying offices, there must be degrees and ranks. The differences of power and gift make degrees, and in every society there will be leaders. Of course there is no commanding authority in the Churches. Its leaders are brethren, whose most imperative highest word is, 'We beseech you.'

Of course, too, these varieties and degrees do not mean real superiority or inferiority in the eye of God. From the highest point of view nothing is great or small, there is no higher or lower. The only measure is quality, the only gauge is motive. 'Small service is true service while it lasts.' He that receiveth a prophet in the name of a prophet, shall receive a prophet's reward. But yet there are, so far as our work here is concerned, degrees and orders, and we need a hearty and ungrudging recognition of superiority wherever we find it. If the 'brother of high degree' needs to be exhorted to beware of arrogance and imposing his own will on his fellows, the 'brother of low degree' needs not less to be exhorted to beware of letting envy and self-will hiss and snarl in his heart at those who are in higher positions than himself. If the chief of all needs to be reminded that in Christ's household pre-eminence means service, the lower no less needs to be reminded that in Christ's household service means pre-eminence.

So much, then, for organisation. It is perfectly reconcilable with democracy that is not mob-ocracy. In fact, democracy needs it most. If I may venture to speak to the members of the Free Churches, with which I am best acquainted, I would take upon myself to say that there is nothing which they need more than that they should show their polity to be capable of reconciling the freest development of the individual with the most efficient organisation of the community. The object is work for Christ, the bond of their fellowship is brotherly union with Christ. Many eyes are on them to-day, and the task is in their hands of showing that they can keep rank. The most perfect discipline in war in old times was found, not amongst the subjects of Eastern despots who were not free enough to learn to submit, but amongst the republics of Greece, where men were all on a level in the city, and fell into their places in the camp, because they loved liberty enough to know the worth of discipline, and so the slaves of Xerxes were scattered before the resistless onset of the phalanx of the free. The terrible legion which moved 'altogether when it moved at all,' and could be launched at the foe like one javelin of steel, had for its units free men and equals. There needs freedom for organisation. There needs organisation for freedom. Let us learn the lesson. 'God is not the author of confusion, but of order, in all churches of saints.'

II. Enthusiastic devotion.

These men came to bring David up to Hebron with one single purpose in their hearts. They had no sidelong glances to their own self-interest, they had no wavering loyalty, they had no trembling fears, so we may take their spirit as expressing generally the deepest requirements for prosperity in a church.

The foundation of all prosperity is a passion of personal attachment to Christ our King.

Christ is Christianity objective. Love to Christ is Christianity subjective. The whole stress of Christian character is laid on this. It is the mother of all grace and goodness, and in regard to the work of the Church, it is the ardour of a soul full of love to Jesus that conquers. The one thing in which all who have done much for Him have been alike is that single-hearted devotion.

But such love is the child of faith. It rests upon belief of truth, and is the response of man to God. Dwelling in the truth is the means of it. How our modern Christianity fails in this strong personal bond of familiar love!

Consider its effect on the individual.

It will give tenacity of purpose, will brace to strenuous effort, will subdue self, self-regard, self-importance, will subdue fear. It is the true anæsthetic. The soldier is unconscious of his wounds, while the glow of devotion is in his heart and the shout of the battle in his ears. It will give fertility of resource and patience.

Consider its effect on the community.

It will remove all difficulties in the way of discipline arising from vanity and self which can be subdued by no other means. That flame fuses all into one glowing mass like a stream that pours from the blast furnace. What a power a church would be which had this! It is itself victory. The men that go into battle with that one firm resolve, and care for nothing else, are sure to win. Think what one man can do who has resolved to sell his life dear!

Consider the worthlessness of discipline without this.

It is a poor mechanical accuracy. How easy to have too much machinery! How the French Revolution men swept the Austrian martinets before them! David was half-smothered in Saul's armour. On the other hand, this fervid flame needs control to make it last and work. Spirit and law are not incompatible. Valour may be disciplined, and the combination is irresistible.

And so here, till we exchange the close array of the battlefield for the open ranks of the festal procession on the Coronation day, and lay aside the helmet for the crown, the sword for the palm, the breastplate for the robe of peace, and stand for ever before the throne, in the peaceful ranks of 'the solemn troops and sweet societies' of the unwavering armies of the heavens who serve Him with a perfect heart, and burn unconsumed with the ardours of an immortal and ever brightening love, let us see to it that we too are **'men that can keep rank and are not of double heart.'**

DAVID'S PROHIBITED DESIRE AND PERMITTED SERVICE

'Then he called for Solomon his son, and charged him to build an house for the Lord God of Israel. 7. And David said to Solomon, My son, as for me, it was in my mind to build an house unto the name of the Lord my God: 8. But the word of the Lord came to me, saying, Thou hast shed blood abundantly, and hast made great wars: thou shalt not build an house unto My name, because thou hast shed much blood upon the earth in My sight. 9. Behold, a son shall be born to thee, who shall be a man of rest; and I will give him rest from all his enemies round about: for his name shall be Solomon, and I will give peace and quietness unto Israel in his days. 10. He shall build an house for My name; and he shall be My son, and I will be his Father; and I will establish the throne of his kingdom over Israel for ever. 11. Now, my son, the Lord be with thee; and prosper thou, and build the house of the Lord thy God as He hath said of thee. 12. Only the Lord give thee wisdom and understanding, and give thee charge concerning Israel, that thou mayest keep the law of the Lord thy God. 13. Then shalt thou prosper, if thou takest heed to fulfil the statutes and judgments which the Lord charged Moses with concerning Israel: be strong, and of good courage; dread not, nor be dismayed. 14. Now, behold, in my trouble I have prepared for the house of the Lord an hundred thousand talents of gold, and a thousand thousand talents of silver; and of brass and iron without weight; for it is in abundance: timber also and stone have I prepared and thou mayest add thereto. 15. Moreover, there are workmen with thee in abundance, hewers and workers of stone and timber, and all manner of cunning men for every manner of work. 16. Of the gold, the silver, and the brass, and the iron, there is no number. Arise, therefore, and be doing, and the Lord be with thee.'
—1 CHRON. xxii. 6-16.

THIS passage falls into three parts. In verses 6-10 the old king tells of the divine prohibition which checked his longing to build the Temple; in verses 11-13 he encourages his more fortunate successor, and points him to the only source of strength for his happy task; in verses 14-16 he enumerates the preparations which he had made, the possession of which laid stringent obligations on Solomon.

I. There is a tone of wistfulness in David's voice as he tells how his heart's desire had been prohibited. The account is substantially the same as we have in 2 Samuel vii. 4-16, but it adds as the reason for the prohibition David's warlike career. We may note the earnestness and the motive of the king's desire to build the Temple. 'It was in my heart'; that implies earnest longing and fixed purpose. He had brooded over the wish till it filled his mind, and was consolidated into a settled resolve. Many a musing, solitary moment had fed the fire before it burned its way out in the words addressed to Nathan. So should our whole souls be occupied with our parts in God's service, and so should our desires be strongly set towards carrying out what in solitary meditation we have felt borne in on us as our duty.

The moving spring of David's design is beautifully suggested in the simple words 'unto the name of the Lord my God.' David's religion was eminently a personal bond between him and God. We may almost say that he was the first to give utterance to that cry of the devout heart, 'My God,' and to translate the generalities of the name 'the God of Israel' into the individual appropriation expressed by the former designation. It occurs in many of the psalms attributed to him, and may fairly be regarded as a characteristic of his ardent and individualising devotion. The sense of a close, personal relation to God naturally prompted the impulse to build His house. We must claim our own portion in the universal blessings shrined in His name before we are moved to deeds of loving sacrifice. We must feel that Christ 'loved me, and gave Himself for me,' before we are melted into answering surrender.

The reason for the frustrating of David's desire, as here given, is his career as a warrior king. Not only was it incongruous that hands which had been reddened with blood should rear the Temple, but the fact that his reign had been largely occupied with fighting for the existence of the kingdom showed that the time for engaging in such a work, which would task the national resources, had not yet come. We may draw two valuable lessons from the prohibition. One is that it indicates the true character of the kingdom of God as a kingdom of peace, which is to be furthered, not by force, but in peace and gentleness. The other is that various epochs and men have different kinds of duties in relation to Christ's cause, some being called on to fight, and others to build, and that the one set of tasks may be as sacred and as necessary for the rearing of the Temple as the other. Militant epochs are not usually times for building. The men who have to do destructive work are not usually blessed with the opportunity or the power to carry out constructive work. Controversy has its sphere, but it is mostly preliminary to true 'edification.' In the broadest view all the activity of the Church on earth is militant, and we have to wait for the coming of the true 'Prince of peace' to build up the true Temple in the land of peace, whence all foes have been cast out for ever. To serve God in God's way, and to give up our cherished plans, is not easy; but David sets us an example of simple-hearted, cheerful acquiescence in a Providence that thwarted darling designs. There is often much self-will in what looks like enthusiastic perseverance in some form of service.

II. The charge to Solomon breathes no envy of his privilege, but earnest desire that he may be worthy of the honour which falls to him. Petitions and exhortations are closely blended in it, and, though the work which Solomon is called to do is of an external sort, the qualifications laid down for it are spiritual and moral. However 'secular' our work in connection with God's service may be, it will not be rightly done unless the highest motives are brought to bear on it, and it is performed as worship. The basis of all successful work is God's presence with us, so David prays for that to be granted to Solomon as the beginning of all his fitness for his task.

Next, David recalls to his son God's promise concerning him, that it may hearten him to undertake and to carry on the great work. A conviction that our service is appointed for us by God is essential for vigorous and successful Christian work. We must have, in some way or other, heard Him 'speak concerning us,' if we are to fling ourselves with energy into it.

The petitions in verse 12 seem to stretch beyond the necessities of the case, in so far as building the Temple is concerned. Wisdom and understanding, and a clear consciousness of the duty enjoined on him by God in reference to Israel, were surely more than that work required. But the qualifications for God's service, however the manner of service may be concerned with 'the outward business of the house of God,' are always these which David asked for Solomon. The highest result of true 'wisdom and understanding' given by God is keeping God's law; and keeping it is the one condition on which we shall obtain and retain that presence of God with us which David prayed for Solomon, and without which they labour in vain that build. A life conformed to God's will is the absolutely indispensable condition of all prosperity in direct Christian effort. The noblest exercise of our wisdom and understanding is to obey every word that we hear proceeding out of the mouth of God.

III. There is something very pathetic in the old king's enumeration of the treasures which, by the economies of a lifetime, he had amassed. The amount stated is enormous, and probably there is some clerical error in the numbers specified. Be that as it may, the sum was very large. It represented many an act of self-denial, many a resolute shearing off of superfluities and what might seem necessaries. It was the visible token of long years of fixed attention to one object. And that devotion was all the more noble because the result of it was never to be seen by the man who exercised it.

Therein David is but a very conspicuous example of a law which runs through all our work for God. None of us are privileged to perform completed tasks. 'One soweth and another reapeth.' We have to be content to do partial work, and to leave its completion to our successors. There is but one Builder of whom it can be said that His hands 'have laid the foundation of this house; His hands shall also finish it.' He who is the 'Alpha and Omega,' and He alone, begins and completes the work in which He has neither sharers nor predecessors nor successors. The rest of us do our little bit of the great work which lasts on through the ages, and, having inherited unfinished tasks, transmit them to those who come after us. It is privilege enough for any Christian to lay foundations on which coming days may build. We are like the workers on some great cathedral, which was begun long before the present generation of masons were born, and will not be finished until long after they have dropped trowel and mallet from their dead hands. Enough for us if we can lay one course of stones in that great structure. The greater our aims, the less share has each man in their attainment. But the division of labour is the multiplication of joy, and all who have shared in the toil will be united in the final triumph. It would be poor work that was capable of being begun and perfected in a lifetime. The labourer that dug and levelled the track and the engineer that drives the locomotive over it are partners. Solomon could not have built the Temple unless, through long, apparently idle, years, David had been patiently gathering together the wealth which he bequeathed. So, if our work is but preparatory for that of those who come after, let us not think it of slight importance, and let us be sure that all who have had any portion in the toil shall share in the victory, that 'he that soweth and he that reapeth may rejoice together.'

DAVID'S CHARGE TO SOLOMON

'And David assembled all the princes of Israel, the princes of the tribes, and the captains of the companies that ministered to the king by course, and the captains over the thousands, and captains over the hundreds, and the stewards over all the substance and possession of the king, and of his sons, with the officers, and with the mighty men, and with all the valiant men, unto Jerusalem. 2. Then David the king stood up upon his feet, and said, Hear me, my brethren, and my people: As for me, I had in mine heart to build an house of rest for the ark of the covenant of the Lord, and for the footstool of our God, and had made ready for the building: 3. But God said unto me, Thou shalt not build an house for My name, because thou hast been a man of war, and hast shed blood. 4. Howbeit the Lord God of Israel chose me before all the house of my father to be king over Israel for ever: for He hath chosen Judah to be the ruler; and of the house of Judah, the house of my father; and among the sons of my father He liked me to make me king over all Israel: 5. And of all my sons, (for the Lord hath given me many sons,) he hath chosen Solomon my son to sit upon the throne of the kingdom of the Lord over Israel. 6. And He said unto me, Solomon thy son, he shall build My house and My courts: for I have chosen him to be My son, and I will be his father. 7. Moreover I will establish his kingdom for ever, if he be constant to do My commandments and My judgments, as at this day. 8. Now therefore in the sight of all Israel the congregation of the Lord, and in the audience of our God, keep and seek for all the commandments of the Lord your God; that ye may possess this good land, and leave it for an inheritance for your children after you for ever. 9. And thou, Solomon my son, know thou the God of thy father, and serve Him with a perfect heart and with a willing mind: for the Lord searcheth all hearts, and understandeth all the imaginations of the thoughts: if thou seek Him, He will be found of thee; but if thou forsake Him, He will cast thee off for ever. 10. Take heed now; for the Lord hath chosen thee to build an house for the sanctuary: be strong, and do it.'—1 CHRON. xxviii. 1-10.

DAVID had established an elaborate organisation of royal officials, details of which occupy the preceding chapters and interrupt the course of the narrative. The passage picks up again the thread dropped at chapter xxiii. 1. The list of the members of the assembly called in verse 1 is interesting as showing how he tried to amalgamate the old with the new. The princes of Israel, the princes of the tribes, represented the primitive tribal organisation, and they receive precedence in virtue of the antiquity of their office. Then come successively David's immediate attendants, the military officials, the stewards of the royal estates, the 'officers' or eunuchs attached to the palace, and the faithful 'mighty men' who had fought by the king's side in the old days. It was an assembly of officials and soldiers whose adherence to Solomon it was all-important to secure, especially in regard to the project for building the Temple, which could not be carried through without their active support. The passage comprises only the beginning of the proceedings of this assembly of notables. The end is told in the next chapter; namely, that the Temple-building scheme was unanimously and enthusiastically adopted, and large donations given for it, and that Solomon's succession was accepted, and loyal submission offered by the assembly to him.

David's address to this gathering is directed to secure these two points. He begins by recalling his own intention to build the Temple and God's prohibition of it. The reason for that prohibition differs from that alleged by Nathan, but there is no contradiction between the two narratives, and the chronicler has already reported Nathan's words (chap. xvii. 3, etc.), so that the motive which is ascribed to many of the variations in this book, a priestly desire to exalt Temple and ritual, cannot have been at work here. Why should there not have been a divine communication to David as well as Nathan's message? That hands reddened with blood, even though it had been shed in justifiable war, were not fitted to build the Temple, was a thought so far in advance of

David's time, and flowing from so spiritual a conception of God, that it may well have been breathed into David's spirit by a divine voice. Sword in one hand and trowel in the other are incongruous, notwithstanding Nehemiah's example. The Temple of the God of peace cannot be built except by men of peace. That is true in the widest and highest application. Jesus builds the true Temple. Controversy and strife do not. And, on a lower level, the prohibition is for ever valid. Men do not atone for a doubtful past by building churches, founding colleges, endowing religious or charitable institutions.

The speech next declares emphatically that the throne belongs to David and his descendants by real 'divine right,' and that God's choice is Solomon, who is to inherit both the promises and obligations of the office, and, among the latter, that of building the Temple. The unspoken inference is that loyalty to Solomon would be obedience to Jehovah. The connection between the true heavenly King and His earthly representative is strongly expressed in the remarkable phrase: 'He hath chosen Solomon . . . to sit upon the throne of the kingdom of Jehovah,' which both consecrates and limits the rule of Solomon, making him but the viceroy of the true king of Israel. When Israel's kings remembered that, they flourished; when they forgot it, they destroyed their kingdom and themselves. The principle is as true to-day, and it applies to all forms of influence, authority, and gifts. They are God's, and we are but stewards.

The address to the assembly ends with the exhortation to these leaders to 'observe,' and not merely to observe, but also to 'seek out' God's commandments, and so to secure to the nation, whom they could guide, peaceful and prosperous days. It is not enough to do God's will as far as we know it; we must ever be endeavouring after clearer, deeper insight into it. Would that these words were written over the doors of all Senate and Parliament houses! What a different England we should see!

But Solomon was present as well as the notables, and it was well that, in their hearing, he should be reminded of his duties. David had previously in private taught him these, but this public 'charge' before the chief men of the kingdom bound them more solemnly upon him, and summoned a cloud of witnesses against him if he fell below the high ideal. It is pitched on a lofty key of spiritual religion, for it lays 'Know thou the God of thy fathers' as the foundation of everything. That knowledge is no mere intellectual apprehension, but, as always in Scripture, personal acquaintanceship with a Person, which involves communion with Him and love towards Him. For us, too, it is the seed of all strenuous discharge of our life's tasks, whether we are rulers or nobodies, and it means a much deeper experience than understanding or giving assent to a set of truths about God. We know one another when we summer and winter with each other, and not unless we love one another, and we know God on no other terms.

After such knowledge comes an outward life of service. Active obedience is the expression of inward communion, love, and trust. The spring that moves the hands on the dial is love, and, if the hands do not move, there is something wrong with the spring. Morality is the garment of religion; religion is the animating principle of morality. Faith without works is dead, and works without faith are dead too.

But even when we 'know God' we have to make

efforts to have our service correspond with our knowledge, for we have wayward hearts and obstinate wills, which need to be stimulated, sometimes to be coerced and forcibly diverted from unworthy objects. Therefore the exhortation to serve God 'with a perfect heart and with a willing mind' is always needful and often hard. Entire surrender and glad obedience are the Christian ideal, and continual effort to approximate to it will be ours in the degree in which we 'know God.' There is no worse slavery than that of the half-hearted Christian whose yoke is not padded with love. Reluctant obedience is disobedience in God's sight.

David solemnly reminds Solomon of those 'pure eyes and perfect judgment,' not to frighten, but to enforce the thought of the need for whole-hearted and glad service, and of the worthlessness of external acts of apparent worship which have not such behind them. What a deal of seeming wheat would turn out to be chaff if that winnowing fan which is in Christ's hand were applied to it! How small our biggest heaps would become!

The solemn conditions of the continuance of God's favour and of the fulfilment of His promises are next plainly stated. God responds to our state of heart and mind. We determine His bearing to us. The seeker finds. If we move away from Him, He moves away from us. That is not, thank God! all the truth, or what would become of any of us? But it is true, and in a very solemn sense God is to us what we make Him. 'With the pure Thou wilt show Thyself pure; and with the perverse Thou wilt show Thyself froward.'

The charge ends with recalling the high honour and office to which Jehovah had designated Solomon, and with exhortations to 'take heed' and to 'be strong, and do it.' It is well for a young man to begin life with a high ideal of what he is called to be and do. But many of us have that, and miserably fail to realise it, for want of these two characteristics, which the sight of such an ideal ought to stamp on us. If we are to fulfil God's purposes with us, and to be such tools as He can use for building His true Temple, we must exercise self-control and 'take heed to our ways,' and we must brace ourselves against opposition and crush down our own timidity. It seems to be commanding an impossibility to say to a weak creature like any one of us, 'Be strong,' but the impossible becomes a possibility when the exhortation takes the full Christian form: 'Be strong in the Lord, and in the power of His might.'

THE WAVES OF TIME

'The times that went over him.'—1 CHRON. xxix. 30.

THIS is a fragment from the chronicler's close of his life of King David. He is referring in it to other written authorities in which there are fuller particulars concerning his hero; and he says, 'the acts of David the King, first and last, behold they are written in the book of Samuel the seer . . . with all his reign and his might, and the times that went over him, and over all Israel, and over all the kingdoms of the countries.'

Now I have ventured to isolate these words, because they seem to me to suggest some very solemn and stimulating thoughts about the true nature of life. They refer, originally, to the strange vicissitudes and extremes of fortune and condition which characterised, so dramatically and remarkably, the life of King David. Shepherd-boy, soldier, court favourite, outlaw, freebooter and all but brigand; rebel, king, fugitive, saint, sinner, psalmist, penitent—he lived a life full of strongly marked alternations, and 'the times that went over him' were singularly separate and different from each other. There are very few of us who have such chequered lives as his. But the principle which dictated the selection by the chronicler of this somewhat strange phrase is true about the life of every man.

I. Note, first, 'the times' which make up each life.

Now, by the phrase here the writer does not merely mean the succession of moments, but he wishes to emphasise the view that these are epochs, sections of 'time,' each with its definite characteristics and its special opportunities, unlike the rest that lie on either side of it. The great broad field of time is portioned out, like the strips of peasant allotments, which show a little bit here, with one kind of crop upon it, bordered by another little morsel of ground bearing another kind of crop. So the whole is patchy, and yet all harmonises in effect if we look at it from high enough up. Thus each life is made up of a series, not merely of successive moments, but of well-marked epochs, each of which has its own character, its own responsibilities, its own opportunities, in each of which there is some special work to be done, some grace to be cultivated, some lesson to be learned, some sacrifice to be made; and if it is let slip it never comes back any more. 'It might have been once, and we missed it, and lost it for ever.' The times pass over us, and every single portion has its own errand to us. Unless we are wide awake we let it slip, and are the poorer to all eternity for not having had in our heads the eyes of the wise man which 'discern both time and judgment.' It is the same thought which is suggested by the well-known words of the cynical book of Ecclesiastes—'To every thing there is a season and a time'—an opportunity, and a definite period—'for every purpose that is under the sun.' It is the same thought which is suggested by Paul's words, 'As we have therefore opportunity, let us do good to all men. In due season we shall reap if we faint not.' There is 'a time for weeping and a time for laughing, a time for building up and a time for casting down.' It is the same thought of life, and its successive epochs of opportunity never returning, which finds expression in the threadbare lines about 'a tide in the affairs of men, which, taken at the flood, leads on to fortune,' and neglected, condemns the rest of a career to be hemmed in among creeks and shallows.

Through all the variety of human occupations, each moment comes to us with its own special mission, and yet, alas! to far too many of us the alternations do not suggest the question, what is it that I am hereby called upon to be or to do? what is the lesson that present circumstances are meant to teach, and the grace that my present condition is meant to force me to cultivate or exhibit? There is one point, as it were, upon the road where we may catch a view far away into the distance, and, if we are not on the lookout when we come there, we shall never get that glimpse at any other point along the path. The old alchemists used to believe that there was what they called the 'moment of projection,' when, into the heaving molten mass in their crucible, if they dropped the magic powder, the whole would turn into gold; an instant later and there would be explosion and death; an instant earlier and there would be no effect. And so God's moments come to us; every one of them—if we had eyes to see and hands to grasp—a crisis, affording opportunity for something for which all eternity will not afford a second opportunity, if the moment be let pass. 'The times went over him,' and your life and mine is parcelled out into seasons which have their special vocation for and message to us.

How solemn that makes our life! How it destroys the monotony that we sometimes complain of! How it heightens the low things and magnifies the apparently small ones! And how it calls upon us for a sharpened attention, that we miss not any of the blessings and gifts which God is meaning to bestow upon us through the ministry of each moment! How it calls upon us for not only sharpened attention, but for a desire to know the meaning of each of the hours and of every one of His providences! And how it bids us, as the only condition of understanding the times, so as to know what we ought to do, to keep our hearts in close union with Him, and ourselves ever standing, as becomes servants, girded and ready for work; and with the question on our lips and in our hearts, 'Lord, what wouldst Thou have me to do? and what wouldst Thou have me to do *now*?' The lesson of the day has to be learned in a day, and at the moment when it is put in practice.

II. Another thought suggested by this text is, the Power that moves the times.

As far as my text represents—and it is not intended to go to the bottom of everything—these times flow on over a man, as a river might. But is there any power that moves the stream? Unthinking and sense-bound men—and we are all such, in the measure in which we are unspiritual—are contented simply to accept the mechanical flow of the stream of time. We are all tempted not to look behind the moving screen to see the force that turns the wheel on which the painted scene is stretched. But, Oh! how dreary a thing it is if all that we have to say about life is, 'The times pass over us,' like the blind rush of a stream, or the movement of the sea around our coasts, eating away here and depositing its spoils there, sometimes taking and sometimes giving, but all the work of mere eyeless and purposeless chance or of natural causes.

Oh, brethren! there is nothing more dismal or paralysing than the contemplation of the flow of the times over our heads, unless we see in their flow something far more than that.

It is very beautiful to notice that this same phrase, or at least the essential part of it, is employed in one of the Psalms ascribed to David, with a very significant addition. He says, 'My times are *in Thy hand.*' So, then, the passage of our epochs over us is not merely the aimless flow of a stream, but the movement of a current which God directs. Therefore, if at any time it goes over our heads and seems to overwhelm us, we can look up through the transparent water and say, '*Thy* waves and *Thy* billows have gone over me,' and so I die not of suffocation beneath them. God orders the times, and therefore, though, as the bitter ingenuity of Ecclesiastes, on the lookout for proofs of the vanity of life, complained, in a one-sided view, as an aggravation of man's lot, that there is a time for everything, yet that aspect of change is not its deepest or truest. True it is that sometimes birth and sometimes death, sometimes joy and sometimes sorrow, sometimes building up and sometimes casting down, follow each other with monotonous uniformity of variety, and seem to reduce life to a perpetual heaping up of what is as painfully to be cast down the next moment, like the pitiless sport of the wind amongst the sandhills of the desert. But the futility is only apparent, and the changes are not meant to occasion 'man's misery' to be 'great upon him,' as Ecclesiastes says they do. The diversity of the 'times' comes from a unity of purpose; and all the various methods of the divine Providence exercised upon us have one unchanging intention. The meaning of all the 'times' is that they should bring us nearer to God, and fill us more full of His power and grace. The web is one, however various may be the pattern wrought upon the tapestry. The resulting motion of the great machine is one, though there may be a wheel turning from left to right here, and another one that fits into it, turning from right to left there. The end of all the opposite motions is straight progress. So the varying times do all tend to the one great issue. Therefore let us seek to pursue, in all varying circumstances, the one purpose which God has in them all, which the Apostle states to be 'even your sanctification,' and let us understand how summer and winter, springtime and harvest, tempest and fair weather, do all together make up the year, and ensure the springing of the seed and the fruitfulness of the stalk.

III. Lastly, let me remind you, too, how eloquently the words of my text suggest the transiency of all the 'times.'

They 'passed over him' as the wind through an archway, that whistles and comes not again. The old, old thought, so threadbare and yet always so solemnising and pathetic, which we know so well that we forget it, and are so sure of that it has little effect on life, the old, old thought, 'this too will pass away,' underlies the phrase of my text.

How blessed it is, brethren! to cherish that wholesome sense of the transiency of things here below, only those who live under its habitual power can fairly estimate. It is thought to be melancholy. We are told that it spoils joys and kills interest, and I know not what beside. It spoils no joys that ought to be joys. It kills no interests that are not on other grounds unworthy to be cherished. Contrariwise, the more fully we are penetrated with the persistent conviction of the transiency of the things seen and temporal, the greater they become, by a strange paradox. For then only are they seen in their true magnitude and nobility, in their true solemnity and importance as having a bearing on the things that are eternal. Time is the 'ceaseless lackey of eternity,' and the things that pass over us may become, like the waves of the sea, the means of bearing us to the unmoving shore. Oh! if only in the midst of joys and sorrows, of heavy tasks and corroding cares, of weary work and wounded spirits, we could feel, 'but for a moment,' all would be different, and joy would come, and strength would come, and patience would come, and every grace would come, in the train of the wholesome conviction that 'here we have no continuing city.'

Cherish the thought. It will spoil nothing the spoiling of which will be a loss. It will heighten everything the possession of which is a gain. It will teach us to trust in the darkness, and to believe in the light. And when the times are dreariest, and frost binds the ground, we shall say, 'If winter comes, can spring be far behind?' The times roll over us, like the seas that break upon some isolated rock, and when the tide has fallen and the vain flood has subsided, the rock is there. If the world helps us to God, we need not mind though it passes, and the fashion thereof.

But do not let us forget that this text in its connection may teach us another thought. The transitory 'times that went over' Israel's king are all recorded imperishably on the pages here, and so, though condensed into narrow space, the record of the fleeting moments lives for ever, and 'the books shall be opened, and men shall be judged according to their works.' We are writing an imperishable record by our fleeting deeds. Half a dozen pages carry all the story of that stormy life of Israel's king. It takes a thousand rose-trees to make a vial full of essence of roses. The record and issues of life will be condensed into small compass, but the essence of it is eternal. We shall find it again, and have to drink as we have brewed when we get yonder. 'Be not deceived, God is not mocked, for whatsoever a man soweth that shall he also reap.' 'There is a time to sow,' and that is the present life; 'and there is a time to gather the fruits' of our sowing, and that is the time when times have ended and eternity is here.

THE SECOND BOOK OF CHRONICLES

THE DUTY OF EVERY DAY

'Then Solomon offered burnt offerings unto the Lord . . . Even after a certain rate every day.'—(A. V.)
'Then Solomon offered burnt offerings unto the Lord, even as the duty of every day required it.'—2 CHRON. viii. 12-13 (R. V.).

THIS is a description of the elaborate provision, in accordance with the commandment of Moses, which Solomon made for the worship in his new Temple. The writer is enlarging on the precise accordance of the ritual with the regulations laid down in the law. He expresses, by the phrase which we have taken as our text, not only the accordance of the worship with the commandment, but its unbroken continuity, and also the variety in it, according to the regulations for different days. For the verse runs on, 'on the Sabbaths, and on the new moons, and on the solemn feasts, three times in the year, even in the Feast of unleavened bread, and in the Feast of weeks, and in the Feast of Tabernacles.' There were, then, these characteristics in the ritual of Solomon's Temple, precise compliance with the Divine commandment, unbroken continuity, and beautiful flexibility and variety of method.

But passing altogether from the original application of the words, I venture to do now what I very seldom do, and that is, to take this verse as a kind of motto. 'Even according as the duty of every day required'; the phrase may suggest three thoughts: that each day has its own work, its own worship, and its own supplies, 'even as the duty of every day required.'

Each day has its own work.

Of course there is a great uniformity in our lives, and many of us who are set down to one continuous occupation can tell twelve months before what, in all probability, we shall be doing at each hour of each day in the week. But for all that, there is a certain individual physiognomy about each new day as it comes to us; and the oldest, most habitual, and therefore in some degree easiest and least stimulating, work has its own special characteristics as it comes again to us day by day for the hundredth time.

So there are three pieces of practical wisdom that I would suggest, and one is—be content to take your work in little bits as it comes. There is a great deal of practical wisdom in taking short views of things, for although we have often to look ahead, yet it is better on the whole that a man should, as far as he can, confine his anticipations to the day that is passing, and leave the day that is coming to look after itself. Take short views and be content to let each day prescribe its tasks, and you have gone a long way to make all your days quiet and peaceful. For it is far more the anticipation of difficulties than the realisation of them that wears and wearies us. If a man says to himself, 'This sorrow that I am carrying, or this work that I have to do, is going to last for many days to come,' his heart will fail. If he said to himself, 'It will be no worse to-morrow than it is at this moment, and I can live through it, for am I not living through it at this moment, and getting power to endure or do at this moment? and to-morrow will probably be like to-day,' things would not be so difficult.

You remember the homely old parable of the clock on the stair that gave up ticking altogether because it began to calculate how many thousands of seconds there are in the year, and that twice that number of times it would have to wag backwards and forwards. The lesson that it learned was—tick one tick and never mind the next. You will be able to do it when the time to do it comes. Let us act 'as the duty of every day requireth.' 'Sufficient for the day is the work thereof.'

Then there is another piece of advice from this thought of each day having its own work, and that is —keep your ears open, and your eyes too, to learn the lesson of what the day's work is. There is generally abundance of direction for us if only we are content with the one-step-at-a-time direction, which we get, and if another condition is fulfilled, if we try to suppress our own wishes and the noisy babble of our own yelping inclinations, and take the whip to them until they cease their barking, that we may hear what God says. It is not because He does not speak, but because we are too anxious to have our own way to listen quietly to His voice, that we make most of our blunders as to what the duty of every day requires. If we will be still and listen, and stand in the attitude of the boy-prophet before the glimmering lamp in the sacred place, saying, 'Speak, Lord! for Thy servant heareth,' we shall get sufficient instruction for our next step.

Another piece of practical wisdom that I would suggest is that if every day has its own work, we should buckle ourselves to do the day's work before night falls and not leave any over for to-morrow, which will be quite full enough. 'Do the duty that lies nearest thee,' was the preaching of one of our sages, and it is wholesome advice. For when we do that duty, the doing of it has a wonderful power of opening up further steps, and showing us more clearly what is the next duty. Only let us be sure of this, that no moment comes from God which has not in it boundless possibilities; and that no moment comes from God which has not in it stringent obligations. We neither avail ourselves of the one, nor discharge the other, unless we come, morning by morning, to the new day that is dawning upon us, with some fresh consciousness of the large issues that may be wrapped in its unseen hours, and the great things for Him that we may do ere its evening falls.

Each day has its tasks, and if we do not do the tasks of each day in its day, we shall fling away life. If a man had £100,000 for a fortune, and turned it all into halfpence, and tossed them out of the window, he could soon get rid of his whole fortune. And if you fling away your moments or live without the consciousness of their solemn possibilities and mystic awfulness, you will find at the last that you have made 'ducks and drakes' of your years, and have flung them away in moments without knowing what you were doing, and without possibility of recovery. 'Take care of the pence, the pounds will take care of themselves.' Take care of the days, and the years will show a fair record.

Secondly, we have here the suggestion that every day has its own worship.

As I remarked at the beginning of my observations, the chronicler dwells, with a certain kind of satisfaction, in accordance with the tone of his whole writings, upon the external ritual of the Temple; and points out its entire conformity with the divine precept, and the unbroken continuity of worship day after day, year in year out, and the variation of the characteristics of that worship according as the day was more or less ritually important. From his words we may deduce a very needful though obvious and commonplace lesson. What we want is every-day religion, and that every-day religion is the only thing that will enable us to do what the duty of every day requires. But that every-day religion which will be our best ally, and power for the discharge of the obligations that each moment brings with it, must have its points of support, as it were, in special moments and methods of worship.

So, then, take that first thought: What we want is a religion that will go all through our lives. A great many of you keep your religion where you keep your best clothes: putting it on on Sunday and locking it away on the Sunday night in a wardrobe because it is not the dress that you go to work in. And some of you keep your religion in your pew, and lock it up in the little box where you put your hymn-books and your Bibles, which you read only once a week, devoting yourselves to ledgers or novels and newspapers for the rest of your time. We want a religion that will go all through our life; and if there is anything in our life that will not stand its presence, the sooner we get rid of that element the better. A mountain road has generally a living brooklet leaping and flashing by the side of it. So our lives will be dusty and dead and cold and poor and prosaic unless that river runs along by the roadside and makes music for us as it flows. Take your religion wherever you go. If you cannot take it in to any scenes or company, stop you outside.

There is nothing that will help a man to do his day's work so much as the realisation of Christ's Presence. And that realisation, along with its certain results, devotion of heart to Him and submission of will to His commandment, and desire to shape our lives to be like His, will make us masters of all circumstances and strong enough for the hardest work that God can lay upon us.

There is nothing so sure to make life beautiful, and noble, and pure, and peaceful, and strong as this—the application to its monotonous trifles of religious principles. If you do not do little things as Christian men and women, and under the influence of Christian principle, pray *what* are you going to do under the influence of Christian principle? If you are keeping your religion to influence the crises of your lives, and are content to let the trifles be ruled by the devil or the world and yourselves, you will find out, when you come to the end, that there were perhaps three or four crises in your experience, and that all the rest of life was made of trifles, and that when the crises came you could not lay your hand on the religious principle that would have enabled you to deal with them. The sword had got so rusty in its scabbard because it had never been drawn for long years, that it could not be readily drawn in the moment of sudden peril; and if you could have drawn it, you would have found its edge blunted. Use your religion on the trifles, or you will not be able to make much of it in the crises. 'He that is faithful in that which is least is faithful also in much.' The worship of every day is the preparation for the work of that day.

Further, that worship, that religion, wearing its common, modest suit of workaday clothes, must also, if there is to be any power in it, have a certain variety in its methods. 'Solomon offered burnt offerings ... on the Sabbaths, on the new moons,' which had a little more ceremonial than the Sabbaths, 'and on the solemn feasts three times in a year,' which had still more ceremonial than the new moons, 'even in the Feast of unleavened bread, and in the Feast of weeks, and in the Feast of tabernacles.' These were spring-tides when the sea of worship rose beyond its usual level, and they kept it from stagnating. We, too, if we wish to have this every-day religion running with any strength of scour and current through our lives, will need to have moments when it touches high-water mark, else it will not flush the foulness out of our hearts and our lives.

Lastly, take the other suggestion, that every day has its own supplies.

That does not lie in the text properly, but for the sake of completeness I add it. Every day has its own supplies. The manna fell every day, and was gathered and consumed on the day on which it fell. God gives us strength measured accurately by the needs of the day. You will get as much as you require, and if ever you do not get as much as you require, which is very often the case with Christian people, that is not because God did not send enough manna, but because their *omer* was not ready to catch it as it fell. The day's supply is measured by the day's need. Suppose an Israelite had sat in his tent and said, 'I am not going out to gather,' would he have had any in his empty vessel? Certainly not. The manna lay all around the tent, but each man had to go out and gather it. God makes no mistakes in His weights and measures. He gives us each sufficient strength to do His will and to walk in His ways; and if we do not do His will or walk in His ways, or if we find our burden too heavy, our sorrows too sharp, our loneliness too dreary, our difficulties too great, it is not because 'the Lord's hand is shortened that it cannot' supply, but because our hands are so slack that they will not take the sufficiency which He gives. In the midst of abundance we are starving. We let the water run idly through the open sluice instead of driving the wheels of life.

My friend! God's measure of supply is correct. If we were more faithful and humble, and if we understood better and felt more how deep is our need and how little is our strength, we should more continually be able to rejoice that He has given, and we have received, 'even as the duty of every day required.'

CONTRASTED SERVICES

'They shall be his servants: that they may know My service, and the service of the kingdoms of the countries.'—2 CHRON. xii. 8.

REHOBOAM was a self-willed, godless king who, like some other kings, learned nothing by experience. His kingdom was nearly wrecked at the very beginning of his reign, and was saved much more by the folly of his rival than by his own wisdom. Jeroboam's religious revolution drove all the worshippers of God among the northern kingdom into flight. They might have endured the separate monarchy, but they could not endure the separate Temple. So all priests and Levites in Israel, and all the adherents of the ancestral worship in the Temple at Jerusalem, withdrew to the southern kingdom and added much to its strength.

Rehoboam's narrow escape taught him neither

moderation nor devotion, his new strength turned his head. He forsook the law of the Lord. The dreary series, so often illustrated in the history of Israel, came into operation. Prosperity produced irreligion; irreligion brought chastisement; chastisement brought repentance; repentance brought the removal of the invader—and then, like a spring released, back went king and nation to their old sin.

So here—Rehoboam's sins take visible form in Sheshak's army. He has sown the dragon's teeth and they spring up armed men. Shemaiah the prophet, the first of the long series of noble men who curbed the violence of Jewish monarchs, points the lesson of invasion in plain, blunt words: 'Ye have forsaken Me.' Then follow penitence and confession—and the promise that Jerusalem shall not be destroyed, but at the same time they are to be left as vassals and tributaries of Egypt—an anomalous position for them—and the reason is given in these words of our text.

I. The contrasted Masters.

Judah was too small to be independent of the powerful warlike states to its north and south, unless miraculously guarded and preserved. So it must either keep near God, and therefore free and safe from invasion, or else, departing from God and following its own ways, fall under alien dominion. Its experience was a type of that of universal humanity. Man is not independent. His mass is not enough for him to do without a central orb round which he may revolve. He has a choice of the form of service and the master that he will choose, but one or other must dominate his life and sway his motions. 'Ye cannot serve God and Mammon'; ye must serve God *or* Mammon. The solemn choice is presented to every man, but the misery of many lives is that they drift along, making their election unawares, and infallibly choosing the worse by the very act of lazily or weakly allowing accident to determine their lives. Not consciously and strongly to will the right, not resolutely and with coercion of the vagrant self to will to take God for our aim, is to choose the low, the wrong. Perhaps none, or very few of us, would deliberately say 'I choose Mammon, having carefully compared the claims of the opposite systems of life that solicit me, and with open-eyed scrutiny measured their courses, their goods and their ends.' But how many of us there are who have in effect made that choice, and never have given one moment's clear, patient examination of the grounds of our choice! The policy of drift is unworthy of a man and is sure to end in ruin.

It is not for me to attempt here to draw out the contrast between man's chief end and all other rival claimants of our lives. Each man must do that for himself, and I venture to assert that the more thoroughly the process of comparison is carried out, and the more complete the analysis not only of the rival claims and gifts, but of our capacities and needs, the more sun-clear will be the truth of the old, well-worn answer: 'Man's chief end is to glorify God and to enjoy Him for ever.' The old woman by her solitary fireside who has learned that and practises it, has chosen the better part which will last when many shining careers have sunk into darkness, and many will-o'-the-wisps, which have been pursued with immense acclamations, have danced away into the bog, and many a man who has been envied and admired has had to sum up his successful career in the sad words, 'I have played the fool and erred exceedingly.' I cannot pretend to conduct the investigation for you, but I can press on every one who does not wish to let accidents mould him, at least to recognise that there is a choice to be made, and to make it deliberately and with eyes open to the facts of the case. It is a shabby way of ruining yourself to do it for want of thought. The rabble of competitors of God catch more souls by accident than of set purpose. Most men are godless because they have never fairly faced the question: what does my soul require in order to reach its highest blessedness and its noblest energy?

II. The contrasted experience of the servants.

Judah learned that the yoke of obedience to God's law was a world lighter than the grinding oppression of the Egyptian invader.

God's service is freedom; the world's is slavery.

Liberty is unrestrained power to do what we ought. Man must be subject to law. The solemn imperative of duty is omnipresent and sovereign. To do as we like is not freedom, but bondage to self, and that usually our worst self, which means crushing or coercing the better self. The choice is to chain the beast in us or to clip the wings of the angel in us, and he is a fool who conceits himself free because he lets his inferior self have its full swing, and hustles his better self into bondage to clear the course for the other. There is but one deliverance from the sway of self, and it is realised in the liberty wherewith Christ has made us free. To make self our master inevitably leads to setting beggars on horseback and princes walking. Passion, the 'flesh' is terribly apt to usurp the throne within when once God is dethroned. Then indulgence feeds passion, and deeper draughts become necessary in order to produce the same effects, and cravings, once allowed free play, grow in ravenousness, while their pabulum steadily loses its power to satisfy. The experience of the undevout sensualist is but too faithful a type of that of all undevout livers, in the failure of delights to delight and of acquisitions to enrich, and in the bondage, often to nothing more worthy to be obeyed than mere habit, and in the hopeless incapacity to shake off the adamantine chains which they have themselves rivetted on their limbs. There are endless varieties in the forms which the service of self assumes, ranging from gross animalism, naked and unashamed, up to refined and cultured godlessness, but they are one in their inmost character, one in their disabling the spirit from a free choice of its course, one in the limitations which they impose on its aspirations and possibilities, one in the heavy yoke which they lay on their vassals. The true liberty is realised only when for love's dear sake we joyously serve God, and from the highest motive enrol ourselves in the household of the highest Person, and by the act become 'no more servants but sons.' Well may we all pray—

> 'Lord! bind me up, and let me lie
> A prisoner to my liberty,
> If such a state at all can be
> As an imprisonment, serving Thee.'

God's service brings solid good, the world's is vain and empty.

God's service brings an approving conscience, a calm heart, strength and gladness. It is in full accord with our best selves. Tranquil joys attend on it. 'In keeping Thy commandments there is great reward,' and that not merely bestowed after keeping, but realised and inherent in the very act. On the other side, think of the stings of conscience, the illusions on which those feed who will not eat of the heavenly food, the husks of the swine-trough, the ashes for bread, that self and the world, in all their forms set before men. A pathetic character in modern fiction says, 'If you make believe very much it is nice.' It takes a tremendous amount of make-believe to keep up an appetite for the world's dainties or to find its meats palatable, after a little while. No sin ever yields the fruit it was expected to produce, or if it does it brings something which was not expected, and the bitter tang of the addition spoils the whole. It may be wisely adapted to secure a given end, but that end is only a means to secure the real end, our substantial blessedness, and that is never attained but by one course of life, the life of service of God. We may indeed win a goodly garment, but the plague is in the stuff and, worn, it will burn into the bones like fire. I read somewhere lately of thieves who had stolen a cask of wine, and had their debauch, but they sickened and died. The cask was examined and a huge snake was found dead in it. Its poison had passed into the wine and killed the drinkers. That is how the world serves those who swill its cup. 'What fruit had ye *then* in those things whereof ye are *now* ashamed?' The threatening pronounced against Israel's disobedience enshrines an eternal truth: 'Because thou servedst not the Lord thy God with joyfulness, and with gladness of heart, by reason of the abundance of all things; therefore shalt thou serve thine enemies . . . in hunger and in thirst, and in nakedness and in want of all things.'

God's service has final issues and the world's service has final issues.

Only fools try to blink the fact that all our doings have consequences. And it augurs no less levity and insensibility to blink the other fact that these consequences show no indications of being broken short off at the end of our earthly life. Men die into another life, as they have ever, dimly and with many foolish accompaniments, believed; and dead, they are the men that they have made themselves while living. Character is eternal, memory is eternal, death puts the stamp of perpetuity on what life has evolved. Nothing human ever dies. The thought is too solemn to be vulgarised by pulpit rhetoric. Enough to say here that these two tremendous alternatives, Life and Death, express some little part of the eternal issues of our fleeting days. Looking fixedly into these two great symbols of the ultimate issues of these contrasted services, we can dimly see, as in the one, a wonder of resplendent glories moving in a sphere 'as calm as it is bright,' so, in the other, whirling clouds and jets of vapour as in the crater of a volcano. One shuddering glance over the rim of it should suffice to warn from lingering near, lest the unsteady soil should crumble beneath our feet.

But the true Lord of our lives loves us too well to let us experience all the bitter issues of our foolish rebellion against His authority, and yet He loves us too well not to let us taste something of them that we may 'know and see that it is an evil thing *and a bitter*, that thou hast forsaken the Lord thy God.' The experiences of the consequences of godless living are in some measure allowed to fall on us by God's love, lest we should persist in the evil and so bring down on ourselves still more fatal issues. It is mercy that here chastises the evildoer with whips, in hope of not having to chastise him with scorpions. God desires to teach us, by the pains and heartaches of an undevout life, by disappointments, foiled plans, wrecked hopes, inner poverty, the difference between His service and that of 'the kingdoms of the countries,' if haply He may not be forced to let the full flood of fatal results overwhelm us. It is best to be drawn to serve Him by the cords of love, but it is possible to have the beginnings of the desire so to serve roused by the far lower motives of weariness and disgust at the world's wages, and by dread of what these may prove when they are paid in full. Self-interest may sicken a man of serving Mammon, and may be transformed into the self-surrender which makes God's service possible and blessed. The flight into the city of refuge may be quickened by the fear of the pursuer, whose horse's hoofs are heard thundering on the road behind the fugitive, and whose spear is all but felt a yard from his back, but once within the shelter of the city wall, gratitude for deliverance will fill his heart and 'perfect love will cast out fear.'

The king concerning whom our text was spoken had to suffer humiliation by the Egyptian invasion. His sufferings were meant to be educational, and when they in some measure effected their purpose, God curbed the invader and granted some measure of deliverance. So is it with us, if, moved by whatever impulse, we betake ourselves to Jesus to save us from the bitter fruits of our evil lives. The extreme severity of the results of our sins does not fall on penitent, believing spirits, but some do fall. As the Psalmist says: 'Thou wast a God that forgavest them though Thou tookest vengeance of their inventions.' A profligate course of life may be forgiven, but health or fortune is ruined all the same. In brief, the so-called 'natural' consequences are not removed, though the sin which caused them is pardoned. Polluted memories, indulged habits, defiled imaginations, are not got rid of, though the sins that inflicted them are forgiven.

Is it not, then, the part of wise men to lay to heart the lessons of experience, and to let what we have learned of the bitter fruit of godless living turn us away from such service, and draw us by merciful chastisement to yield ourselves to God, whom to serve accords with our deepest needs and brings first fruits and pre-libations of blessedness and peace here, and fullness of joy with pleasures for evermore hereafter?

THE SECRET OF VICTORY

'The children of Judah prevailed, because they relied upon the Lord God of their fathers.'—2 CHRON. xiii. 18.

THESE words are the summing-up of the story of a strange old-world battle between Jeroboam, the adventurer who rent the kingdom, and Abijah, the son of the foolish Rehoboam, whose unseasonable blustering had played into the usurper's hands. The son was a wiser and better man than his father. It is characteristic of the ancient world, that before battle was joined Abijah made a long speech to the enemy, recounting the ritual deficiencies of the Northern kingdom, and proudly contrasting the punctilious correctness of the Temple service with the irregular cult set up by Jeroboam. He confidently pointed to the priests 'with their trumpets' in his army as the visible sign that 'God is with us at our head,' and while charging Israel with having 'forsaken the Lord our God,' to whom he and his people had kept true, besought them not to carry their rebellion to the extreme of fighting against their fathers' God, and assured them that no success could attend their weapons in such a strife. The passionate appeal had no effect, but while Abijah was orating, Jeroboam was carrying out a ruse, and planting part of his troops behind Judah, so as to put them between two fires and draw a net round the outnumbered and outmanœuvred enemy.

Abijah and his men suddenly detected their desperate position, and did the only wise thing. When, with a shock of surprise, they saw that 'behold! the battle was before and behind them,' they 'cried unto the Lord, and the priests sounded with the trumpets.' The sharp, short cry from thousands of agitated men ringed round by foes, and the blare of the trumpets were both prayers, and heartened the suppliants for their whirlwind charge, before which the men of Israel, double in number as they were, broke and fled. The defeat was thorough, and, for a while, Rehoboam and his kingdom were 'brought under,' and a comparatively long peace followed. Our text gathers up the lesson taught, not to Judah or Israel alone, by victory and defeat, when it declares that to rely upon the Lord is to prevail. It opens for us the secret of victory, in that old far-off struggle and in to-day's conflicts.

I. We note the faith of the fighters.

'They relied,' says the chronicler, 'upon the Lord.' Now the word rendered 'relied' is one of several picturesque words by which the Old Testament, which we are sometimes told, with a great flourish of learning, has no mention of 'faith,' expresses 'trust,' by metaphors drawn from bodily actions which symbolise the spiritual act. The word here literally signifies to lean on, as a feeble hand might on a staff, or a tremulous arm on a strong one. And does not that picture carry with it much insight into what the essence of Old Testament 'trust' or New Testament 'faith' is? If we think of faith as leaning, we shall not fall into that starved misconception of it which takes it to be nothing more than intellectual assent. We shall see there is a far fuller pulse of feeling than that beating in it. A man who leans on some support, does so because he knows that his own strength is insufficient for his need. The consciousness of weakness is the beginning of faith. He who has never despaired of himself has scarcely trusted in God. Abijah's enemies were two to one of his own men. No wonder that they cried unto the Lord, and felt a stound of despair shake their courage. And who of us can face life with its heavy duties, its thick-clustering dangers and temptations, its certain struggles, its possible failures, and not feel the cold touch of dread gripping our hearts, though strong and brave? Surely he has had little experience, or has learned little wisdom from the experience he has had, who has yet to discover his own weakness. But the consciousness of weakness is by itself debilitating, and but increases the weakness of which it is painfully aware. There is no surer way to sap what strength we have than to tell ourselves what poor creatures we are. The purpose and end of self-contemplation which becomes aware of our own feebleness is to lead us to the contemplation of God, our immortal strength. Abijah's assurance that 'God is with us at our head' rang out triumphantly. Faith has an upper and an under side: the under side is self-distrust; the upper, trust in God. He will never lean all his weight on a prop, who fancies that he can stand alone, or has other stays to hold him up.

But Abijah's example teaches us another lesson—that for a vigorous faith, there must be obedience to all God's known will. True, thank God! faith often springs in its power in a soul that is conscious but of sin, but a continuance in disobedience will inevitably kill faith. It was because Abijah and his people had kept 'the charge of the Lord our God,' that they were sure that God was with them. We can only be sure of God to lean on when we are doing His will, and we shall do His will only as we are sure that we lean on Him. Our trust in Him will be strong and operative in the measure in which our lives are conformed to His commandments. Much elaborate dissertation has been devoted to expounding what faith is, and the strong, vivid Scriptural conception of it has been wofully darkened and overlaid with cobwebs of theology, but surely this eloquent metaphor of our text tells us more than do many learned volumes. It bids us lean on God, rest the whole weight of our needs, our weaknesses, and our sins on Him. Like any human friend or helper, He is better pleased when we lean hard on Him than when we gingerly put a finger on His arm, and lay no pressure on it, as we do when in ceremonial fashion we seem to accept another's support, and hold ourselves back from putting a weight on the offered arm. We cannot rely too utterly on Him. We honour Him most when we repose our whole selves on His strong arm.

II. The increase of faith by sudden fear.

'When Judah looked back, behold, the battle was before and behind them.' The shock of seeing the flashing spears in the rear would make the bravest hold their breath for one overwhelming moment, but the next moment their faith in God surged back with tenfold force, increased by the sudden new peril. The sharp collision of flint and steel struck out a spark of faith. 'What time I am afraid, I will trust in Thee,' said an expert in the genesis and growth of trust. Peril kills a feeble trust, but vivifies it, if strong. The recognition of danger is meant to drive us to God. If each fresh difficulty or danger makes us tighten our clasp of Him, and lean the harder on Him, it has done its highest service to us, and we have conquered it, and are the stronger because of it. The storm that makes the traveller, fighting with the wind and the rain in his face, clasp his cloak tighter round him, does him no harm. The purpose of our trials is to drive us to God, and a fair-weather faith which had all but fallen asleep is often roused to energy that works wonders, by the sudden dash of danger flung into and disturbing a life. It is wise seamanship to make a run to get snugly behind the breakwater when a sudden gale springs up.

III. The expression of faith in appeal to God.

When the ambush was unmasked, the surrounded men of Judah 'cried unto the Lord, and the priests sounded with the trumpets,' before they flung themselves on the enemy. We may be sure that their cry was short and sharp, and poignant with appeal to God. There would be no waste words, nor perfunctory petitions without wings of desire, in that cry. Should we not look for the essential elements of prayer rather to such cries, pressed from burdened hearts by a keen sense of absolute helplessness, and very careless of proprieties so long as they were shrill enough to pierce God's ear and touch His heart, than to the formal petitions of well-ordered worship? A single ejaculation flung heavenward in a moment of despair or agony is more precious in God's sight than a whole litany of half-hearted devotions.

The text puts in a striking form another lesson well worth learning, that, in the greatest crises, no time is better spent than time used for prayer. A rush on the enemy would not have served Abijah's purpose nearly so well as that moment's pause for crying to the Lord, before his charge. Hands lifted to heaven are nerved to clutch the sword and strike manfully. It is not only that Christ's soldiers are to fight and pray, but that they fight by praying. That is true in the small conflicts and antagonisms of the lives of each of us, and it is true in regard to the agelong battle against ignorance and sin. Christian's sword was named 'All-prayer.'

The priests, too, blew a prayer through their trumpets, for the ordinance had appointed that 'when ye go to war . . . then shall ye sound an alarm with the trumpets; and ye shall be remembered before the Lord your God, and ye shall be saved from your enemies.' The clear, strident blare was not intended to hearten warriors, or to sing defiance, but to remind God of His promises, and to bring Him on to the battlefield, as He had said that He would be. The truest prayer is that which but picks up the arrows of promise shot from heaven to earth, and casts them back from earth to heaven. He prays best who fills his mouth with God's words, turning every 'I will' of His into 'Do Thou!'

IV. The strength that comes through faith.

'As the men of Judah shouted, it came to pass that God smote Jeroboam and all Israel before Abijah and Judah.' There is no such quickener of all a man's natural force as even the lowest forms of faith. He who throws himself into any enterprise sure of success will often succeed just because he was sure he would. The world's history is full of instances where men, with every odds against them, have plucked the flower safety out of the nettle danger, just because they trusted in their star, or their luck, or their destiny. We all know how a very crude faith turned a horde of wild Arabs into a conquering army, that in a century dominated the world from Damascus to Seville. The truth that is in 'Christian Science' is that many forms of disease yield to the patient's firm persuasion of recovery. And from these and many other facts the natural power of faith is beginning to dawn on the most matter-of-fact and unspiritual people. They are beginning to think that perhaps Christ was right after all in saying 'All things are possible to him that believeth,' and that it is not such a blunder after all to make faith the first step to all holiness and purity, and the secret of victory in life's tussle. Leaving out of view for the moment the supernatural effects of faith, which Christianity alleges are its constant consequences, it is clear that its natural effects are all in the direction of increasing the force of the trusting man. It calms, it heartens for all work, effort, and struggle. It imparts patience, it brightens hope, it forbids discouragement, it rebukes and cures despondency. And besides all this, there is the supernatural communication of a strength not our own, which is the constant result of Christian faith. Christian faith knits the soul and the Saviour in so close a union, that all that is Christ's becomes the Christian's, and every believer may hear His Lover's voice whispering to him what one of His servants once heard in an hour of despondency, 'My grace is sufficient for thee, for My power is made perfect in weakness.'

Faith joins us to the Lord, and 'he that is joined to the Lord is one spirit'; and that Lord has said to all His disciples, 'I give thee Myself, and in Myself all that is Mine.' We do not go to warfare at our own charges, but there will pass into and abide in our hearts the warlike might of the true King and Captain of the Lord's host, and we shall hear the ring of His encouraging voice saying, 'Be of good cheer! I have overcome the world.'

ASA'S REFORMATION, AND CONSEQUENT PEACE AND VICTORY

'And Asa did that which was good and right in the eyes of the Lord his God: 3. For he took away the altars of the strange gods, and the high places, and brake down the images, and cut down the groves: 4. And commanded Judah to seek the Lord God of their fathers, and to do the law and the commandment. 5. Also he took away out of all the cities of Judah the high places and the images: and the kingdom was quiet before him. 6. And he built fenced cities in Judah: for the land had rest, and he had no war in those years; because the Lord had given him rest. 7. Therefore he said unto Judah, Let us build these cities, and make about them walls, and towers, gates, and bars, while the land is yet before us; because we have sought the Lord our God, we have sought Him, and He hath given us rest on every side. So they built and prospered. 8. And Asa had an army of men that bare targets and spears, out of Judah three hundred thousand; and out of Benjamin, that bare shields and drew bows, two hundred and fourscore thousand: all these were mighty men of valour.'—2 CHRON. xiv. 2-8.

ASA was Rehoboam's grandson, and came to the throne when a young man. The two preceding reigns had favoured idolatry, but the young king had a will of his own, and inaugurated a religious revolution, with which and its happy results this passage deals.

I. It first recounts the thorough clearance of idolatrous emblems and images which Asa made. 'Strange altars,'—that is, those dedicated to other gods; 'high places,'—that is, where illegal sacrifice to Jehovah was offered, 'pillars,'—that is, stone columns; and 'Asherim,'—that is, trees or wooden poles, survivals of ancient stone- or tree-worship; 'sun-images,'—that is, probably, pillars consecrated to Baal as sun-god, were all swept away. The enumeration vividly suggests the incongruous rabble of gods which had taken the place of the one Lord. How vainly we try to make up for His absence from our hearts by a multitude of finite delights and helpers! Their multiplicity proves the insufficiency of each and of all.

1 Kings xv. 13 adds a detail which brings out still more clearly Asa's reforming zeal; for it tells us that he had to fight against the influence of his mother, who had been prominent in supporting disgusting and immoral forms of worship, and who retained some authority, of which her son was strong enough to take the extreme step of depriving her. Remembering the Eastern reverence for a mother, we can estimate the effort which that required, and the resolution which it implied. But 1 Kings differs from our narrative in stating that the 'high places' were not taken away—the explanation of the variation probably being that the one account tells what Asa attempted and commanded, and the other records the imperfect way in which his orders were carried out. They would be obeyed in Jerusalem and its neighbourhood, but in many a secluded corner the old rites would be observed.

It is vain to force religious revolutions. Laws which are not supported by the national conscience will only be obeyed where disobedience will involve penalties. If men's hearts cleave to Baal, they will not be turned into Jehovah-worshippers by a king's commands. Asa could command Judah to 'seek the Lord God of their fathers, and to do the law,' but he could not make them do it.

II. The chronicler brings out strongly the truth which runs through his whole book,—namely, the connection between honouring Jehovah and national prosperity. He did not import that thought into his narrative, but he insisted on it as moulding the history of Judah. Modern critics charge him with writing with a bias, but he learned the 'bias' from God's own declarations, and had it confirmed by observation, reflection, and experience. The whole history of Israel and Judah was one long illustration of the truth which he is constantly repeating. No doubt, the divine dealings with Israel brought obedience and well-being into closer connection than exists now; but in deepest truth the sure defence of our national prosperity is the same as theirs, and it is still the case that 'righteousness exalteth a nation.' 'The kingdom was quiet,' says the chronicler, 'and he had no war in those years; because the Lord had given him rest.' 1 Kings makes more of the standing enmity with the northern kingdom, and records scarcely anything of Asa's reign except the war which, as it says, was between him and Baasha of Israel 'all their days.' But, according to 2 Chronicles xvi. 1, Baasha did not proceed to war till Asa's thirty-sixth year, and the halcyon time of peace evidently followed immediately on the religious reformation at its very beginning.

Asa's experience embodies a truth which is substantially fulfilled in nations and in individuals; for obedience brings rest, often outward tranquillity, always inward calm. Note the heightened earnestness expressed in the repetition of the expression 'We have sought the Lord' in verse 7, and the grand assurance of His favour as the source of well-being in the clause which follows, 'and He hath given us rest on every side.' That is always so, and will be so with us. If we seek Him with our whole hearts, keeping Him ever before us amid the distractions of life, taking Him as our aim and desire, and ever stretching out the tendrils of our hearts to feel after Him and clasp Him, all around and within will be tranquil, and even in warfare we shall preserve unbroken peace.

Asa teaches us, too, the right use of tranquillity. He clearly and gratefully recognised God's hand in it, and traced it not to his own warlike skill or his people's prowess, but to Him. And he used the time of repose to strengthen his defences, and exercise his soldiers against possible assaults. We do not yet dwell in the land of peace, where it is safe to be without bolts and bars, but have ever to be on the watch for sudden attacks. Rest from war should give leisure for building not only fortresses, but temples, as was the case with Solomon. The time comes when, as in many an ancient fortified city of Europe, the ramparts may be levelled, and flowers bloom where sentries walked; but to-day we have to be on perpetual guard, and look to our fortifications, if we would not be overcome.

ASA'S PRAYER

'And Asa cried unto the Lord his God, and said, Lord, it is nothing with Thee to help, whether with many, or with them that have no power: help us, O Lord our God; for we rest on Thee, and in Thy Name we go against this multitude. O Lord, Thou art our God; let not man prevail against Thee.'—2 CHRON. xiv. 11.

THIS King Asa, Rehoboam's grandson, had had a long reign of peace, which the writer of the Book of Chronicles traces to the fact that he had rooted out idolatry from Judah. 'The land had rest, and he had no war . . . because the Lord had given him rest.'

But there came a time when the war-cloud began to roll threateningly over the land, and a great army—the numbers of which, from their immense magnitude, seem to be erroneously given—came up against him. Like a wise man he made his military dispositions first, and prayed next. He set his troops in order, and then he fell down on his knees, and spoke to God.

Now, it seems to me that this prayer contains the very essence of what ought to be the Christian attitude in reference to all the conditions and threatening dangers and conflicts of life; and so I wish to run over it, and bring out the salient points of it, as typical of what ought to be our disposition.

I. The wholesome consciousness of our own impotence.

It did not take much to convince Asa that he had 'no power.' His army, according to the numbers given of the two hosts, was outnumbered two to one; and so it did not require much reflection to say, 'We have no might.' But although perhaps not so sufficiently obvious to us, as truly as in the case in our text, if we look fairly in the face our duties, our tasks, our dangers, the possibilities of life and its certainties, the more humbly we think of our own capacity, the more wisely we shall think about God, and the more truly we shall estimate ourselves. The world says, 'Self-reliance is the conquering virtue'; Jesus says to us, 'Self-distrust is the condition of all victory.' And that does not mean any mere shuffling off of responsibility from our own shoulders, but it means looking the facts of our lives, and of our own characters, in the face. And if we will do that, however apparently easy may be our course, and however richly endowed in mind, body, or estate we may be, if we all do that honestly, we shall find that we each are like 'the man with ten thousand' that has to meet 'the King that comes against him with twenty thousand'; and we shall not 'desire conditions of peace' with our enemy, for that is not what in this case we have to do, but we shall look about us, and not keep our eyes on the horizon, and on the levels of earth, but look up to see if there is not there an Ally that we can bring into the field to redress the balance, and to make our ten as strong as the opposing twenty. Zerah the Ethiopian, who was coming down on Asa, is said to have had a million fighting-men at his back, but that is probably an erroneous figure, because Old Testament numbers are necessarily often unreliable. Asa had only half the number; so he said, 'What can I do?' And what *could* he do? He did the only thing possible, he 'grasped at God's skirts, and prayed,' and that made all the difference.

Now all that is true about the disproportion between the foes we have to face and fight and our own strength. It is eminently true about us Christian people, if we are doing any work for our Master. You hear people say, 'Look at the small number of professing Christians in this country, as compared with the numbers on the other side. What is the use of their trying to convert the world?' Well, think of the assembled Christian people, for instance, of Manchester, on the most charitable supposition, and the shallowest interpretation of that word 'Christian.' What are they among so many? A mere handful. If the Christian Church had to undertake the task of Christianising the world by its own strength, we might well despair of success and stop altogether. 'We have no might.' The disproportion both numerically and in all things that the world estimates as strength (which are many of them good things), is so great that we are in a worse case than Asa was. It is not two to one; it is twenty to one, or an even greater disproportion. But we are not only numerically weak. A multitude of non-effectives, mere camp followers, loosely attached, nominal Christians, have to be deducted from the muster-roll, and the few who are left are so feeble as well as few that they have more than enough to do in holding their own, to say nothing of dreaming of charging the wide-stretching lines of the enemy. So a profound self distrust is our wisdom. But that should not paralyse us, but lead to something better, as it led Asa.

II. Summoning God into the field should follow wholesome self-distrust.

Asa uses a remarkable expression, which is, perhaps, scarcely reproduced adequately in our Authorised Version: 'It is nothing with Thee to help, whether with many or with them that have no power.' It is a strange phrase, but it seems most probable that the suggested rendering in the Revised Version is nearer the writer's meaning, which says, 'Lord! there is none beside Thee to help between the mighty and them that have no power,' which to our ears is a somewhat cumbrous way of saying that God, and God only, can adjust the difference between the mighty and the weak; can redress the balance, and by the laying of His hand upon the feeble hand can make it strong as the mailed fist to which it is opposed. If we know ourselves to be hopelessly outnumbered, and send to God for reinforcements, He will clash His sword into the scale, and make it go down. Asa turns to God and says, 'Thou only canst trim the scales and make the lighter of the two the heavier one by casting Thy might into it. So help us, O Lord our God!'

One man with God at his back is always in the majority; and, however many there may be on the other side, 'there are more that be with us than they that be with them.' *There* is encouragement for people who have to fight unpopular causes in the world, who have been accustomed to be in minorities all their days, in the midst of a wicked and perverse generation. Never mind about the numbers; bring God into the field, and the little band, which is compared in another place in these historical Books to 'two flocks of kids' fronting the enemy, that had flowed all over the land, is in the majority. 'God with us'; then we are strong.

The consciousness of weakness may unnerve a man; and that is why people in the world are always patting each other on the back and saying 'Be of good cheer, and rely upon yourself.' But the self-distrust that turns to God becomes the parent of a far more reliable self-reliance than that which trusts to men. My consciousness of need is my opening the door for God to come in. Just as you always find the lakes in the hollows, so you will always find the grace of God coming into men's hearts to strengthen them and make them victorious, when there has been the preparation of the lowered estimate of one's self. Hollow out your heart by self-distrust, and God will fill it with the flashing waters of His strength bestowed. The more I feel myself weak, the more I am meant not to fold my hands and say, 'I never can do that thing; it is of no use my trying to attempt it, I may as well give it up'; but to say, 'Lord! there is none beside

Thee that can set the balance right between the mighty and him that hath no strength.' 'Help me, O Lord my God!' Just as those little hermit-crabs that you see upon the seashore, with soft bodies unprotected, make for the first empty shell they can find, and house in that and make it their fortress, our exposed natures, our unarmoured characters, our sense of weakness, ought to drive us to Him. As the unarmed population of a land invaded by the enemy pack their goods and hurry to the nearest fortified place, so when I say to myself I have no strength, let me say, 'Thou art my Rock, my Strength, my Fortress, and my Deliverer. My God, in whom I trust, my Buckler, and the Horn of my Salvation, and my high Tower.'

Now, there is one more word about this matter, and that is, the way by which we summon God into the field. Asa prays, 'Help us, O Lord our God! for we *rest* on Thee'; and the word that he employs for 'rest' is not a very frequent one. It carries with it a very striking picture. Let me illustrate it by a reference to another case where it is employed. It is used in that tragical story of the death of Saul, when the man that saw the last of him came to David and drew in a sentence the pathetic picture of the wearied, wounded, broken-hearted, discrowned, desperate monarch, *leaning on* his spear. You can understand how hard he leaned, with what a grip he held it, and how heavily his whole languid, powerless weight pressed upon it. And that is the word that is used here. 'We lean on Thee' as the wounded Saul leaned upon his spear. Is that a picture of your faith, my friend? Do you lean upon God like that, laying your hand upon Him till every vein on your hand stands out with the force and tension of the grasp? Or do you lean lightly, as a man that does not feel much the need of a support? Lean hard if you wish God to come quickly. 'We rest on Thee; help us, O Lord!'

III. Courageous advance should follow self-distrust and summoning God by faith.

It is well when self-distrust leads to confidence, when, as Charles Wesley has it in his great hymn:

'... I am weak,
But confident in self-despair.'

But that is not enough. It is better when self-distrust and confidence in God lead to courage, and as Asa goes on, 'Help us, for we rely on Thee, and in Thy name we go against this multitude.' Never mind though it is two to one. What does that matter? Prudence and calculation are well enough, but there is a great deal of very rank cowardice and want of faith in Christian people, both in regard to their own lives and in regard to Christian work in the world, which goes masquerading under much too respectable a name, and calls itself 'judicious caution' and 'prudence.' There is little ever done by that, especially in the Christian course; and the old motto of one of the French republicans holds good; 'Dare! dare! always dare!' You have more on your side than you have against you, and creeping prudence of calculation is not the temper in which the battle is won. 'Dash' is not always precipitate and presumptuous. If we have God with us, let us be bold in fronting the dangers and difficulties that beset us, and be sure that He will help us.

IV. And now the last point that I would notice is this—the all-powerful plea which God will answer.

'Thou art my God, let not man prevail against Thee.' That prayer covers two things. You may be quite sure that if God is your God you will not be beaten; and you may be quite sure that if you have made God's cause yours He will make your cause His, and again you will not be beaten.

'Thou art our God.' 'It takes two to make a bargain,' and God and we have both to act before He is truly ours. He gives Himself to us, but there is an act of ours required too, and you must take the God that is given to you, and make Him yours because you make yourselves His. And when I have taken Him for mine, and not unless I have, He is mine, to all intents of strength-giving and blessedness. When I can say, 'Thou art my God, and it is impossible that Thou wilt deny Thyself,' then nothing can snap that bond; and 'neither life nor death, nor angels, nor principalities, nor powers, nor things present, nor things to come, nor height, nor depth, nor any *other* creature' can do it. But there is a creature that can, and that is I. For I can separate *myself* from the love and the guardianship of God, and He can say to a man, 'I am thy God,' and the man *not* answer, 'Thou art my God.'

And then there is another plea here. 'Let not man prevail against Thee.' What business had Asa to identify his little kingdom and his victory with God's cause and God's conquest? Only this, that he had flung himself into God's arms, and because he had, and was trying to do what God would have him do, he was quite sure that it was not Asa but Jehovah that the million of Ethiopians were fighting against. People warn us against the fanaticism of taking for granted that our cause is God's cause. Well, we need the warning sometimes, but we may be quite sure of this, that if we have made God's cause ours, He will make our cause His, down to the minutest point in our daily lives.

And then, if thus we say in the depths of our hearts, and live accordingly, 'There is none other that fighteth for us, but only Thou, O God!' it will be with us as it was with Asa in the story before us, 'the enemy fled, and could not recover themselves, for they were destroyed before the Lord and before His hosts.'

THE SEARCH THAT ALWAYS FINDS

'They ... sought Him with their whole desire; and He was found of them: and the Lord gave them rest round about.'—2 CHRON. xv. 15.

THESE words occur in one of the least familiar passages of the Old Testament. They describe an incident in the reign of Asa, who was the grandson of Solomon's foolish son Rehoboam, and was consequently the third king of Judah after the secession of the North. He had just won a great victory, and was returning with his triumphant army to Jerusalem, when there met him a prophet, unknown otherwise, who poured out fiery words, exhorting Asa and his people to cleave to God and to cast away their idols. Asa, encouraged by the prophetic words of this bold speaker for God, screwed himself up, and was able to induce also his people, to effect a great religious reformation. He made a clean sweep of the idols, and gathered the sadly-dwindled nation together in Jerusalem, where they renewed the covenant with the Lord God of their fathers. The text sums up their work and its result. 'They sought Him with their whole heart, and He was found of them; and the Lord gave them rest round about.' The words express in simplest form what should be the chief desire of our hearts and occupation of our lives, and what will then be our peaceful experience. We shall best bring out these points if we take the words just as they lie, and consider the seeking, the finding which certainly crowns that seeking, and the rest which ensues on finding God.

I. The seeking.

Now, of course, there is no doubt that what the chronicler meant to describe by the phrase, 'seeking the Lord,' was largely the mere external acts of ritual worship, the superficial turning from idols to a purely external recognition of God as the God of Israel. But while there may have been nothing deeper than a change in the nominal object of nominal worship, so far as many were concerned, no doubt a very real turning of heart to God underlay the external change in many other cases, of which the destruction of idols and the renewed observance of the form of Jehovah's worship were the consequence and sign. That turning of mind, will, and affection towards God must be ours if we are to be among those wise and happy seekers who are sure to find that which—or rather Him whom—they seek and to rest in Him whom they find. That search is not after a lost treasure, nor does it imply ignorance of where its object is to be found. We seek that which we know, and which we may be assured of finding. Therefore there need be no tremors of uncertainty in our quest, and the blessedness of the search is as real as, though different from, the blessedness of the possession which ends it. The famous saying which prefers the search after, to the possession of truth, is more proud than wise; but the comparison which it institutes is so far true that there is a joy in the aspiration after and the efforts towards truth only less joyous than that which attends its attainment. But truth divorced from

God is finite and may pall, become familiar and lose its radiance, like a gathered flower; and hence the preference for the search is intelligible though one-sided. But God does not pall, and the more we find Him the more we delight in Him; the highest bliss is to find Him, the next highest is to seek Him; and, since seeking and finding Him are never wholly separate, these kindred joys blend their lights in the experience of all His children.

But our text lays emphasis on the whole-heartedness of the people's seeking of God. The search must be earnest and engaged in with the whole energy of our whole being, if any blessing is to come from it. Why! one reason why the great mass of professing Christians make so little of their religion is because they are only half-hearted in it. If you divide a river into two streams the force of each is less than half the power of the original current; and the chances are that you will make a stagnant marsh where there used to be a flowing stream. 'All in all, or not at all,' is the rule for life, in all departments. It is the rule in daily business. A man that puts only half himself in his profession or trade, while the other half of his wits is gone woolgathering and dreaming, is predestined from all eternity to fail. The same is true about our religion. If you and I attend to it as a kind of by-occupation; if we give the balance of our time and the superfluity of our energy, after we have done a hard day's work—say, an hour upon a Sunday—to seeking God, and devote all the rest of the week to seeking worldly prosperity, it is no wonder if our religion languishes, and is mainly a matter of forms, as it is with such hosts of people that call themselves Christians.

Oh! dear brethren, I do believe there is more unconscious unreality in the average Christian man's endeavour to be a better Christian than there is in almost anything else in the world:—

> 'One foot on sea, and one on shore,
> To one thing constant never.'

That is why so many of us know nothing of a progressive strengthening of our faith, and an increasing conquest of ourselves, and a firmer grasp of God, and a fuller realisation of the blessedness of walking in His ways.

'They sought Him with all their heart.' That does not mean, remember, that there are to be no other desires, for it is a great mistake to pit religion against other things which are meant to be its instruments and its helps. We are not required to seek nothing else in order to seek God wholly. He demands no impossible and fantastic detachment of ourselves from the ordinary and legitimate occupations, affections, and duties of human life, but He does ask that the dominant desire after Him should be powerful enough to express itself through all our actions, and that we should seek for God in them, and for them in God.

Whilst thus we are to give the right interpretation to that whole-heartedness in our seeking God, on which the text lays stress, do not let us forget that the one token of it which the text specifies is, casting out our idols. There must be detachment if there is to be attachment. If some climbing plant, for instance, has twisted itself round the unprofitable thorns in the hedge, the gardener, before he can get it to go up the support that it is meant to encircle, has carefully to detach it from the stays to which it has wantonly clung, taking care that in the process he does not break its tendrils and destroy its power of growth. So, to train our souls to cleave to God, and to grow up round the great Stay that is provided for us, there is needed, as an essential part of the process, the voluntary, conscious, conscientious, and constant guarding of ourselves from the vagrancies of our desires, which send out their shoots away from Him; and when the objects of these become idols, then there is nothing for it but that, like Asa and his people, we should hew them to pieces and make a bonfire of them; and then renew our covenant before God. I desire to press that upon you and upon myself. The heart must be emptied of baser liquors, if the new wine of the Kingdom is to be poured into it.

True it is, of course—and thank God for it!—that the most powerful agent in effecting that detachment of ourselves from lower things is our fruition of higher. It is when God comes into the temple that Dagon falls on the threshold. It is when a new affection begins to spring in the heart that old loves are thrust out of it. But whilst that is true, it is also true that the two processes run on simultaneously; and that whilst, on the one hand, if we are ever to overcome our love of the world it must be through the love of God, on the other hand, if we are ever to be confirmed in a whole-hearted love of God, it must be through our conquest of our love of the world. 'Unite my heart to fear Thy name' was the profound prayer of the old Psalmist; and the 'heart,' according to Old Testament usage, is the central fountain from which flow all the streams of conscious life. To seek Him with the whole heart is to engage the whole self in the quest, and that is the only kind of seeking which has the certainty of success.

II. The finding which crowns such seeking.

'He was found of them.' Yes; anything is possible rather than that a whole-hearted search after God should be a vain search. For there are, in that case, *two* seekers—God is seeking for us more truly than we are seeking for Him. And if the mother is seeking her child, and the child its mother, it will be a very wide desert where they will not meet. 'The Father seeketh such to worship Him,' that is—the divine activity is going about the world, searching for the heart that turns to Him, and it cannot but be that they that seek Him shall find Him, or 'shall be found of Him.' Open the windows, and you cannot keep out the sunshine; open your lungs and you cannot keep out the air. 'In Him we live and move and have our being,' and if our desires turn, however blindly, to Him, and are accompanied with the appropriate action, heaven and earth are more likely to rush to ruin than such a searching to be frustrated of its aim.

Brethren! is there anything else in the world of which you can say, 'Seek, and ye shall find'? You, with white hairs on your heads, have you found anything else in which the chase was sure to result in the capture; in which capture was sure to yield all that the hunter had wished? There is only one direction for a man's desires and aims, in which disappointment is an impossibility. In all other regions the most that can be promised is 'Seek, and *perhaps* you will find'; and, when you have found, perhaps you will feel that the prize was not worth the finding. Or it is, 'Seek, and *possibly* you will find; and after you have found and kept for a little while, you will lose.' Though it may be

> 'Better to have loved and lost,
> Than never to have loved at all,'

a treasure that slips out of our fingers is not the best treasure that we can search for. But here the assurance is, 'Seek, and ye *shall* find; and shall never lose. Find, and you shall always possess.'

What would you think of a company of gold-seekers, hunting about in some exhausted claim, for hypothetical grains, ragged, starving—and all the while in the next gully were lying lumps of gold for the picking up? And that figure fairly represents what people do and suffer who seek for good and do not seek for God.

III. The rest which ensues on finding God.

'The Lord gave them rest round about.' We believe that the Jewish nation was under special supernatural guidance, so that national adherence to the Law was always followed by external prosperity. That is not, of course, the case with us. But which is the better thing, 'rest round about' or rest within? We have no immunity from toil or conflict. Seeking God does not cover our heads from the storm of external calamities, nor arm our hearts against the darts and daggers of many a pain, anxiety, and care, but disturbance around is a very small matter if there be a better thing, rest within.

Do you remember who it was that said, 'In the world ye shall have tribulation . . . but in Me ye shall have peace'? Then we have, as it were, two abodes—one, as far as regards the life of sense, in the world of sense —another, as far as regards the inmost self, which may, if we will, be in Christ. A vessel with an outer casing and a layer of air between it and the inner will keep its contents hot. So we may have round us the very opposite of repose, and, if God so wills, let us not kick against His will; we may have conflict and stir and strife, and yet a better rest than that of my text may be ours. 'Rest round about' is sometimes good and sometimes bad. It is often bad, for it is the people that 'have no changes' who most usually 'do not fear God.' But rest within, that is sure to come when a man has sought with all his desire for God, whom he has found in all His fullness, is only good and best of all.

We all know, thank God! in worldly matters and in inferior degree, how blessed and restful it is when some strong affection is gratified, some cherished desire fulfilled. Though these satisfactions are not perpetual, nor perfect, they may teach us what a depth of blessed and calm repose, incapable of being broken by any storms or by any tasks, will come to and abide with the man whose deepest love is satisfied in God, and whose most ardent desires have found more than they sought for in Him. Be sure of this, dear friends! that if we do thus seek, and thus find, it is not in the power of anything 'that is at enmity with joy' utterly to 'abolish or destroy' the quietness of our hearts. 'Rest in the Lord, and wait patiently for Him.' They who thus repose will have peace in their hearts, even whilst tasks and temptations, changes and sorrows, disturb their outward lives. 'In the world ye shall have tribulation.' Be it so; it may be borne with submission and thankfulness if in Christ we have peace.

Thus we may have the peace of God, rest in and from Him, entering into us, and in due time, by His gracious guidance and help, we shall enter into eternal rest. Whilst to seek is to find Him, in a very deep and blessed sense, even in this life; in another aspect all our earthly life may be regarded as seeking after Him, and the future as the true finding of Him. That future will bring to those whose hearts have turned from the shows and vanities of time to God a possession of Him so much fuller than was experienced here that the lesser discoveries and enjoyments of Him which are experienced here, scarcely deserve in comparison to be called by the same name. So my text may be taken, as in its first part, a description of the blessed life here—'They sought Him with all their heart'—and in its second, as a shadowy vision of the yet more blessed life hereafter, 'He was found of them, and the Lord gave them rest round about,' as well as within, in the land of peace, where sorrow and sighing, and toil and care, shall pass from memory; and they that warred against us shall be far away.

JEHOSHAPHAT'S REFORM

'And Jehoshaphat his son reigned in his stead, and strengthened himself against Israel. 2. And he placed forces in all the fenced cities of Judah, and set garrisons in the land of Judah, and in the cities of Ephraim, which Asa his father had taken. 3. And the Lord was with Jehoshaphat, because he walked in the first ways of his father David, and sought not unto Baalim; 4. But sought to the Lord God of his father, and walked in His commandments, and not after the doings of Israel. 5. Therefore the Lord established the kingdom in his hand; and all Judah brought to Jehoshaphat presents; and he had riches and honour in abundance. 6. And his heart was lifted up in the ways of the Lord: moreover he took away the high places and groves out of Judah. 7. Also in the third year of his reign he sent to his princes, even to Ben-hail, and to Obadiah, and to Zechariah, and to Nethaneel, and to Michaiah, to teach in the cities of Judah. 8. And with them he sent Levites, even Shemaiah, and Nethaniah, and Zebadiah, and Asahel, and Shemiramoth, and Jehonathan, and Adonijah, and Tobijah, and Tobadonijah, Levites: and with them Elishama and Jehoram, priests. 9. And they taught in Judah, and had the book of the law of the Lord with them, and went about throughout all the cities of Judah, and taught the people. 10. And the fear of the Lord fell upon all the kingdoms of the lands that were round about Judah, so that they made no war against Jehoshaphat.'—2 CHRON. xvii. 1-10.

THE first point to be noted in this passage is that Jehoshaphat followed in the steps of Asa his father. Stress is laid on his adherence to the ancestral faith, 'the first ways of his father David,'—before his great fall,—and the paternal example, 'he sought to the God of his father.' Such carrying on of a predecessor's work is rare in the line of kings of Judah, where father and son were seldom of the same mind in religion. The principle of hereditary monarchy secures peaceful succession, but not continuity of policy. Many a king of Judah had to say in his heart what Ecclesiastes puts into Solomon's mouth, 'I hated all my labour, . . . seeing that I must leave it unto the man that shall be after me. And who knoweth whether he shall be a wise man or a fool?'

But it is not only in kings' houses that that experience is realised. Many a home is saddened to-day because the children do not seek the God of their fathers. 'Instead of the fathers' should 'come up thy children'; but, alas! grandmother Lois and mother Eunice do not always see the boy who has known the Scriptures from a child grow up into a Timothy, in whom their unfeigned faith lives again. The neglect of religious instruction in professedly Christian families, the inconsistent lives of parents or their too rigid restraints, or, sometimes, their too lax discipline, are to be blamed for many such cases. But there are many instances in which not the parents, but the children, are to be blamed. An earnest Sunday-school teacher may do much to lead the children of godly parents to their father's God. Blessed is the home where the golden chain of common faith binds hearts together, and family love is elevated and hallowed by common love of God!

Jehoshaphat's religion was, further, resolutely held in the face of prevailing opposition. 'The Baalim' were popular; it was fashionable to worship them. They were numerous, and all varieties of taste could find a Baal to please them. But this young king turned from the tempting ways that opened flower-strewn before him, and chose the narrow road that led upwards. 'So did not I, because of the fear of God,' might have been his motto. A similar determined setting of our faces God-ward, in spite of the crowd of tempting false deities around us, must mark us, if we are to have any religion worth calling by the name. This king recoiled from the example of the neighbouring monarchy, and walked 'not after the doings of Israel.' His seeking to God was very practical, for it was not shown simply by professed beliefs or by sentiment, but by ordering his life in obedience to God's will. The test of real religion is, after all, a life unlike the lives of the men who do not share our faith, and moulded in accordance with God's known will. It is vain to allege that we are seeking the Lord unless we are walking in His commandments.

Prosperity followed godliness, in accordance with the divinely appointed connection between them which characterised the Old Dispensation. 'Prosperity is the blessing of the Old Testament; adversity is the blessing of the New,' says Bacon. But the epigram is too neat to be entirely true, for the Book of Job and many a psalm show that the eternal problem of suffering innocence was raised by facts even in the old days, and in our days there are forms of well-being which are the natural fruits of well-doing. Still, the connection was closer in Judah than with us, and, in the case before us, the establishment of Jehoshaphat in the kingdom, his subjects' love, which showed itself in voluntary gifts over and above the taxes imposed, and his wealth and honour, were the direct results of his true religion.

A really devout man must be a propagandist. True faith cannot be hid nor be dumb. As certainly as light must radiate must faith strive to communicate itself.

So the account of Jehoshaphat's efforts to spread the worship of Jehovah follows the account of his personal godliness. 'His heart was lifted up in the ways of the Lord.' There are two kinds of lifted-up hearts; one when pride, self-sufficiency, and forgetfulness of God, raise a man to a giddy height, from which God's judgments are sure to cast him down and break him in the fall; one when a lowly heart is raised to high courage and devotion, and 'set on high,' because it fears God's name. Such elevation is consistent with humility. It fears no fall; it is an elevation above earthly desires and terrors, neither of which can reach it, so as to hinder the man from walking in 'the ways of the Lord.' This king was lifted to it by his happy experience of the blessed effects of obedience. These encouraged him to vigorous efforts to spread the religion which had thus gladdened and brightened his own life. Is that the use we make of the ease which God gives us?

Jehoshaphat had to destroy first, in order to build up. The 'high places and Asherim' had to be taken out of Judah before the true worship could be established there. So it is still. The Christian has to carry a sword in the one hand, and a trowel in the other. Many a rotten old building, the stones of which have been cemented in blood, has to be swept away before the fair temple can be reared. The Devil is in possession of much of the world, and the lawful owner has to dispossess the 'squatter.' No one can suppose that society is organised on Christian principles even in so-called 'Christian countries'; and there is much overturning work to be done before He whose right it is to reign is really king over the whole earth. We, too, have our 'high places and Asherim' to root out.

But that destructive work is not to be done by force.

Institutions can only be swept away when public opinion has grown to see their evils. Forcible reformations of manners, and, still more, of religion, never last, but are sure to be followed by violent rebounds to the old order. So, side by side with the removal of idolatry, this king took care to diffuse the knowledge of the true worship, by sending out a body of influential commissioners to teach in Judah. That was a new departure of great importance. It presents several interesting features. The composition of the staff of instructors is remarkable. The principal men in it are five court officers, next to whom, and subordinate, as is shown not only by the order of enumeration, but by the phrase 'with them,' were nine Levites, and, last and lowest of all, two priests. We might have expected that priests should be the most numerous and important members of such a body, and we are led to suspect that the priesthood was so corrupted as to be careless about religious reformation. A clerical order is not always the most ardent in religious revival. The commissioners were probably chosen, without regard to their being priests, Levites, or 'laymen,' because of their zeal in the worship of Jehovah; and the five 'princes' head the list in order to show the royal authority of the commission.

Another point is the emphasis with which their function of teaching is thrice mentioned in three verses. Apparently the bulk of the nation knew little or nothing of 'the law of the Lord,' either on its spiritual and moral or its ceremonial side; and Jehoshaphat's object was to effect an enlightened, not a forcible and superficial, change. God's way of influencing actions is to reveal Himself to the understanding and the heart, that these may move the will, and that may shape the deeds. Wise men will imitate God's way. Jehoshaphat did not issue royal commands, but sent out teachers. In chapter xix. we find him despatching 'judges' in similar fashion throughout Judah. They had the power to punish, but these teachers had only authority to explain and to exhort.

The present writer accepts the chronicler's statement that the teachers had 'the Book of the Law' with them, though he recognises it as possible that that 'Book' was not identical with the complete collection of documents which now bears the name. But, be that as it may, the incident of our text is remarkable as being the only recorded systematic and complete attempt to diffuse the remedy against idolatry throughout the kingdom, as putting religious reformation on its only sure ground, and as hinting at deep and widespread ignorance among the masses.

'When a man's ways please the Lord, He maketh even his enemies to be at peace with him.' So Judah found. 'A terror of the Lord fell upon all the kingdoms' around. No doubt, the news filtered to them of how Jehovah was exerting His might on the nation, and a certain indefinable awe of this so potent god, who was defeating the Baalim, made them think that peace was the best policy. Each nation was supposed to have its own god, and the national god was supposed to fight for his worshippers; so that war was a struggle of deities as well as of men, and the stronger god won. Here was a god who had reconquered his territory, and had cast out usurpers. Prudence dictated keeping on good terms with him. But it never occurred to any of these peoples that their own gods were any less real than Judah's, or that Judah's God could ever become theirs.

AMASIAH

'Amasiah, the son of Zichri, who willingly offered himself unto the Lord.'—2 CHRON. xvii. 16.

THIS is a scrap from the catalogue of Jehoshaphat's 'mighty men of valour'; and is Amasiah's sole record. We see him for a moment and hear his eulogium and then oblivion swallows him up. We do not know what it was that he did to earn it. But what a fate, to live to all generations by that one sentence!

I. Cheerful self-surrender the secret of all religion.

The words of our text contain a metaphor naturally drawn from the sacrificial system. It comes so easily to us that we scarcely recognise the metaphorical element, but the clear recognition of it gives great additional energy to the words. Amasiah was both sacrificer and sacrifice. His offering was self-immolation. As in all love, so in that noblest kind of it which clasps God, its perfect expression is, 'I give Thee my living, loving self.' Nor is it only sacrifice and sacrificer that are seen in deepest truth in the experience of the Christian life, but the reality of the Temple is also there, for 'Ye also . . . are built up a spiritual house, to be a holy priesthood, to offer up spiritual sacrifices.' Only when God dwells in us, shall we have the nerve and the firmness of hand to take the knife and 'slay before the Lord,' the awful Guest in the sanctuary within, the most precious of the children of our spirits.

The essence of the sacrifice of self is the sacrifice of will. In the Christian experience 'willingly offered' is almost tautology, for unwilling offerings are a contradiction and in fact there are no such things. The quality of unwillingness destroys the character of the offering and robs it of all sacredness. Reluctant Christianity is not Christianity. That noun and that adjective can never be buckled together.

The submission of will and the consequent surrender of myself and my powers, opportunities, and possessions, so that I do all, enjoy all, use all, and when need is, endure all with glad thankful reference to God is only possible to me in the measure in which my will is made flexible by love, and such will-subduing love comes only when we 'know and believe the love that God hath to us.' There is the point at which not a few moral and religious teachers go wrong and bewilder themselves and their disciples. There, too, is the point at which Christ and the Gospel of salvation through faith in Him stand forth as emancipating humanity from the dreary round of efforts and vain attempts to work up the condition needful for achieving the height of self-surrender, which is seen to be indispensable to all true nobleness of living, but is felt to be beyond the reach of the ordinary man. There, too, is the point at which many good people mar their lives as Christians. They waste their strength in trying to bring the jibbing horse up to the leap. They try to blow up a fire of devotion and to make themselves priests to offer themselves, but all the while the mutinous self recoils from the leap, and the fire burns smokily, and their sacrifice is laid on the altar with little joy, because they have not been careful and wise enough to begin at the beginning and to follow God's way of melting their wills, by love, the reflection of the Infinite love of God to them. God's priests offer themselves because they offer their wills; they offer their wills because they love God; they love God because they know that God loves them. That is the divine order. It is vain to try to accomplish the end by any other.

II. This willing offering hallows all life.

No syllable is left to tell us what Amasiah did to win this praise. Probably the words enshrine some now forgotten memory of his cheerful courage, some heroic feat on an unrecorded battlefield. Particulars are not given nor needed. Specific actions are unimportant; the spirit of a life can be told with very incomplete details, and it, not the details, is the important thing. Sometimes, as in many modern biographies, one 'cannot see the wood for the trees,' and misses the main drift and aim of a life in the chaos of a bewildering mass of nothings. How much more happy the lot of this man of whom we have only the generalised expression of the text, unweighted and undisturbed by petty incidents! It takes tons of rose leaves to make a tiny phial of otto of roses, but the fragrance is far more pungent in a drop of the distillation than in armfuls of leaves. Every life shrinks into very small compass, and the centuries do not tolerate long biographies. Shall we not seek to order our life so that Amasiah's epitaph may serve for us? It will be blessed if this—and nothing else—is known about us, that we 'willingly offered ourselves to the Lord.' My friend! will that be a true epitome of your life?

III. This willing offering is accepted by God.

We may hear a mightier voice behind the chronicler's, and the judgment of the Judge of all pronounced by His lips. It matters little what men say of one another, but it matters everything what God says of us. We are but too apt to forget that He is now saying something as to each of us, and that we have not to wait for death to put a final period to our activities, before our lives become fit subjects for God's judgment. Moment by moment we are writing our own sentences. But while it is good for us to remember the continuous judgment of God on each deed, it is not good to let dark thoughts of the principles of that judgment paralyse our activity or chill our confidence in His forgiving and accepting mercy. There is often a dark suspicion, like that of the one-talented servant, which blackens God's fair fame as being 'an austere Man,' making demands rather than imparting power, and the effect of such an ugly conception of Him is to cut the nerve of service and bury the talent, carefully folded up, it may be, but none the less earning nothing. 'If we call on Him as Father, who without respect of persons judgeth according to every man's work,' let us be sure that it will be a Fatherly judgment that He will pass upon us and our offerings. There is a wonderful collection on His altar of what many people would think rubbish, just as many a mother has laid away among her treasures some worthless article which her child had once given her—a weed plucked by the roadside in a long past summer day, some trifle of rare preciousness in the child's eyes, and of none in any others than her own. She opens her drawer and brings out the poor little thing, and her eyes fill and her heart fills as she looks. And does not God keep His children's gifts as lovingly, and set them in places of honour in the day when He 'makes up His jewels'? There are cups of cold water and widows' mites and much else that a supercilious world would call 'trash' stored there. Thank God! He accepts imperfect service, faltering faith, partial consecration, a little love. Even our poor offering may be an 'odour of a sweet smell,' ministering fragrance that is a delight to Him, if it is offered with the much incense of the great Sacrifice and through the mediation of the great High Priest.

The world forgot Amasiah, or never knew him, an obscure soldier in an obscure kingdom, but God did not forget, and here is his epitaph, and this is his memorial to all generations. Men's chronicles have no room for all the names that their wearers are eager to have inscribed on their crumbling and crowded pages, 'but the Lamb's Book of Life' has ample space on its radiant pages for all who desire to set their names there, and if ours are there, we need not envy the proudest whose titles and deeds fill the most conspicuous pages in the world's records. 'Then shall every man have praise of Christ,' and he who wins that guerdon needs nothing more, and can have nothing more to swell his blessedness.

'A MIRROR FOR MAGISTRATES'

'And Jehoshaphat the king of Judah returned to his house in peace to Jerusalem. 2. And Jehu the son of Hanani the seer went out to meet him, and said to king Jehoshaphat, Shouldest thou help the ungodly, and love them that hate the Lord? therefore is wrath upon thee from before the Lord. 3. Nevertheless there are good things found in thee, in that thou hast taken away the groves out of the land, and hast prepared thine heart to seek God. 4. And Jehoshaphat dwelt at Jerusalem: and he went out again through the people from Beer-sheba to mount Ephraim, and brought them back unto the Lord God of their fathers. 5. And he set judges in the land throughout all the fenced cities of Judah, city by city. 6. And said to the judges, Take heed what ye do: for ye judge not for man, but for the Lord, who is with you in the judgment. 7. Wherefore now let the fear of the Lord be upon you; take heed and do it: for there is no iniquity with the Lord our God, nor respect of persons, nor taking of gifts. 8. Moreover in Jerusalem did Jehoshaphat set of the Levites, and of the priests, and of the chief of the fathers of Israel, for the judgment of the Lord, and for controversies, when they returned to Jerusalem. 9. And he charged them, saying, Thus shall ye do in the fear of the Lord, faithfully, and with a perfect heart. 10. And what cause soever shall come to you of your brethren that dwell in their cities, between blood and blood, between law and commandment, statutes and judgments, ye shall even warn them that they trespass not against the Lord, and so wrath come upon you, and upon your brethren: this do, and ye shall not trespass. 11. And, behold, Amariah the chief priest is over you in all matters of the Lord; and Zebadiah the son of Ishmael, the ruler of the house of Judah, for all the king's matters: also the Levites shall be officers before you. Deal courageously, and the Lord shall be with the good.'—2 CHRON. xix. 1-11.

JEHOSHAPHAT is distinguished by two measures for his people's good: one, his sending out travelling preachers through the land (2 Chron. xvii. 7-9); another, this provision of local judges and a central court in Jerusalem. The former was begun as early as the third year of his reign, but was probably interrupted, like other good things, by his ill-omened alliance with Ahab. The prophet Jehu's plain speaking seems to have brought the king back to his better self, and its fruit was his going 'among the people,' from south to north, as a missionary, 'to bring them back to Jehovah.' The religious reformation was accompanied by his setting judges throughout the land. Our modern way of distinguishing between religious and civil concerns is foreign to Eastern thought, and was especially out of the question in a theocracy. Jehovah was the King of Judah; therefore the things that are Caesar's and the things that are God's coalesced, and these two objects of Jehoshaphat's journeyings were pursued simultaneously. We have travelled far from his simple institutions, and our course has not been all progress. His supreme concern was to deal out even-handed justice between man and man; is not ours rather to give ample doses of law? To him the judicial function was a copy of God's, and its exercise a true act of worship, done in His fear, and modelled after His pattern. The first impression made in one of our courts is scarcely that judge and counsel are engaged in worship.

There had been local judges before Jehoshaphat—elders in the villages, the 'heads of the fathers' houses' in the tribes. We do not know whether the great secession had flung the simple old machinery somewhat out of gear, or whether Jehoshaphat's action was simply to systematise and make universal the existing arrangements. But what concerns us most is to note that all the charge which he gives to these peasant magistrates bears on the religious aspect of their duties. They are to think themselves as acting for Jehovah and with Jehovah. If they recognise the former, they may be confident of the latter. They are to 'let the fear of Jehovah be upon you,' for that awe resting on a spirit will, like a burden or water-jar on a woman's shoulder, make the carriage upright and the steps firm. They are not only to act for and with Jehovah, but to do like Him, avoiding injustice, favouritism, and corruption, the plague-spots of Eastern law-courts. In such a state of society, the cases to be adjudicated were mostly such as mother-wit, honesty and the fear of God could solve; other times call for other qualifications. But still, let us learn from this charge that even in our necessarily complicated legal systems and political life, there is room and sore need for the application of the same principles. What a different world it would be if our judges and representatives carried some tincture of Jehoshaphat's simple and devout wisdom into their duties! Civic and political life ought to be as holy as that of cloister and cell. To judge righteously, to vote honestly, is as much worship as to pray. A politician may be 'a priest of the Most High God.'

And for us all the spirit of Jehoshaphat's charge is binding, and every trivial and secular task is to be discharged for God, with God, in the fear of God. 'On the bells of the horses shall be Holiness unto Jehovah.'

If our religion does not drive the wheels of daily life, so much the worse for our life and our religion. But, above all, this charge reminds us that the secret of right living is to imitate God. These peasants were to find direction, as well as inspiration, in gazing on Jehovah's character, and trying to copy it. And we are to be 'imitators of God, as beloved children,' though our best efforts may only produce poor results. A masterpiece may be copied in some wretched little newspaper blotch, but the great artist will own it for a copy, and correct it into complete likeness.

The second step was to establish a 'supreme court' in Jerusalem, which had two divisions, ecclesiastical and civil, as we should say, the former presided over by the chief priest, and the latter by 'the ruler of the house of Judah.' Murder cases and the graver questions involving interpretation of the law were sent up thither, while the village judges had probably to decide only points that shrewdness and integrity could settle. But these superior judges, too, received charges as to moral, rather than intellectual or learned qualifications. Religiously, uprightly, 'with a perfect heart,' courageously, they were to act, 'and Jehovah be with the good!' That may be a prayer, like the old invocation with which heralds sent knights to tilt at each other, and with which, in some legal proceedings, the pleas are begun, 'God defend the right!' But more probably it is an assurance that God will guide the judges to favour the good cause, if they on their parts will bring the aforesaid qualities to their decisions. And are not these qualities just such as will, for the most part, give similar results to us, if in our various activities we exercise them? And may we not see a sequence worth our practically putting to the proof in these characteristics enjoined on Jehoshaphat's supreme court? Begin with 'the fear of the Lord'; that will help us to 'faithfulness and a perfect heart'; and these again by taking away occasions of ignoble fear, and knitting together the else tremulous and distracted nature, will make the fearful brave and the weak strong.

But another thought is suggested by Jehoshaphat's language. Note how this court does not seem to have inflicted punishments, but to have had only counsels and warnings to wield. It was a board of conciliation rather than a penal tribunal. Two things it had to do—to press upon the parties the weighty consideration that crimes against men were sins against God, and that the criminal drew down wrath on the community. This remarkable provision brings out strongly thoughts that modern society will be the better for incorporating. The best way to deal with men is to get at their hearts and consciences. The deeper aspect of civil crimes or wrongs to men should be pressed on the doer; namely, that they are sins against God. Again, all such acts are sins against the mystical sacred bond of brotherhood. Again, the solidarity of a nation makes it inevitable that 'one sinner destroyeth much good,' and pulls down with him, when God smites him, a multitude of innocents. So finely woven is the web of the national life that, if a thread run in any part of it, a great rent gapes. If one member sins, all the members suffer with it. And lastly, the cruellest thing that we can do is to be dumb when we see sin being committed. It is not public men, judges and the like, alone, who are called on thus to warn evil-doers, but all of us in our degree. If we do not, we are guilty along with a guilty nation; and it is only when, to the utmost of our power, we have warned our brethren as to national sins, that we can wash our hands in innocency. 'This do, and ye shall not be guilty.'

A STRANGE BATTLE

'We have no might against this great company that cometh against us; neither know we what to do: but our eyes are upon Thee.'—2 CHRON. xx. 12.

A FORMIDABLE combination of neighbouring nations, of which Moab and Ammon, the ancestral enemies of Judah, were the chief, was threatening Judah. Jehoshaphat, the king, was panic-stricken when he heard of the heavy war-cloud that was rolling on, ready to burst in thunder on his little kingdom. His first act was to muster the nation, not as a military levy but as suppliants, 'to seek help of the Lord.' The enemy was camping down by the banks of the Dead Sea, almost within striking distance of Jerusalem. It seemed a time for fighting, not for praying, but even at that critical moment, the king and the men, whom it might have appeared that plain duty called to arms, were gathered in the Temple, and, hampered by their wives and children, were praying. Would they not have done better if they had been sturdily marching through the wilderness of Judah to front their foes? Our text is the close and the climax of Jehoshaphat's prayer, and, as the event proved, it was the most powerful weapon that could have been employed, for the rest of the chapter tells the strangest story of a campaign that was ever written. No sword was drawn. The army was marshalled, but Levites with their instruments of music, not fighters with their spears, led the van, and as 'they began to sing and to praise,' sudden panic laid hold on the invading force, who turned their arms against each other. So when Judah came to some rising ground, on which stood a watch-tower commanding a view over the savage grimness of 'the wilderness,' it saw a field of corpses, stark and stiff and silent. Three days were spent in securing the booty, and on the fourth, Jehoshaphat and his men 'assembled themselves in the Valley of Blessing,' and thence returned a joyous multitude praising God for the victory which had been won for them without their having struck a blow. The whole story may yield large lessons, seasonable at all times. We deal with it, rather than with the fragment of the narrative which we have taken as our text.

I. We see here the confidence of despair.

Jehoshaphat's prayer had stayed itself on God's self-revelation in history, and on His gift of the land to their fathers. It had pleaded that the enemy's hostility was a poor 'reward' for Israel's ancient forbearance, and now, with a burst of agony, it casts down before God, as it were, Judah's desperate plight as outnumbered by the swarm of invaders and brought to their last shifts—'we have no might against this great company . . . neither know we what to do.' But the very depth of despair sets them to climb to the height of trust. That is a mighty 'But,' which buckles into one sentence two such antitheses as confront us here. 'We know not what to do, but our eyes are upon Thee'—blessed is the desperation which catches at God's hand; firm is the trust which leaps from despair!

The helplessness is always a fact, though most of us manage to get along for the most part without discovering it. We are all outnumbered and overborne by the claims, duties, hindrances, sorrows, and entanglements of life. He is not the wisest of men who, facing all that life may bring and take away, all that it must bring and take away, knows no quiver of nameless fear, but jauntily professes himself ready for all that life can inflict. But there come moments in every life when the false security in which shallow souls wrap themselves ignobly is broken up, and then often a paroxysm of terror or misery grips a man, for which he has no anodyne, and his despair is as unreasonable as his security. The meaning of all circumstances that force our helplessness on us is to open to us Jehoshaphat's refuge in his—'our eyes are upon Thee.' We need to be driven by the crowds of foes and dangers around to look upwards. Our props are struck away that we may cling to God. The tree has its lateral branches hewed off that it may shoot up heavenward. When the valley is filled with mist and swathed in evening gloom, it is the time to lift our gaze to the peaks that glow in perpetual sunshine. Wise and happy shall we be if the sense of helplessness begets in us the energy of a desperate faith. For these two, distrust of self and glad confidence in God, are not opposites, as naked distrust and trust are, but are complementary. He does not turn his eyes to God who has not turned them on himself, and seen there nothing to which to cling, nothing on which to lean. Astronomers tell us that there are double stars revolving round one axis and forming a unity, of which the one is black and the other brilliant. Self-distrust and trust in God are thus knit together and are really one.

II. We see here the peaceful assurance of victory that attends on faith.

A flash of inspiration came to one of the Levitical

singers who had, no doubt, been deeply moved and had unconsciously fitted himself for receiving it. Divinely breathed confidence illuminated his waiting spirit, and a great message of encouragement poured from his lips. His words heartened the host more than a hundred trumpets braying in their ears. How much one man who has drunk in God's assurance of victory can do to send a thrill of his own courage through more timorous hearts! Courage is no less contagious than panic. This Levite becomes the commander of the army, and Jehoshaphat and his captains 'bow their heads' and accept his plan for to-morrow, hearing in his ringing accents a message from Jehovah. The instructions given and at once accepted are as unlike those of ordinary warfare as is the whole incident; for there is to be no sword drawn nor blow struck, but they are to 'stand still and see the salvation of the Lord.' They are told where to find the enemy and are bid to go forth in order of battle against them, and they are assured 'that the battle is not theirs, but God's.' No wonder that the message was hailed as from heaven, and put new heart into the host, or that, when the messenger's voice ceased, his brother Levites broke into shrill praise as for a victory already won. With what calm, triumphant hearts the camp would sleep that night!

May we not take that inspired Levite's message as one to ourselves in the midst of our many conflicts both in the outward life and in the inward? If we have truly grasped God's hands, and are fighting for what is accordant with His will, we have a right to feel that 'the battle is not ours but God's,' and to be sure that therefore we shall conquer. Of course we are not to say to ourselves, 'God will fight for us, and we need not strike a blow.' Jehoshaphat's example does not fit our case in that respect, and we may thank God that it does not. We have a better lot than to 'stand still and see the salvation of God,' for we are honoured by being allowed to share the stress of conflict and the glow of battle as well as in the shout of victory. But even in the struggles of outward life, and much more in those of our spiritual nature, every man who watches his own career will many a time have to recognise God's hand, unaided by any act of his own, striking for him and giving him victory; and in the spiritual life every Christian man knows that his best moments have come from the initiation of the Spirit who 'bloweth where He listeth.' How often we have been surprised by God's help; how often we have been quickened by God's inbreathed Spirit, and have been taught that the passivity of faith draws to us greater blessings than the activity of effort! 'They also serve who only stand and wait,' and they also conquer who in quietness and confidence keep themselves still and let God work for them and in them. The first great blessing of trust in God is that we may be at peace on the eve of battle, and the second is that in every battle it is, in truth, not we that fight, but God who fights for and in us.

III. We learn here the best preparation for the conflict.

When the morning dawned, the array was set in order and the march begun, and a strange array it was. In the van marched the Temple singers singing words that are music to us still: 'Give thanks unto the Lord, for His mercy endureth for ever,' and behind them came the ranks of Judah, no doubt swelling the volume of melody, that startled the wild creatures of the wilderness, and perhaps travelled through the still morning as far as the camp of the enemy. The singers had no armour nor weapons. They were clad in 'the beauty of holiness,' the priestly dress, and for sword and spear they carried harps and timbrels. Our best weapons are like their equipment.

We are most likely to conquer if we lift up the voice of thanks for victory in advance, and go into the battle expecting to triumph, because we trust in God. The world's expectation of success is too often a dream, a will-o'-the-wisp that tempts to bogs where the beguiled victim is choked, though even in the world it is often true; 'screw your courage to the sticking point, and we'll not fail.' But faith, that is the expectation of success based on God's help and inspiring to struggles for things dear to His heart, is wont to fulfil itself, and by bringing God into the fray, to secure the victory. A thankful heart not seldom brings into existence that for which it is thankful.

IV. We see here the victory and the praise for it.

The panic that laid hold on the enemy, and turned their swords against each other, was more natural in an undisciplined horde such as these irregular levies of ancient times, than it would be in a modern army. Once started, the infection would spread, so we need not wonder that by the time that Judah arrived on the field all was over. How often a like experience attends us! We quiver with apprehension of troubles that never attack us. We dread some impending battle-field, and when we reach it, Jehoshaphat's surprise is repeated, 'and, behold they were dead bodies, fallen to the earth.' Delivered from foes and fears, Judah's first impulse was to secure the booty, for they were keen after wealth, and their 'faith' was not very pure or elevating. But their last act was worthier, and fitly ended the strange campaign. They gathered in some wâdy among the grim cliffs of the wilderness of Judah, which broke the dreariness of that savage stretch of country with perhaps verdure and a brook, and there they 'blessed the Lord.' The chronicler gives a piece of popular etymology, in deriving the name, 'the valley of blessing,' from that morning's worship. Perhaps the name was older than that, and was given from a feeling of the contrast between the waste wilderness, which in its gaunt sterility seemed an accursed land, and the glen which with its trees and stream was indeed a 'valley of blessing.' If so, the name would be doubly appropriate after that day's experience. Be that as it may, here we have in vivid form the truth that all our struggles and fightings may end in a valley of blessing, which will ring with the praise of the God who fights for us. If we begin our warfare with an appeal to God, and with prayerful acknowledgment of our own impotence, we shall end it with thankful acknowledgment that we are 'more than conquerors through Him that loved us' and fought for us, and our choral song of praise will echo through the true Valley of Blessing, where no sound of enemies shall ever break the settled stillness, and the host of the redeemed, like that army of Judah, shall bear 'psalteries and harps and trumpets,' and shall need spear and sword no more at all for ever.

HOLDING FAST AND HELD FAST

'As they went forth Jehoshaphat stood and said, Believe in the Lord your God, so shall ye be established.'—2 CHRON. xx. 20.

CERTAINLY no stronger army ever went forth to victory than these Jews, who poured out of Jerusalem that morning with no weapon in all their ranks, and having for their van, not their picked men, but singers who 'praised the beauty of holiness' and chanted the old hymn, 'Give thanks unto the Lord, for His mercy endureth for ever.' That was all that men had to do in the battle, for as the shrill song rose in the morning air 'the Lord set liers in wait for the foe,' and they turned their swords against one another, so that when Jehoshaphat and his troops came in sight of the enemy the battle was over and the field strewn with corpses— so great and swift is the power of devout recognition of God's goodness and trust in His enduring mercy, even in the hour of extremest peril.

The exhortation in our text which is Jehoshaphat's final word to his army, has, in the original, a beauty and emphasis that are incapable of being preserved in translation. There is a play of words which cannot be reproduced in another language, though the sentiment of it may be explained. The two expressions for 'believing' and 'being established' are two varying forms of the same root-word; and although we can only imitate the original clumsily in our language, we might translate in some such way as this: 'Hold fast by the Lord your God, and you will be held fast,' or 'stay yourselves on Him and you will be stable.' These attempts at reproducing the similarity of sound between the two verbs in the two clauses of our text, rude as they are, preserve what is lost, so far as regards form, in the English translation, though that is correct as to the meaning of the command and promise. If we note this connection of the two clauses we just come to the general principle which lies here, that the true source of steadfastness in character and conduct, of victory over temptation, and of standing fast in slippery places, is simple reliance, or, to use the New Testament word, 'faith.' 'Believe and ye shall be established.' Put out your hand and clasp Him, and He puts out His hand and steadies you. But all the steadfastness and strength come from the mighty Hand that is outstretched, not from the tremulous one that grasps it.

So, then, keeping to the words of my text, let me suggest to you the large lessons that this saying teaches us, in regard to three things, which I may put as being the object, the nature, and the issues of faith; or, in other words, to whom we are to cling, how we are to cling, and what the consequence of the clinging is.

I. To whom we must cling.

'Stay yourselves on the Lord your God.' Well, then, faith is not believing a number of theological articles, nor is it even accepting the truth of the Gospel as it lies in Jesus Christ, but it is accepting the Christ whom the truth of the Gospel reveals to us. And, although we have to come to Him through the word that declares what He is, and what He has done for us, the act of believing on Him is something that lies beyond the mere understanding of, or giving credence to, the message that tells us who He is and what He has done. A man may have not the ghost of a doubt or hesitation about one tittle of revealed truth, and if you were to cross-question him, could answer satisfactorily all the questions of an orthodox inquisitor, and yet there may not be one faintest flicker of faith in that man's whole being, for all the correctness of his creed, and the comprehensiveness of it, too. Trust is more than assent. If it is a Person on whom our faith leans, then from that there follows clearly enough that the bond which binds us to Him must be something far warmer, far deeper, and far more under the control of our own will than the mere consent or assent of our brains to a set of revealed truths. 'The Lord your God,' and not even the Bible that tells you about Him; 'the Lord your God,' and not even the revealed truths that manifest Him, but Him as revealed by the truths—it is He that is the Object to which our faith clings.

Jehoshaphat, in the same breath in which he exhorted his people to 'believe in the Lord, that they might be established,' also said, 'Believe His prophets, so shall ye prosper.' The immediate reference, of course, was to the man who the day before had assured them of victory. But the wider truth suggested is, that the only way to get to God is through the word that speaks of Him, and which has come from the lips either of prophets or of the Son who has spoken more, and more sweetly and clearly, than all the prophets put together. If we are to believe God, we must believe the prophets that tell us of Him.

And then there is another suggestion that may be made. The Object of faith proposed to Judah is not only 'the Lord,' but 'the Lord *your* God.' I do not say that there can be no faith without the 'appropriating' action which takes the whole Godhead for mine, but I doubt very much whether there is any. And it seems to me that to a very large extent the difference between mere nominal, formal Christians and men who really are living by the power of faith in God as revealed in Jesus Christ, lies in that one little word, 'the Lord *your* God.' That a man shall put out a grasping hand, and say, 'I take for my own—for my very own—the universal blessing, I claim as my possession that God of the spirits of all flesh, I believe that He does stand in a real individualising relation to me, and I to Him,' is surely of the very essence of faith. There is no presumption, but the truest wisdom and lowliness in enclosing, if I may so say, a part of this great common for ours, and putting a hedge about it, as it were, and saying, 'That is mine.' We shall not have understood the sweetness and the power of the Gospel of Jesus Christ until we have pointed and condensed the general declaration, 'He so loved the world,' into the individualising and appropriating one, 'He loved me, and gave Himself for me.' Oh! if we could only apply that process thoroughly to all the broad glorious words and promises of Scripture, and feel that the whole incidence of them was meant to fall upon us, one by one, and that just as the sun, up in the heavens there, sends all his beams into the tiniest daisy on the grass, as if there was nothing else in the whole world, but only its little petals to be smoothed out and opened, I think our Christianity would be more real, and we should have more blessings in our hands. God in Christ and I, the only two beings in the universe, and all His fullness mine, and all my weakness supported and supplemented by Him—that is the view that we should sometimes take. We should set ourselves apart from all mankind, and claim Him as our very own, and so be filled with the fullness of God.

This, then, is the Object of faith, a Person who is all mine and all yours too. The beam of light that falls on my eye falls on yours, and no man makes a sunbeam the smaller because he sees by it; and in like manner we may each possess the whole of God for our very own property.

II. How we cling.

The metaphor, I suppose, is more eloquent than all explanations of it. 'Believe in the Lord'; hold fast by

Him with a tight grip, continually renewed when it tends to slacken, as it surely will, and then you will be established.

We might run out into any number of figurative illustrations. Look at that little child beginning to learn to walk, how it fastens its little dimpled hands into its mother's apron, and so the tiny tottering feet get a kind of steadfastness into them. Look at that man lying at the door of the Temple, who never had walked since his mother's womb, and had lain there for forty years, with his poor weak ankles all atrophied by reason of their disuse. 'He *held* Peter and John.' Would not his grasp be tight? Would he not clasp their hands as his only stay? He had not become accustomed to the astounding miracle of walking, nor learned to balance himself and accomplish the still more astounding feat of standing steady. So he clutched at the two Apostles and was 'established.' Look at that man walking by a slippery path which he does not know, holding by the hand the guide who is able to direct and keep him up. See this other in some wild storm, with an arm round a steadfast tree-stem, to keep him from being blown over the precipice, how he clings like a limpet to a rock. And that is how we are to hold on to God, with what would be despair if it were not the perfection of confidence, with the clear sense that the only thing between us and ruin is the strong Hand that we clasp.

And what do we mean by clasping God? I mean making daily efforts to rivet our *love* on Him, and not to let the world, with all its delusive and cloying sweets, draw us away from Him. I mean continual and strenuous efforts to fix our *thoughts* upon Him, and not to allow the trivialities of life, or the claims of culture, or the necessities of our daily position so to absorb our minds as that thoughts of God are comparative strangers there, except, perhaps, sometimes on a Sunday, and now and then at the sleepy end, or the half-awake beginning, of a day. I mean continually repeated and strenuous efforts to cleave to Him by the submission of our *will*, letting Him 'do what seemeth Him good,' and not lifting ourselves up against Him, or perking our own inclinations, desires, and fancies in His face, as if we would induce Him to take them for His guides! And I mean that we should try to commit our *way* unto the Lord, 'to rest in the Lord, and wait patiently for Him.' The submissive will which cleaves to God's commandments, the waiting heart that clings to His love, the regulated thoughts that embrace His truth, and the childlike confidence that commits its path to Him—these are the elements of that steadfast adherence to the Lord which shall not be in vain.

III. The blessed effects of this clinging to God.

'So shall ye be established.' That follows, as a matter of course. The only way to make light things stable is to fasten them to something that is stable. And the only way to put any kind of calmness and fixedness, and yet progress—stability in the midst of progress, and progress in the midst of stability—into our lives, is by keeping firm hold of God. If we grasp His hand, then a calm serenity will be ours. In the midst of changes, sorrows, losses, disappointments, we shall not be blown about here and there by furious winds of fortune, nor will the heavy currents of the river of life sweep us away. We shall have a holdfast and a mooring. And although, like some light-ship anchored in the Channel, we may heave up and down with the waves, we shall keep in the same place, and be steadfast in the midst of mobility, and wholesomely mobile although anchored in the one spot where there is safety. As the issue of faith, of this throwing the responsibility for ourselves upon God, there will be quietness of heart, and continuance and persistence in righteousness, and steadfastness of purpose and continuity of advancement in the divine life. 'The law of the Lord is in his heart,' says one of the Psalms, 'none of his steps shall slide.' The man who walks holding God's hand can put down a firm foot, even when he is walking in slippery places. There will be decision, and strength, and persistence of continuous advance, in a life that derives its impulse and its motive power from communion with God in Jesus Christ.

There will be victory, not indeed after the fashion of that in this story before us. In it, of course, men had to do nothing but 'stand still and see the salvation of God.' That is the law for us, in regard to the initial blessings of acceptance, and forgiveness, and the communication of the divine life from above. We have to be simple recipients, and we have no co-operating share in that part of the work of our own salvation. But for the rest we have to help God. 'Work out your own salvation with fear and trembling, for it is God that worketh in you.' But none the less, 'This is the victory that overcometh the world, even our faith,' and if we give heed to Jehoshaphat's commandment, and go out to battle as his people did, with the love and trust of God in our hearts, then we shall come back as they did, laden with spoil, and shall name the place which was the field of conflict 'the valley of blessing,' and return to Jerusalem 'with psalteries, and harps, and trumpets,' and 'God will give us rest from all our enemies round about us.'

JOASH

'And Joash did that which was right in the sight of the Lord all the days of Jehoiada the priest. . . . 17. Now after the death of Jehoiada came the princes of Judah, and made obeisance to the king. Then the king hearkened unto them.
—2 CHRON. xxiv. 2, 17.

HERE we have the tragedy of a soul. Joash begins life well and for the greater part of it remains faithful to his conscience and to his duty, and then, when outward circumstances change, he casts all behind him, forgets the past and commits moral suicide. It is the sad old story, a bright commencement, an early promise all scattered to the winds. It is a strange story, too. This seven-year-old king had been saved when his father had been killed, and that true daughter of Jezebel, as well by nature as by blood, Athaliah, had murdered all his brothers and sisters, and made herself queen. He had been saved by the courage of a woman who might worthily stand by the side of Deborah and other Jewish heroines. By this woman, who was his aunt, he was hidden and brought up in the Temple until, whilst yet a mere boy, he came to the throne, the High Priest Jehoiada, the husband of his aunt, being his guardian during his nonage. He reigns well till the lad of seven becomes a mature man of thirty or thereabouts, and then Jehoiada dies, full of years and honours, and they fitly lay him among the kings of Judah, a worthy resting-place for one who had 'done good in Israel.' And now the weakling on the throne is left alone without the strong arm to guide him and keep him right, and we read that 'the princes of Judah came and made obeisance to him.' They take him on his weak side, and I dare say Jehoiada had been too true and too noble to do that, and though we are not told what means they took to flatter and coax him, we see very plainly what they were conspiring to do, for we read that 'they left the house of the Lord their God, the God of their fathers, and served groves and idols,' the groves here mentioned being symbols of Ashtaroth the goddess of the Sidonians. And so all the past is wiped out and Joash takes his place amongst the apostates. The story has solemn lessons.

I. Note the change from loyal adhesion to apostasy.

The strong man on whom Joash used to lean was away, and the poor, weak king went just where the wicked princes led him. It was probably out of sheer imbecility that he passed from the worship of God to the acknowledgment and service of idols.

The first point that I would insist upon is a well-worn and familiar one, as I am well aware, but I urge it upon you, and especially upon the younger portion of my audience. It is this, that there is no telling the amount of mischief that pure weakness of character may lead into. The worst men we come across in the Bible are not those who begin with a deliberate intention of doing evil. They are weak creatures, 'reeds shaken by the wind,' who have no power of resisting the force of circumstances. It is a truth which every one's experience confirms, that the mother of all possible badness is weakness, and that, not only as Milton's Satan puts it, 'To be weak is to be miserable,' but that weakness is wickedness sooner or later. The man who does not bar the doors and windows of his senses and his soul against temptation, is sure to make shipwreck of his life and in the end to become 'a fool.' There is so much wickedness lying round us in this world that any man who lets himself be shaped and coloured by that with which he comes in contact, is sure to go to the bad in the long run. Where a man lays himself open to the accidents of time and circumstances, the majority of these influences will be contrary to what is right and good. Therefore, he must gather himself together and learn to say 'No!' There is no foretelling the profound abysses into which a 'good, easy' nature, with plenty of high and pure impulses, perhaps, but which are written in water, may fall. 'Thou, therefore, young man! be strong in the grace that is in Christ Jesus.' Learn to say No! or else you will be sure to say Yes! in the wrong place, and then down you will go, like this Joash whose goodness depended on Jehoiada, and when *he* died, all the virtue that had characterised this life hitherto was laid with him in the dust.

Let us learn from this story in the next place, how little power of continuance there is in a merely traditional religion. Many of you call yourselves Christian people mainly because other people do the same. It is customary to respect and regard Christianity. You have been brought up in the midst of it. Our country is always considered a Christian land, and so, naturally, you tacitly accept the truth of a religion which is so influential. The lowest phase of this attitude is that which seeks some advantage from a church connection, like the foolish man in the Old Testament who thought he would do well because he had a Levite for his priest. Religion is the most personal thing about a man. To become a Christian is the most personal act one can perform. It is a thing that a man has to do for himself, and however friends and guides may help us in other matters, in trials and perplexities and difficulties, by their sympathy and experience, they are useless here. A man has here to act as if there were no other beings in the universe but a solitary God and himself, and unless we have ourselves done that act in the depths of our own personality, we have not done it at all. If you young people are good, just because you have pious parents who make you go to church or chapel on a Sunday, and keep you out of mischief during the week, your goodness is a sham. One great result of personal Christianity is to make a minister, a teacher, a guide, superfluous, and when such an one becomes so, his work has been successful and not till then. Unless you put forth for yourself the hand of faith and for yourself yield up the devotion and love of your own heart, your religion is nought.

However much active effort about the outside of religion there may be, it is of itself useless. It is without bottom and without reality. Here we have Joash busy with the externals of worship and actually deceiving himself thereby. It was a great deal easier to make that chest for contributions to a Temple Repairing Fund, and to get it well filled, and to patch up the house of the Lord, than for him to get down on his knees and pray, and he may have thought that to be busy about the house of God was to be devout. So it may be with many Sunday-school teachers and Church workers. Their religion may be as merely superficial and as little personal as this man's was. It is not for me to say so about A, B, or C. It is for you to ask of yourselves if it is so as to you. But I do say that there is nothing that masks his own soul from a man more than setting him to do something for Christianity and God's Church, while in his inmost self he has not yet yielded himself to God.

I look around and I see the devil slaying his thousands by setting them to work in Christian associations and leaving them no time to think about their own

Christianity. My brother! if the cap fits, go home and put it on.

We see in Joash's life for how long a time a man may go on in this self-delusion of external and barren service and never know it. Joash came to the throne at the age of seven. Up till that age he had lived in the Temple in concealment. Until he was one and thirty he went on in a steady, upright course, never knowing that there was anything hollow in his life. Apparently, Jehoiada's long life of one hundred and thirty years extended over the greater part of Joash's reign, during most of which he had Jehoiada to direct him and keep him right, and all this tragedy comes at the fag end of it.

So he went on apparently all right, like a tree that has become quite hollow, till during some storm it is blown down and falls with a crash, and it is seen that for years it has been only the skin of a tree, bark outside, and inside—emptiness.

II. We come now to the second stage in the later life of Joash: His resistance to the divine pleading.

'And they left the house of the Lord God of their fathers, and served groves and idols, and wrath came upon Judah and Jerusalem for their trespass, yet He sent prophets to them to bring them again unto the Lord.' He sent with endless pity, with long-suffering patience. He would not be put away, and as they increased the distance between Him and them, He increased His energies to bring them back. But they lifted themselves up, Joash and his princes, and with that strange, awful power of resisting the attraction of the divine pleading, and hardening their hearts against the divine patience—'they would not.' And then comes the affecting episode of the death of the high priest Zechariah, who had succeeded to his father's place and likewise to his heroism, and who, with the Spirit of God upon him, stands up and pointing out his wickedness, rebukes the fallen monarch for his apostasy. Joash, doubtless stung to the quick by Zechariah's just reproaches, allowed the truculent princes to slay him in the court of the Temple, even between the very shrine and the altar.

What a picture we have here of the divine love which follows every wanderer with its pleadings and beseechings! It came to this man through the lips of a prophet. It comes to us all in daily blessings, sometimes in messages, like these poor words of mine. God will not let us ruin ourselves without pleading with us and wooing us to love Him and cling to Him. 'He rises up early' and daily sends us His messages, sometimes rebukes and voices in our conscience, sometimes sunset glows and starry heavens lifting our thoughts above this low earth, sometimes sorrows that are meant to 'drive us to His breast,' and above all, the 'Gospel of our salvation' in Christ, ever, in such a land as ours, sounding in our ears.

Still further, we see in Joash what a strange, awful strength of obstinate resistance, a character weak as regards its resistance to man, can put forth against God. He never attempted to say 'No!' to the princes of Judah, but he could say it again and again to his Father in heaven. He could not but yield to the temptations which were level with his eyes, and this poor creature, easily swayed by human allurements and influences, could gather himself together, standing, as it were, on his little pin point, and say to God, 'Thou dost call and I refuse.' What a paradox, and yet repetitions of it are sitting in these pews, only half aware that it is about them that I am speaking!

The ever-deepening evil which began with forsaking the house of the Lord and serving Ashtaroth, ends with Joash steeping his hands in blood. The murder of Zechariah was beyond the common count of crimes, for it was a foul desecration of the Temple, an act of the blackest ingratitude to the man who had saved his infant life, and put him on the throne, an outrage on the claims of family connections, for Joash and Zechariah were probably blood relations. My brother! once get your foot upon that steep incline of evil, once forsake the path of what is good and right and true, and you are very much like a climber who misses his footing up among the mountain peaks, and down he slides till he reaches the edge of the precipice and then in an instant is dashed to pieces at the bottom. Once put your foot on that slippery slope and you know not where you may fall to.

III. Last comes the final scene: The retribution.

We have that picture of Zechariah, solemnly lifting up his eyes to heaven and committing his cause to God. 'The Lord look upon it and require it,' says the martyr priest in the spirit of the old Law. The dying appeal was soon answered in the invasion of the Syrian army, a comparatively small company, into whose hands the Lord delivered a very great host of the Israelites. The defeat was complete, and possibly Joash's 'great diseases,' of which the narrative speaks, refer to wounds received in the fight. The end soon comes, for two of his servants, neither of them Hebrews, one being the son of an Ammonitess and the other the son of a Moabitess, who were truer to his religion than he had been, and resolved to revenge

Zechariah's death, entered the room of the wounded king in the fortress whither he had retired to hide himself after the fight, and 'slew him on his bed.' Imagine the grim scene—the two men stealing in, the sick man there on the bed helpless, the short ghastly struggle and the swift end. What an end for a life with such a beginning!

Now I am not going to dwell on this retribution, inflicted on Joash, or on that which comes to us if we are like him, through a loud-voiced conscience, and a memory which, though it may be dulled and hushed to sleep at present, is sure to wake some day here or yonder. But I beseech you to ask yourselves what your outlook is. 'Be not deceived, God is not mocked; for whatsoever a man soweth that shall he also reap.' Is that all? Zechariah said, 'The Lord look upon it and require it.' The great doctrine of retribution is true for ever. Yes; but our Zechariah lifts up his eyes to heaven and he says, 'Father! forgive them, for they know not what they do.' And so, dear brother! you and I, trusting to that dear Lord, may have all our apostasy forgiven, and be brought near by the blood of Christ. Let us say with the Apostle Peter, 'Lord, to whom shall we go but to Thee? Thou hast the words of eternal life.'

GLAD GIVERS AND FAITHFUL WORKERS

'And it came to pass after this, that Joash was minded to repair the house of the Lord. 5. And he gathered together the priests and the Levites, and said to them, go out unto the cities of Judah, and gather of all Israel money to repair the house of your God from year to year, and see that ye hasten the matter. Howbeit the Levites hastened it not. 6. And the king called for Jehoiada the chief, and said unto him, Why hast thou not required of the Levites to bring in out of Judah and out of Jerusalem the collection, according to the commandment of Moses the servant of the Lord, and of the congregation of Israel, for the tabernacle of witness? 7. For the sons of Athaliah, that wicked woman, had broken up the house of God;

and also all the dedicated things of the house of the Lord did they bestow upon Baalim. 8. And at the king's commandment they made a chest, and set it without at the gate of the house of the Lord. 9. And they made a proclamation through Judah and Jerusalem, to bring in to the Lord the collection that Moses the servant of God laid upon Israel in the wilderness. 10. And all the princes and all the people rejoiced, and brought in, and cast into the chest, until they had made an end. 11. Now it came to pass, that at what time the chest was brought unto the king's office by the hand of the Levites, and when they saw that there was much money, the king's scribe and the high priest's officer came and emptied the chest, and took it, and carried it to his place again. Thus they did day by day, and gathered money in abundance. 12. And the king and Jehoiada gave it to such as did the work of the service of the house of the Lord, and hired masons and carpenters to repair the house of the Lord, and also such as wrought iron and brass to mend the house of the Lord. 13. So the workmen wrought, and the work was perfected by them, and they set the house of God in his state, and strengthened it. 14. And when they had finished it, they brought the rest of the money before the king and Jehoiada, whereof were made vessels for the house of the Lord, even vessels to minister, and to offer withal, and spoons, and vessels of gold and silver. And they offered burnt offerings in the house of the Lord continually all the days of Jehoiada.'— 2 CHRON. xxiv. 4-14.

JOASH owed his life and his throne to the high-priest Jehoiada, who was his uncle by marriage with the sister of Ahaziah, his father. Rescued by his aunt when an infant, he 'was with them, hid in the house of God six years,' and, when seven years old, was made king by Jehoiada's daring revolt against 'that wicked woman, Athaliah. Jehoiada's influence was naturally paramount, and was as wholesome as strong. It is remarkable, however, that this impulse to repair the Temple seems to have originated with the king, not with the high-priest, though no doubt the spirit which conceived the impulse was largely moulded by the latter. The king, whose childhood had found a safe asylum in the Temple, might well desire its restoration, even apart from considerations of religion.

I. The story first brings into strong contrast the eager king, full of his purpose, and the sluggards to whom he had to entrust its execution. We can only guess the point in his reign at which Joash summoned the priests to his help. It was after his marriage (ver. 3), and considerably before the twenty-third year of his reign, at which time his patience was exhausted (2 Kings xii. 6). Some years were apparently wasted by the dawdling sluggishness of the priests, who, for some reason or other, did not go into the proposed restoration heartily. Joash seems to have suspected that they would push the work languidly; for there is a distinct tinge of suspicion and 'whipping up' in his injunction to 'hasten the matter.'

The first intention was to raise the funds by sending out the priests and Levites to collect locally the statutory half-shekel, as well as other contributions mentioned in 2 Kings xii. There we learn that each collector was to go to 'his acquaintance.' The subscription was to be spread over some years, and for a while Joash waited quietly; but in the twenty-third year of his reign (see 2 Kings), he could stand delay no longer. Whether the priests had been diligent in collecting or not, they had done nothing towards repairing. Perhaps they found it difficult to determine the proportion of the money which was needed for the ordinary expenses of worship, and for the restoration fund; and, as the former included their own dues and support, they would not be likely to set it down too low. Perhaps they did not much care to carry out a scheme which had not begun with themselves; for priests are not usually eager to promote ecclesiastical renovations suggested by laymen. Perhaps they did not care as much about the renovation as the king did, and smiled at his earnestness as a pious imagining. Possibly there was even deliberate embezzlement. But, at any rate, there was half-heartedness, and that always means languid work, and that always means failure. The earnest people are fretted continually by the indifferent. Every good scheme is held back, like a ship with a foul bottom, by the barnacles that stick to its keel and bring down its speed. Professional ecclesiastics in all ages have succumbed to the temptation of thinking that 'church property' was first of all to be used for their advantage, and, secondarily, for behoof of God's house. Eager zeal has in all ages to be yoked to torpid indifference, and to drag its unwilling companion along, like two dogs in a leash. Direct opposition is easier to bear than apparent assistance which tries to slow down to half speed.

Joash's command is imperative on all workers for God. 'See that ye hasten the matter,' for time is short, the fruit great, the evening shadows lengthening, the interests at stake all-important, and the Lord of the harvest will soon come to count our sheaves. Whatever work may be done without haste, God's cannot be, and a heavy curse falls on him who 'does the work of the Lord negligently.' The runner who keeps well on this side of fatigue, panting, and sweat, has little chance of the crown.

II. The next step is the withdrawal of the work from the sluggards. They are relieved both of the collection and expenditure of the money. Apparently (2 Kings xii. 9) the contributors handed their donations to the doorkeepers, who put them into the chest with 'a hole in the lid of it,' in the sight of the donors. The arrangement was not flattering to the hierarchy, but as appearances were saved by Jehoiada's making the chest (see 2 Kings) they had to submit with the best grace they could. In our own times, we have seen the same thing often enough. When clergy have maladministered church property, Parliament has appointed ecclesiastical commissioners. Common sense prescribes taking slovenly work out of lazy hands. The more rigidly that principle is carried out in the church and the nation, at whatever cost of individual humiliation, the better for both. 'The tools to the hands that can use them' is the ideal for both. God's dealings follow the same law, both in withdrawing opportunities of service and in giving more of such. The reward for work is more work, and the punishment for sloth is compulsory idleness.

III. We are next shown the glad givers. Probably suspicion had been excited in others than the king, and had checked liberality. People will not give freely if the expenses of the collectors' support swallow up the funds. It is hard to get help for a vague scheme, which unites two objects, and only gives the balance, after the first is provided for, to the second and more important. So the whole nation, both high and low, was glad when the new arrangement brought a clear issue, and secured the right appropriation of the money.

No doubt, too, Joash's earnestness kindled others. Chronicles speaks only of the 'tax,'—that is, the half-shekel,—but Kings mentions two other sources, one of which is purely spontaneous gifts, and these are implied by the tone of verse 10, which lays stress on the gladness of the offerers. That is the incense which adds fragrance to our gifts. Grudging service is no service, and money given for ever so religious a purpose, without gladness because of the opportunity of giving, is not, in the deepest sense, given at all. Love is a longing to give to the beloved, and whoever truly loves God will know no keener delight than surrender for His dear sake. Pecuniary contributions for religious purposes afford a rough but real test of the depth of a man's religion; but it is one available only for himself, since the motive, and not the amount, is the determining element. We all need to bring our hearts more under the influence of God's love to us, that our love to Him may be increased, and then to administer possessions, under the impulse to glad giving which enkindled love will always excite. Super-heated steam has most expansive power and driving force. These glad givers may remind us not only of the one condition of acceptable giving, but also of the need for clear and worthy objects, and of obvious disinterestedness in those who seek for money to help good causes. The smallest opening for suspicion that some of it sticks to the collector's fingers is fatal, as it should be.

IV. Joash was evidently a business-like king. We next hear of the precautions he took to secure the public confidence. There was a rough but sufficient audit. When the chest grew heavy, and sounded full, two officials received it at the 'king's office.' The Levites carried it there, but were not allowed to handle the contents. The two tellers represented the king and the chief priest, and thus both the civil and religious authorities were satisfied, and each officer was a check on the other. Public money should never be handled by a man alone; and an honest one will always wish, like Paul, to have a brother associated with him, that no man may blame him in his administration of it. If we take 'day by day' literally, we have a measure of the liberality which filled the chest daily; but, more probably, the expression simply means 'from time to time,' when occasion required.

V. The application of the money is next narrated. In this Jehoiada is associated with Joash, the king probably desiring to smooth over any slight that might seem to have been put on the priests, as well as being still under the influence of the high-priest's strong character and early kindness. Together they passed over the results of the contribution to the contractors, who in turn paid it in wages to the workmen who repaired the fabric, such as masons and carpenters, and to other artisans who restored other details, such as brass and iron work. The Second Book of Kings tells us that Joash's cautious provision against misappropriation seems to have deserted him at this stage; for no account was required of the workmen, 'for they dealt faithfully.' That is an indication of their goodwill. The humble craftsmen were more reliable than the priests. They had, no doubt, given their half-shekel like others, and now they gladly gave their work, and were not hirelings, though they were hired. We, too, have to give our money and our labour; and if our hearts are right, we shall give both with the same conscientious cheerfulness, and, if we are paid in coin for our work, will still do it for higher reasons and looking for other wages. These Temple workmen may stand as patterns of what religion should do for those of us whose lot is to work with our hands,—and not less for others who have to toil with their brains, and the sweat of whose brow is inside their heads. A Christian workman should be a 'faithful' workman, and will be so if he is full of faith.

Joash knew when to trust and when to keep a sharp eye on men. His experience with the priests had not soured him into suspecting everybody. Cynical disbelief in honesty is more foolish and hurtful to ourselves than even excessive trust. These workmen wrought all the more faithfully because they knew that they were trusted, and in nine cases out of ten men will try to live up to our valuation of them. The Rugby boys used to say, 'It's a shame to tell Arnold a lie, he always believes us.' Better to be cheated once than to treat the nine as rogues,—better for them and better for ourselves.

'Faithful' work is prosperous work. As verse 13 picturesquely says, 'Healing went up upon the work'; and the Temple was restored to its old fair proportions, and stood strong as before. Where there is conscientious effort, God's blessing is not withheld. Labour 'in the Lord' can never be empty labour, though even a prophet may often be tempted, in a moment of weary despondency, to complain, 'I have laboured in vain.' We may not see the results, nor have the workmen's joy of beholding the building rise, course by course, under our hands, but we shall see it one day, though now we have to work in the dark.

There seems a discrepancy between the statements in Chronicles and Kings as to the source from which the cost of the sacrificial vessels was defrayed, since, according to the former, it was from the restoration fund, which is expressly denied by the latter. The explanation seems reasonable, that, as Chronicles says, it was from the balance remaining after all restoration charges were liquidated, that this other expenditure was met. First, the whole amount was sacredly devoted to the purpose for which it had been asked, and then, when the honest overseers repaid the uncounted surplus, which they might have kept, it was found sufficient to meet the extra cost of furnishing. God blesses the faithful steward of his gifts with more than enough for the immediate service, and the best use of the surplus is to do more with it for Him. 'God is able to make all grace abound unto you; that ye, having always all sufficiency in every thing, may abound unto every good work, . . . being enriched in every thing unto all liberality.'

PRUDENCE AND FAITH

'And Amaziah said to the man of God, But what shall we do for the hundred talents which I have given to the army of Israel? And the man of God answered, The Lord is able to give thee much more than this.'—2 CHRON. xxv. 9.

THE character of this Amaziah, one of the Kings of Judah, is summed up by the chronicler in a damning epigram: 'He did that which was right in the sight of the Lord, but not with a perfect heart.' He was one of your half-and-half people, or, as Hosea says, 'a cake not turned,' burnt black on one side, and raw dough on the other. So when he came to the throne, in the buoyancy and insolence of youth, he immediately began to aim at conquests in the neighbouring little states; and in order to strengthen himself he hired 'a hundred thousand mighty men of valour' out of Israel for a hundred talents of silver. To seek help from Israel was, in a prophet's eyes, equivalent to flinging off help from God. So a man of God comes to him, and warns him that the Lord is not with Israel, and that the alliance is not permissible for him. But, instead of yielding to the prophet's advice, he parries it with this misplaced question, 'But what shall we do for the hundred talents that I have given to the army of Israel?' He does not care to ask whether the counsel that he is receiving is right or wrong, or whether what he is intending to do is in conformity with, or in opposition to, the will of God, but, passing by all such questions, at once he fastens on the lower consideration of expediency—'What is to become of me if I do as this prophet would have me do? What a heavy loss one hundred talents will be! It is too much to sacrifice to a scruple of that sort. It cannot be done.'

A great many of us may take a lesson from this man. There are two things in my text—a misplaced question and a triumphant answer: 'What shall we do for the hundred talents?' 'The Lord is able to give thee much more than this.' Now, remarkably enough, both question and answer may be either very right or very wrong, according as they are taken, and I purpose to look at those two aspects of each.

I. A misplaced question.

I call it misplaced because Amaziah's fault, and the fault of a great many of us, was, not that he took consequences into account, but that he took them into account at the wrong time. The question should have come second, not first. Amaziah's first business should have been to see clearly what was duty; and then, and not till then, the next business should have been to consider consequences.

Consider the right place and way of putting this question. Many of us make shipwreck of our lives because, with our eyes shut, we determine upon some grand design, and fall under the condemnation of the man that 'began to build, and was not able to finish.' He drew a great plan of a stately mansion; and then found that he had neither money in the bank, nor stones in his quarry, to finish it, and so it stood—a ruin. All through our Lord's life He was engaged rather in repressing volunteers than in soliciting recruits, and He from time to time poured a douche of cold water upon swiftly effervescing desires to go after Him. When the multitudes followed Him, He turned and said to them, 'If you are counting on being My disciples, understand what it means: take up the cross and follow Me.' When an enthusiastic man, who had not looked consequences in the face, came rushing to

PRUDENCE AND FAITH

Him and said: 'Lord, I will follow Thee whithersoever Thou goest,' His answer to him was another pull at the string of the shower bath: 'The Son of Man hath not where to lay His head.' When the two disciples came to Him and said: 'Grant that we may sit, the one on Thy right hand and the other on Thy left, when Thou comest into Thy kingdom,' He said: 'Are ye able to drink of the cup that I drink of, and to be baptized with the baptism that I am baptized withal?' Look the facts in the face before you make your election. Jesus Christ will enlist no man under false pretences. Recruiting-sergeants tell country bumpkins or city louts wonderful stories of what they will get if they take the shilling and put on the king's uniform; but Jesus Christ does not recruit His soldiers in that fashion. If a man does not open his eyes to a clear vision of the consequences of his actions, his life will go to water in all directions. And there is no region in which such clear insight into what is going to follow upon my determinations and the part that I take is more necessary than in the Christian life. It is just because in certain types of character, 'the word is received with joy,' and springs up immediately, that when 'the sun is risen with a burning heat'—that is, as Christ explains, when the pinch of difficulty comes —'immediately they fall away,' and all their grand resolutions go to nothing. 'Lightly come, lightly go.' Let us face the facts of what is involved, in the way of sacrifice, surrender, loss, if we determine to be on Christ's side; and then, when the anticipated difficulties come, we shall neither be perplexed nor swept away, but be able quietly to say, 'I discounted it all beforehand; I knew it was coming.' The storm catches the ship that is carrying full sail and expecting nothing but light and favourable breezes; while the captain that looked into the weather quarter and saw the black cloud beginning to rise above the horizon, and took in his sails and made his vessel snug and tight, rides out the gale. It is wisdom that becomes a man, to ask this question, if first of all he has asked, 'What ought I to do?'

But we have here an instance of a right thing in a wrong place. It was right to ask the question, but wrong to ask it at that point. Amaziah thought nothing about duty. There sprang up in his mind at once the cowardly and ignoble thought: 'I cannot afford to do what is right, because it will cost me a hundred talents,' and that was his sin. Consequences may be, must be, faced in anticipation, or a man is a fool. He that allows the clearest perception of disagreeable consequences, such as pain, loss of ease, loss of reputation, loss of money, or any other harmful results that may follow, to frighten him out of the road that he knows he ought to take, is a worse fool still, for he is a coward and recreant to his own conscience.

We have to look into our own hearts for the most solemn and pressing illustrations of this sin, and I daresay we all of us can remember clear duties that we have neglected, because we did not like to face what would come from them. A man in business will say, 'I cannot afford to have such a high standard of morality; I shall be hopelessly run over in the race with my competitors if I do not do as they do,' or he will say, 'I durst not take a stand as an out-and-out Christian; I shall lose connections, I shall lose position. People will laugh at me. What am I to do for the hundred talents?'

But we can find the same thing in Churches. I do not mean to enter upon controversial questions, but as an instance, I may remind you that one great argument that our friends who believe in an Established Church are always bringing forward, is just a modern form of Amaziah's question, 'What shall we do for the hundred talents? How could the Church be maintained, how could its ministrations be continued, if its State-provided revenues were withdrawn or given up?' But it is not only Anglicans who put the consideration of the consequences of obedience in the wrong place. All the Churches are but too apt to let their eyes wander from reading the plain precepts of the New Testament to looking for the damaging results to be expected from keeping them. Do we not sometimes hear, as answer to would-be reformers, 'We cannot afford to give up this, that, or the other practice? We should not be able to hold our ground, unless we did so-and-so and so-and-so.'

But not only individuals or Churches are guilty in this matter. The nation takes a leaf out of Amaziah's book, and puts aside many plain duties, for no better reason than that it would cost too much to do them. 'What is the use of talking about suppressing the liquor traffic or housing the poor? Think of the cost.' The 'hundred talents' block the way and bribe the national conscience. For instance, the opium traffic; how is it defended? Some attempt is made to prove either that we did not force it upon China, or that the talk about the evils of opium is missionary fanaticism, but the sheet-anchor is: 'How are we ever to raise the Indian revenue if we give up the traffic?' That is exactly Amaziah over again, come from the dead, and resurrected in a very ugly shape.

So national policy and Church action, and—what is of far more importance to you and me than either the one or the other,—our own personal relation to Jesus Christ and discipleship to Him, have been hampered, and are being hampered, just by that persistent and unworthy attitude of looking at the consequences of doing plain duties, and permitting ourselves to be frightened from the duties because the consequences are unwelcome to us.

Prudence is all right, but when prudence takes command and presumes to guide conscience, then it is all wrong. In some courts of law and in certain cases, the judge has an assessor sitting beside him, an expert about some of the questions that are involved. Conscience is the judge, prudence the assessor. But if the assessor ventures up on the judgment-seat, and begins to give the decisions which it is not his business to give—for *his* only business is to give advice—then the only thing to do with the assessor is to tell him to hold his tongue and let the judge speak. It is no answer to the prophet's prohibition to say, 'But what shall I do for the hundred talents?' A yet better answer than the prophet gave Amaziah would have been, 'Never mind about the hundred talents; do what is right, and leave the rest to God.' However, that was not the answer.

II. The triumphant answer.

'The Lord is able to give thee much more than this.' Now, this answer, like the question, may be right or wrong, according as it is taken. In what aspect is it wrong? In what sense is it not true? I suppose this prophet did not mean more than the undeniable truth that God was able to give Amaziah more than a hundred talents. He was not thinking of the loftier meanings which we necessarily, as Christian people, at a later stage of Revelation, and with a clearer vision of many things, attach to the words. He simply meant, 'You will very likely get more than the hundred talents that you have lost, if you do what pleases God.' He was speaking from the point of view of the Old Testament; though even in the Old Testament we have instances enough that prosperity did not always attend righteousness. In the Old Testament we find the Book of Job, and the Book of Ecclesiastes, and many a psalm, all of which were written in order to grapple with the question, 'How is it that God does *not* give the good man more than the hundred talents that he has lost for the sake of being good?' It is not true, and it is a dangerous mistake to suggest that it is true, that a man in this world never loses by being a good, honest, consistent Christian. He often does lose a great deal, as far as this world is concerned; and he has to make up his mind to lose it, and it would be a very poor thing to say to him, 'Now, live like a Christian man, and if you are flinging away money or anything else because of your Christianity, you will get it back.' No; you will not, in a good many cases. Sometimes you will, and sometimes you will not. It does not matter whether you do or do not.

But the sense in which the triumphant answer of the prophet is true is a far higher one. 'The Lord is able to give thee much more than this,'—what is 'more'? a thousand talents? No; the 'much more' that Christianity has educated us to understand is meant in the depths of such a promise as this is, first of all, character. Every man that sacrifices anything to convictions of duty gains more than he loses thereby, because he gains in inward nobleness and strength, to say nothing of the genial warmth of an approving conscience. And whilst that is true in all regions of life, it is most especially true in regard to sacrifices made from Christian principle. No matter how disastrous may be the results externally, the inward results of faithfulness are so much greater and sweeter and nobler than all the external evil consequences that may follow, that it is 'good policy' for a man to beggar himself for Christ's sake, for the sake of the durable riches—which our Lord Himself explains to be synonymous with righteousness—which will come thereby. He that wins strength and Christ-likeness of character by sacrificing for Christ has won far more than he can ever lose.

He wins not only character, but a fuller capacity for a fuller possession of Jesus Christ Himself, and that is infinitely more than anything that any man has ever sacrificed for the sake of that dear Lord. Do you remember when it was that there was granted to the Apostle John the vision of the throned Christ, and that he felt laid upon him the touch of the vivifying Hand from Heaven? It was 'when I was in Patmos for the Word of God, and for the testimony of Jesus.' He lost Ephesus; he gained an open heaven and a visible Christ. Do you remember who it was that said, 'I have suffered the loss of all things, and do count them but dung, that I may win Christ'? It was a good bargain, Paul! The balance-sheet showed a heavy balance to your credit. Debit, 'all things'; credit, 'Christ.' 'The Lord is able to give thee much more than this.'

Remember the old prophecy: 'For brass I will bring gold; and for iron, silver.' The brass and the iron may be worth something, but if we barter them away and get instead gold and silver, we are gainers by the transaction. Fling out the ballast if you wish the balloon to rise. Let the hundred talents go if you wish to get 'the more than this.' And listen to the New Testament variation of this man of God's promise, 'If thou wilt have treasure in heaven, go and sell all that thou hast, and follow Me.'

JOTHAM

'So Jotham became mighty, because he prepared his ways before the Lord his God.'—2 CHRON. xxvii. 6.

THIS King Jotham is one of the obscurer of the Jewish monarchs, and we know next to nothing about him. The most memorable event in his reign is that 'in the year when King Uzziah,' his father, 'died,' and consequently in Jotham's first year, Isaiah saw the Lord sitting in the Temple on the empty throne, and had the lips which were to utter so many immortal words touched with fire from the altar. Whether it were the effect of the prophet's words, or from other causes, the little that is told of him is good, and he is eulogised as having imitated his father's God-pleasing acts, and not having stained himself by repeating his father's sin. The rest that we hear of him in Chronicles is a mere sketch of campaigns, buildings, and victories, and then he and his reign are summed up in the words of our text, which is the analysis of the man and the disclosure of the secret of his prosperity: 'He became mighty, because he prepared his ways'—and, more than that, 'he prepared them before the Lord his God.'

So then, if we begin, as it were, at the bottom, as we ought to do, in studying a character, taking the deepest thing first, and laying hold upon the seminal and germinal principle of the whole, this text reminds us that—The secret of true strength lies in the continual recognition that life is lived 'Before the Lord our God.'

Now to say, 'Walk thou *before* Me,' the command given to Abraham, suggests a somewhat different modification of the idea from the apparently parallel phrase, 'to walk *with* God,' which is declared to have been the life's habit of Enoch. The one expression suggests simple companionship and communion; the other suggests rather the vivid and continual realisation of the thought that we are 'ever in the great Taskmaster's eye.' To walk before God is to feel thrillingly and continually, and yet without being abased or crushed or discomposed, but rather being encouraged and quickened and calmed and ennobled and gladdened thereby: 'Thou God seest me.' It seems to me that one of the plainest pieces of Christian duty, and, alas! one of the most neglected of them, is the cultivation, definitely and consciously, by effort and by self-discipline, of that consciousness as a present factor in all our lives, and an influencing motive in everything that we do. If once we could bring before the eye of our minds that great, blazing, white throne, and Him that sits upon it, we should want nothing else to burn up the commonplaces of life, and to flash its insignificance into splendour and awfulness. We should want nothing else to lift us to a 'solemn scorn of ills,' and to deliver us from the false sweetnesses and fading delights that grow on the low levels of a sense-bound life! Brethren! our whole life would be transformed and glorified, and we should be different men and women if we ordered our ways as '*before the Lord our*

God.' What meanness could live when we knew that it was seen by those pure Eyes? How we should be ashamed of ourselves, of our complaints, of our murmurings, of our reluctance to do our duty, of our puerile regrets for vanished blessings, and of all the low cares and desires that beset and spoil our lives, if once this thought, 'before God,' were habitual with us, and we walked in it as in an atmosphere!

Why is it not? and might it not be? and if it might not, ought it not to be? And what are we to say to Him whom we profess to love as our Supreme Good, if all the day long the thought of Him seldom comes into our minds, and if any triviality, held near the eye, is large enough and bright enough to shut Him out from our sight? With deep ethical significance and accuracy was the command given to Abraham as the sole, all-sufficient direction for both inward and outward life: 'Walk before Me and (so) be thou perfect.' For indeed the full realisation—adequate and constant and solid enough to be a motive—of 'Thou God seest me,' would be found to contain practical directions in regard to all moral difficulties, and would unfailingly detect the evil, howsoever wrapped up, and would carry in itself not only motive but impulse, not only law but power to fulfil it. The Master's eye makes diligent servants. How schoolboys bend themselves over their slates and quicken their effort when the teacher is walking behind the benches! And how a gang of idle labourers will buckle to the spade and tax their muscles in an altogether different fashion when the overseer appears upon the field! If we realised, as we should do, the presence in all our little daily life of that great, sovereign Lord, there would be less skulking, less superficially performed tasks, less jerry work put into our building; more of our strength cast into all our work, and less of ourselves in any of it.

Remember, too, how connected with this is another piece of effort needful in the religious life, and suggested by the last words of this text, 'Before the Lord *his* God.' Cultivate the habit of narrowing down the general truths of religion to their relation to yourselves. Do not be content with 'the Lord *our* God,' or 'the Lord the God of the whole earth,' but put a 'my' in, and realise not only the presence of a divine Inspector, but the closeness of the personal bond that unites to Him; and the individual responsibility, in all its width and depth and unshiftableness—if I may use such a word—which results therefrom. You cannot shake off or step out of the tasks that 'the Lord *your* God' lays upon you. You and He are as if alone in the world. Make Him your God by choice, by your own personal acceptance of His authority and dependence upon His power, and try to translate into daily life the great truth, 'Thou God seest *me*,' and bring it to bear upon the veriest trifles and smallest details.

Now the text follows the order of observation, so to speak, and mentions the outward facts of Jotham's success before it goes deeper and accounts for them. We have reversed the process and dealt first with the cause. The spring of all lay in his conscious recognition of his relation to God and God's to him. From that, of course, followed that he 'prepared,' according to the Authorised Version, or 'ordered,' according to the Revised Version, 'his ways.' There is an alternative rendering of the word rendered 'prepared' or 'ordered' given in the margin of the Authorised Version, which reads, 'established his ways.' Both the ideas of ordering and establishing are contained in the word.

Now that fact, that the same word means both these, conveys a piece of practical wisdom, which it will do us all good to note clearly and take to heart. For it teaches us that whatever is 'ordered' is firm, and whatever is disorderly, haphazard, done without the exercise of one's mind on the act, being chaotic, is necessarily short-lived.

The ordered life is the established life. The life of impulse, chance, passion, the life that is lived without choice and plan, without reflection and consideration of consequences, the following of nature, which some people tell us is the highest law, and which is wofully likely to degenerate into following the *lower* nature, which ought not to be followed, but covered and kept under hatches—such a life is sure to be a topsy-turvy life, which, being based upon the narrowest point, must, by the laws of equilibrium, topple over sooner or later. If you would have your lives established, they must be ordered. You must bring your brains to bear upon them, and you must bring more than brain, you must bring to bear on every part of them the spiritual instincts that are quickened by contact with the thought of the All-seeing God, and let these have the ordering of them. Such lives, and only such, will endure 'when all that seems shall suffer shock.' 'He that doeth the will of God abideth for ever.'

But the lesson that is pressed upon us by this word, understood in the other meanings of 'prepared' or 'ordered,' is that all our 'ways,' that is, our practical life, our acts, direction of mind, habits, should be regulated by continual consciousness of, and reference to, the All-discerning Eye that looks down upon us, and 'the God in whose hands our breath is, and whose are' —whether we make them so or not—'all our ways.' To translate that into less picturesque, and less forcible, but more modern words, it is just this: You Christian people ought to make it a point of duty to cultivate the habit of referring everything that you do to the will and judgment of God. Take Him into account in everything great or small, and in nothing say, 'Thus I will, thus I command. My will shall stand instead of all other reasons'; but say, 'Lord! by Thee and for Thee I try to do this'; and having done it, say, 'Lord! the seed is sown in Thy name; bless Thou the springing thereof.' Works thus begun, continued and ended, will never be put to confusion, and 'ways' thus ordered will be established. A path of righteousness like that can no more fail to be a way of peace than can God's throne ever totter or fall. An ordered life in which He is consulted, and which is all shaped at His bidding, and by His strength, and for His dear name, will 'stand foursquare to all the winds that blow,' and, being founded upon a rock, will never fall.

But we may also note that in the strength of that thought, that we are before the Lord our God, we shall best establish our ways in the sense that we shall keep on steadily and doggedly on the path. Well begun may be half ended, but there is often a long dreary grind before it is wholly ended, and the last half of the march is the wearisome half. The Bible has a great deal to say about the need of obstinate persistence on the right road. 'Ye did run well, what did hinder you?' 'Cast not away your confidence, which hath great recompense of reward.' 'We are made partakers of Christ if we hold fast the beginning of our confidence firm unto the end.' 'He that overcometh and keepeth My words unto the end, to him will I give authority.' Lives which derive their impulse from communion with

God will not come to a dead stop half-way on their road, like a motor the fuel of which fails; and it will be impossible for any man to 'endure unto the end,' and so to be heir of the promise—'the same shall be saved,' unless he draws his persistency from Him who 'fainteth not, neither is weary,' and who 'reneweth strength to them that have no might,' so that in all the monotonous levels they shall 'walk and not faint,' and in all the crises, demanding brief spurts of energy, 'they shall run and not be weary,' and at last 'shall mount up with wings as eagles.' A path ordered and a path persisted in ought to be the path of every Christian man.

The text finally tells of the prosperity and growing power which attends such a course. 'Jotham became mighty.' That was simple outward blessing. His kingdom prospered, and, according to the theocratic constitution of Judah, faithfulness to God and material well-being went together. You cannot apply these words, of course, to the outward lives of Christians. It is no doubt true that 'Godliness *is* profitable for all things,' but there are a great many other things besides the godliness of the man that does them which determine whether a man's undertakings shall prosper in the world's sense or not. It would be a pitiable thing if the full revelation of God in Christ did not teach us Christians more about the meaning and the worth of outward success and inward prosperity than the Old Testament could teach. I hope we have learned that lesson; at least, it is not the fault of our lesson book if we have not. Although it is true that religion does make the best of both worlds, it does not do so by taking the world's estimate of what its best for to-day is, and giving a religious man *that*. Sometimes it does, and sometimes it does not, and whether it does or no depends on other considerations than the reality of the man's devotion. Good men are often made better by being made sad and unsuccessful. And if they are not bettered by adversity, it is not the fault of the discipline but of the people who undergo it.

But though the husk of my text falls away—and we should thank God that it has fallen away—the kernel of it is ever true. Whosoever will thus root his life in the living thought of a loving, divine Eye being perpetually upon him, and make that thought a motive for holiness and loving obedience and effort after service, will find that the true success, the only success and the only strength that are worth a man's ambition to desire or his effort to secure, will assuredly be his. He may be voted a failure as regards the world's prizes. But a man that 'orders his ways,' and perseveres in ways thus ordered, 'before the Lord' will for reward get more power to order his ways, and a purer and more thrilling, less interrupted and more childlike vision of the Face that looks upon him. God's 'eyes behold the upright,' and the upright behold His eyes, and in the interchange of glances there is power; and in that power is the highest reward for ordered lives. We shall get power to do, power to bear, power to think aright, power to love, power to will, power to behold, power to deny ourselves, 'power to become sons of God.' This is the success of life, when out of all its changes, and by reason of all its efforts, we realise more fully our filial possession of our Father, and our Father's changeless love to us. We shall become mighty with the might that is born of obedience and faith if we order our ways before the Lord our God. 'The path of the just is as the shining light, that shineth more and more until the noontide of the day.'

COSTLY AND FATAL HELP

'He sacrificed unto the gods of Damascus, which smote him: and he said, Because the gods of the kings of Syria help them, therefore will I sacrifice to them, that they may help me. But they were the ruin of him, and of all Israel.'
—2 CHRON. xxviii. 23.

AHAZ came to the throne when a youth of twenty. From the beginning he reversed the policy of his father, and threw himself into the arms of the heathen party. In a comparatively short reign of sixteen years he stamped out the worship of God, and nearly ruined the kingdom.

He did not plunge into idolatry for want of good advice. The greatest of the prophets stood beside him. Isaiah addressed to him remonstrances which might have made the most reckless pause, and promises which might have kindled hope and courage in the bosom of despair. Hosea in the northern kingdom, Micah in Judah, and other less brilliant names were amongst the stars which shone even in that dark night. But their light was all in vain. The foolish lad had got the bit between his teeth, and, like many another young man, thought to show his 'breadth' and his 'spirit' by neglecting his father's counsellors, and abandoning his father's faith. He was ready to worship anything that called itself a god, always excepting Jehovah. He welcomed Baal, Moloch, Rimmon, and many more with an indiscriminate eagerness that would have been ludicrous if it had not been tragical. The more he multiplied his gods the more he multiplied his sorrows, and the more he multiplied his sorrows the more he multiplied his gods.

From all sides the invaders came. From north, north-east, east, south-east, south, they swarmed in upon him.

They tore away the fringes of his kingdom; and hostile armies flaunted their banners beneath the very walls of Jerusalem.

And then, in his despair, like a scorpion in a circle of fire, he inflicted a deadly wound on himself by calling in the fatal help of Assyria. Nothing loth, that warlike power responded, scattered his less formidable foes, and then swallowed the prey which it had dragged from between the teeth of the Israelites and Syrians. The result of Ahaz's frantic appeals to false gods and faithless men may still be read on the cuneiform inscriptions, where, amidst a long list of unknown tributary kings, stands, with a Philistine on one side of him and an Ammonite on the other, the shameful record, 'Ahaz of Judah.'

That was what came of forsaking the God of his fathers. It is a type of what always has come, and always must come, of a godless life. That is the point of view from which I wish to look at the story, and at these words of my text which gather the whole spirit of it into one sentence.

I. First, then, let me ask you to notice how this narrative illustrates for us the crowd of vain helpers to which a man has to take when he turns his back upon God.

If we compare the narrative in our chapter with the parallel in the Second Book of Kings, we get a very vivid picture of the strange medley of idolatries which they introduced. Amongst Ahaz's new gods are, for instance, the golden calves of Israel and the ferocious Moloch of Ammon, to whom he sacrificed, passing through the fire at least one of his own children. The ancient sacred places of the Canaanites, on every high hill and beneath every conspicuous tree, again smoked with incense to half-forgotten local deities. In every open space in Jerusalem he planted a brand-new altar with a brand-new worship attendant upon it. In the Temple, he brushed aside the altar that Solomon had made and put up a new one, copied from one which he had seen at Damascus. The importation of the Damascene altar, I suppose, meant, as our text tells us, the importation of the Damascene gods along with it.

Side by side with that multiplication of false deities went the almost entire neglect of the worship of Jehovah, until at last, as his reign advanced and he floundered deeper into his troubles, the Temple was spoiled, everything in it that could be laid hands upon was sent to the melting-pot, to pay the Assyrian tribute; and then the doors were shut, the lamps extinguished, the fire quenched on the cold altars, and the silent Temple left to the bats and — *the Shekinah*; for God still abode in the deserted house.

Further, side by side with this appealing all round the horizon to whatsoever obscene and foul shape seemed to promise some help, there went the foolish appeal to the northern invaders to come and aid him, which they did, to his destruction. His whole career is that of a godless and desperate man who will grasp at anything that offers deliverance, and will worship any god or devil who will extricate him from his troubles.

Is the breed extinct, think you? Is there any one among us who, if he cannot get what he wants by fair ways, will try to get it by foul? Do none of you ever bow down to Satan for a slice of the kingdoms of this world? Ahaz has still plenty of brothers and sisters in all our churches and chapels.

This story illustrates for us what, alas! is only too true, both on the broad scale, as to the generation in which we live, and on the narrower field of our own individual lives. Look at the so-called cultured classes of Europe to-day; turning away, as so many of them are, from the Lord God of their fathers; what sort of gods are they worshipping instead? Scraps from Buddhism, the Vedas, any sacred books but the Bible; quackeries, and charlatanism, and dreams, and fragmentary philosophies all pieced together, to try and make up a whole, instead of the old-fashioned whole that they have left behind them. There are men and women in many congregations who, in modern fashion, are doing precisely the thing that Ahaz did—having abandoned Christianity, they are trying to make up for it by hastily stitching together shreds and patches that they have found in other systems. 'The garment is narrower than that a man can wrap himself in it,' and a creed patched together so will never make a seamless whole which can be trusted not to rend.

But look, further, how the same thing is true as to the individual lives of godless men.

Many of us are trying to make up for not having the One by seeking to stay our hearts on the many. But no accumulation of insufficiencies will ever make a sufficiency. You may fill the heaven all over with stars, bright and thickly set as those in the whitest spot in the galaxy, and it will be night still. Day needs the sun, and the sun is one, and when it comes the twinkling lights are forgotten. You cannot make up for God by any extended series of creatures, any more than a row of figures that stretched from here to *Sirius* and back again would approximate to infinity.

The very fact of the multitude of helpers is a sign

that none of them is sufficient. There is no end of 'cures' for toothache, that is to say there is none. There is no end of helps for men that have abandoned God, that is to say, every one in turn when it is tried, and the stress of the soul rests upon it, gives, and is found to be a broken staff that pierces the hand that leans upon it.

Consult your own experience. What is the meaning of the unrest and distraction that mark the lives of most of the men in this generation? Why is it that you hurry from business to pleasure, from pleasure to business, until it is scarcely possible to get a quiet breathing time for thought at all? Why is it but because one after another of your gods have proved insufficient, and so fresh altars must be built for fresh idolatries, and new experiments made, of which we can safely prophesy the result will be the old one. We have not got beyond St. Augustine's saying:— 'Oh, God! my heart was made for Thee, and in Thee only doth it find repose.' The many idols, though you multiply them beyond count, all put together will never make the One God. You are seeking what you will never find. The many pearls that you seek will never be enough for you. The true wealth is One, 'One pearl of great price.'

II. So notice again how this story teaches the heavy cost of these helpers' help.

Ahaz had, as he thought, two strings to his bow. He had the gods of Damascus and of other lands on one hand, he had the king of Assyria on another. They both of them exacted onerous terms before they would stir a foot to his aid. As for the northern conqueror, all the wealth of the king and of the princes and of the Temple was sent to Assyria as the price of his hurtful help. As for the gods, his helpers, one of his sons at least went into the furnace to secure their favour; and what other sacrifices he may have made besides the sacrifice of his conscience and his soul history does not tell us. These were considerable subsidies to have to be paid down before any aid was granted.

Do *you* buy this world's help any cheaper, my brother? You get nothing for nothing in that market. It is a big price that you have to pay before these mercenaries will come to fight on your side. Here is a man that 'succeeds in life,' as we call it. What does it cost him? Well! it has cost him the suppression, the atrophy by disuse, of many capacities in his soul which were far higher and nobler than those that have been exercised in his success. It has cost him all his days; it has possibly cost him the dying out of generous sympathies and the stimulating of unwholesome selfishness. Ah! he has bought his prosperity very dear. Political economists have much to say about the 'appreciation of gold.' I think if people would estimate what they pay for it, in an immense majority of cases, in treasure that cannot be weighed and stamped, they would find it to be about the dearest thing in God's universe; and that there are few men who make worse bargains than the men who give *themselves* for worldly success, even when they receive what they give themselves for.

There are some of you who know how much what you call enjoyment has cost you. Some of us have bought pleasure at the price of innocence, of moral dignity, of stained memories, of polluted imaginations, of an incapacity to rise above the flesh: and some of us have bought it at the price of health. The world has a way of getting more out of you than it gives to you.

At the best, if you are not Christian men and women, whether you are men of business, votaries of pleasure, seekers after culture and refinement or anything else, you have given Heaven to get earth. Is that a good bargain? Is it much wiser than that of a horde of naked savages that sell a great tract of fair country, with gold-bearing reefs in it, for a bottle of rum, and a yard or two of calico? What is the difference? You have been fooled out of the inheritance which God meant for you; and you have got for it transient satisfaction, and partial as it is transient. If you are not Christian people, you have to buy this world's wealth and goods at the price of God and of your own souls. And I ask you if that is an investment which recommends itself to your common sense. Oh! my brother; 'what shall it profit a man if he gain the whole world, and lose himself?' Answer the question.

III. Lastly, we may gather from this story an illustration of the fatal falsehood of the world's help.

Ahaz pauperised himself to buy the hireling swords of Assyria, and he got them; but, as it says in the narrative, 'the king came unto him, and distressed him, but strengthened him not.' He helped Ahaz at first. He scattered the armies of which the king of Judah was afraid like chaff, with his fierce and disciplined onset. And then, having driven them off the bleeding prey, he put his own paw upon it, and growled 'Mine!' And where he struck his claws there was little more hope of life for the prostrate creature below him.

Ay! and that is what this world always does. In the case before us there was providential guidance of the politics of the Eastern nations in order to bring about these results; and we do not look for anything of that sort. No! But there are natural laws at work to-day which are God's laws, and which ensure the worthlessness of the help bought so dear.

A godless life has at the best only partial satisfaction, and that partial satisfaction soon diminishes. 'Even in laughter the heart is sorrowful, and the end of that mirth is heaviness.'

That is the experience of all men, and I need not dwell upon the threadbare commonplaces which have survived from generation to generation, because each generation in turn has found them so piteously true, about the incompleteness and the fleetingness of all the joys and treasures of this life. The awful power of habit, if there were no other reason, takes the edge off all gratification except in so far as God is in it. Nothing fully retains its power to satisfy. Nothing has that power absolutely at any moment; but even what measure of it any of our possessions or pursuits may have for a time, soon, or at all events by degrees, passes away. The greater part of life is but like drinking out of empty cups, and the cups drop from our hands. What one of our purest and peacefullest poets said in his haste about all his kind is true in spirit of all godless lives:—

> 'We poets, in our youth, begin in gladness,
> But thereof cometh, in the end, despondency and madness.'

'Vanity of vanities! saith'—not the Preacher only, but the inmost heart of every godless man and woman—'vanity of vanities! all is vanity!'

And do not forget that, partial and transient as these satisfactions of which I have been speaking are, they derive what power of helping and satisfying *is* in them only from the silence of our consciences, and our success in being able to shut out realities. One word, they say, spoken too loud, brings down the avalanche, and beneath its white, cold death, the active form is motionless and the beating heart lies still. One word from conscience, one touch of an awakened reflectiveness, one glance at the end—the coffin and the shroud and what comes after these—slay your worldly satisfactions as surely as that falling snow would crush some light-winged, gauzy butterfly that had been dancing at the cliff's foot. Your jewellery is all imitation. It is well enough for candle-light. Would you like to try the testing acid upon it? Here is a drop of it. 'Know thou that for all these things God will bring thee into judgment.' Does it smoke? or does it stand the test? Here is another drop. 'This night thy soul shall be required of thee.' Does it stand that test? My brother! do not be afraid to take in all the facts of your earthly life, and do not pretend to satisfy yourselves with satisfactions which dare not face realities, and shrivel up at their presence.

These fatal helpers come as friends and allies, and they remain as masters. Ahaz and a hundred other weak princes have tried the policy of sending for a strong foreign power to scatter their enemies, and it has always turned out one way. The foreigner has come and he has stopped. The auxiliary has become the lord, and he that called him to his aid becomes his tributary. Ay! and so it is with all the things of this world. Here is some pleasant indulgence that I call to my help lightly and thoughtlessly. It is very agreeable and does what I wanted with it, and I try it again.

Still it answers to my call. And then after a while I say, 'I am going to give that up,' and I cannot. I have brought in a master when I thought I was only bringing in an ally that I could dismiss when I liked. The sides of the pit are very slippery; it is gay travelling down them, but when the animal is trapped at the bottom there is no possibility of getting up again. So some of you, dear friends! have got masters in your delights, masters in your pursuits, masters in your habits. These are your gods, these are your tyrants, and you will find out that they are so, if ever, in your own strength, you try to break away from them.

So let me plead with you. With some of you, perhaps, my voice, as a familiar voice, that in some measure, however undeservedly, you trust, may have influence. Let me plead with you—do not run after these will-o'-the-wisps that will only lure you into destruction, but follow the light of life which is Jesus Christ Himself. Do not take these tyrants for your helpers, who will master you under pretence of aiding you; and work their will of you instead of lightening your burden. The same unwise and hopeless mode of life, which we have been describing this evening by one symbolic illustration, as calling vain helpers to our aid, was presented by Ahaz's great contemporary Isaiah, in words which Ahaz himself may have heard, as 'striking a covenant with death, and making lies our refuge.' Some of us, alas! have been doing that all our lives. Let such hearken to the solemn words which may have rung in the ears of this unworthy king. 'Judgment also will I lay to the line, and righteousness to the plummet, and the hail shall sweep away the refuge of lies.' I come to you, dear friends! to press on your acceptance the true Guide and Helper—even Jesus

Christ your Brother, in whose single Self you will find all that you have vainly sought dispersed 'at sundry times and in divers manners'—among creatures. Take Him for your Saviour by trusting your whole selves to Him. He is the Sacrifice by whose blood all our sins are washed away, and the Indweller, by whose Spirit all our spirits are ennobled and gladdened. I ask you to take Him for your Helper, who will never deceive you; to call whom to our aid is to be secure and victorious for ever. 'Behold! I lay in Zion for a foundation a stone, a tried stone, a precious corner-stone, a sure foundation: he that believeth shall not make haste.'

A GODLY REFORMATION

'Hezekiah began to reign when he was five and twenty years old, and he reigned nine and twenty years in Jerusalem. And his mother's name was Abijah, the daughter of Zechariah. 2. And he did that which was right in the sight of the Lord, according to all that David his father had done. 3. He in the first year of his reign, in the first month, opened the doors of the house of the Lord, and repaired them. 4. And he brought in the priests and the Levites, and gathered them together into the east street, 5. And said unto them, Hear me, ye Levites; Sanctify now yourselves, and sanctify the house of the Lord God of your fathers, and carry forth the filthiness out of the holy place. 6. For our fathers have trespassed, and done that which was evil in the eyes of the Lord our God, and have forsaken Him, and have turned away their faces from the habitation of the Lord, and turned their backs. 7. Also they have shut up the doors of the porch, and put out the lamps, and have not burnt incense, nor offered burnt-offerings in the holy place unto the God of Israel. 8. Wherefore the wrath of the Lord was upon Judah and Jerusalem, and He hath delivered them to trouble, to astonishment, and to hissing, as ye see with your eyes. 9. For, lo, our fathers have fallen by the sword; and our sons and our daughters and our wives are in captivity for this. 10. Now it is in mine heart to make a covenant with the Lord God of Israel, that His fierce wrath may turn away from us. 11. My sons, be not now negligent: for the Lord hath chosen you to stand before Him, to serve Him, and that ye should minister unto Him, and burn incense.'—2 CHRON. xxix. 1-11.

HEZEKIAH, the best of the later kings, had the worst for his father, and another almost as bad for his son. His own piety was probably deepened by the mad extravagance of his father's boundless idolatry, which brought the kingdom to the verge of ruin. Action and reaction are equal and contrary. Saints grown amidst fashionable and deep corruption are generally strong, and reformers usually arise from the midst of the systems which they overthrow. Hezekiah came to a tottering throne and an all but beggared nation, ringed around by triumphant enemies. His brave young heart did not quail. He sought 'first the kingdom of God, and His righteousness,' and of the two pressing needs for Judah, political peace and religious purity, he began with the last. The Book of Kings tells at most length the civil history; the Book of Chronicles, as usual, lays most stress on the ecclesiastical. The two complete each other. The present passage gives a beautiful picture of the vigorous, devout young king setting about the work of reformation.

We may note, first, his prompt action. Joash had to whip up the reluctant priests with his 'See that ye hasten the matter!' Hezekiah lets no grass grow under his feet, but begins his reforms with his reign. 'The first month' (ver. 3) possibly, indeed, means the first month of the calendar, not of Hezekiah, who may have come to the throne in the later part of the Jewish year; but, in any case, no time was lost. The statement in verse 3 may be taken as a general *résumé* of what follows in detail, but this vigorous speech to the priests was clearly among the new king's first acts. No doubt his purpose had slowly grown while his father was affronting Heaven with his mania for idols. Such decisive, swift action does not come without protracted, previous brooding. The hidden fires gather slowly in the silent crater, however rapidly they burst out at last.

We can never begin good things too early, and when

we come into new positions, it is always prudence as well as bravery to show our colours unmistakably from the first. Many a young man, launched among fresh associations, has been ruined because of beginning with temporising timidity. It is easier to take the right standing at first than to shift to it afterwards. Hezekiah might have been excused if he had thought that the wretched state of political affairs left by Ahaz needed his first attention. Edomites on the east, Philistines on the west and south, Syrians and Assyrians on the north, 'compassed him about like bees,' and worldly prudence would have said, 'Look after these enemies to-day, and the Temple to-morrow.' He was wiser than that, knowing that these were effects of the religious corruption, and so he went at that first. It is useless trying to mend a nation's fortunes unless you mend its morals and religion.

And there are some things which are best done quickly, both in individual and national life. Leaving off bad habits by degrees is not hopeful. The only thing to be done is to break with them utterly and at once. One strong, swift blow, right through the heart, kills the wild beast. Slighter cuts may make him bleed to death, but he may kill you first. The existing state was undeniably sinful. There was no need for deliberation as to that. Therefore there was no reason for delay. Let us learn the lesson that, where conscience has no doubts, we should have no dawdling. 'I made haste, and delayed not to keep thy commandment.'

Note, too, in Hezekiah's speech, the true order of religious reformation. The priests and Levites were not foremost in it, as indeed is only too often the case with ecclesiastics in all ages. Probably many of them had been content to serve Ahaz as priests of his multiform idolatry. At all events, they needed 'sanctifying,' though no doubt the word is here used in reference to merely ceremonial uncleanness. Still the requirement that they should cleanse themselves before they cleansed the Temple has more than ceremonial significance. Impure hands are not fit for the work of religious reformation, though they have often been employed in it. What was the weakness of the Reformation but that the passions of princes and nobles were so soon and generally enlisted for it, and marred it? He that enters into the holy place, especially if his errand be to cleanse it, must have 'clean hands, and a pure heart.' The hands that wielded the whip of small cords, and drove out the money-changers, were stainless, and therefore strong. Some of us are very fond of trying to set churches to rights. Let us begin with ourselves, lest, like careless servants, we leave dirty finger-marks where we have been 'cleaning.'

The next point in the speech is the profound and painful sense of existing corruption. Note the long-drawn-out enumeration of evils in verses 6 and 7, starting with the general recognition of the fathers' trespass, advancing to the more specific sin of forsaking Him and His house, and dwelling, finally, as with fascinated horror, on all the details of closed shrine and quenched lamps and cold altars. The historical truth of the picture is confirmed by the close of the previous chapter, and its vividness shows how deeply Hezekiah had felt the shame and sin of Ahaz. It is not easy to keep clear of the influence of prevailing corruptions of religion. Familiarity weakens abhorrence, and the stained embodiments of the ideal hide its purity from most eyes. But no man will be

God's instrument to make society, the church, or the home, better, unless he feels keenly the existing evils. We do not need to cherish a censorious spirit, but we do need to guard against an unthinking acquiescence in the present state of things, and a self-complacent reluctance to admit their departure from the divine purpose for the church. There is need to-day for a like profound consciousness of evil, and like efforts after new purity. If we individually lived nearer God, we should be less acclimatised to the Church's imperfections. No doubt Hezekiah's clear sight of the sinfulness of the idolatry so universal round him was largely owing to Isaiah's influence. Eyes which have caught sight of the true King of Israel, and of the pure light of His kingdom, will be purged to discern the sore need for purifying the Lord's house.

The clear insight into the national sin gives as clear understanding of the national suffering. Hezekiah speaks, in verses 8 and 9, as the Law and the Prophets had been speaking for centuries, and as God's providence had been uttering in act all through the national history. But so slow are men to learn familiar truths that Ahaz had grasped at idol after idol to rescue him; 'but they were the ruin of him, and of all Israel.' How difficult it is to hammer plain truths, even with the mallet of troubles, into men's heads! How blind we all are to the causal connection between sin and sorrow! Hezekiah saw the iron link uniting them, and his whole policy was based upon that 'wherefore.' Of course, if we accept the Biblical statements as to the divine dealing with Israel and Judah, obedience and disobedience were there followed by reward and suffering more certainly and directly than is now the case in either national or individual life. But it still remains true that it is a 'bitter' as well as an 'evil' thing to depart from the living God. If we would find the cause of our own or of a nation's sorrows, we had better begin our search among our or its sins.

That phrase 'an astonishment, and an hissing' (ver. 8) is new. It appears for the first time in Micah (Micah vi. 16), and he, we know, exercised influence on Hezekiah (Jer. xxvi. 18, 19). Perhaps the king is here quoting the prophet.

The exposition of the sin and its fruit is followed by the king's resolve for himself, and, so far as may be, for his people. The phrase 'it is in my heart' expresses fixed determination, not mere wish. It is used by David and of him, in reference to his resolve to build the Temple. 'To make a covenant' probably means to renew the covenant, made long ago at Sinai, but broken by sin. The king has made up his mind, and announces his determination. He does not consult priests or people, but expects their acquiescence. So, in the early days of Christianity, the 'conversion' of a king meant that of his people. Of course, the power of the kings of Israel and Judah to change the national religion at their pleasure shows how slightly any religion had penetrated, and how much, at the best, it was a matter of mere ceremonial worship with the masses. People who worshipped Ahaz's rabble of gods and godlings to-day because he bade them, and Hezekiah's God to-morrow, had little worship for either, and were much the same through all changes.

Hezekiah was in earnest, and his resolve was none the less right because it was moved by a desire to turn away the fierce anger of the Lord. Dread of sin's consequences and a desire to escape these is no unworthy motive, however some superfine moralists nowadays may call it so. It is becoming unfashionable to preach 'the terror of the Lord.' The more is the pity, and the less is the likelihood of persuading men. But, however kindled, the firm determination (which does not wait for others to concur) that 'As for me, I will serve the Lord,' is the grand thing for us all to imitate. That strong young heart showed itself kingly in its resolve, as it had shown itself sensitive to evil and tender in contemplating the widespread sorrow. If we would brace our feeble wills, and screw them to the sticking-point of immovable determination to make a covenant with God, let us meditate on our departures from Him, the Lover and Benefactor of our souls, and on the dreadfulness of His anger and the misery of those who forsake Him.

Once more the king turns to the priests. He began and he finishes with them, as if he were not sure of their reliableness. His tone is kindly, 'My sons,' but yet monitory. They would not have been warned against 'negligence' unless they had obviously needed it, nor would they have been stimulated to their duties by reminding them of their prerogatives, unless they had been apt to slight these. Officials, whose business is concerned with the things of God, are often apt to drop into an easy-going pace. Negligent work may suit unimportant offices, but is hideously inconsistent with the tasks and aims of God's servants. If there is any work which has to be done 'with both hands, earnestly,' it is theirs. Unless we put all our strength into it, we shall get no good for ourselves or others out of it. The utmost tension of all powers, the utmost husbanding of every moment, is absolutely demanded by the greatness of the task; and the voice of the great Master says to all His servants, 'My sons, be not now negligent.' Ungirt loins and unlit lamps are fatal.

We should meditate, too, on the prerogatives and lofty offices to which Christ calls those who love Him; not to minister to self-complacency, as if we were so much better than other men, but to deepen our sense of responsibility, and stir us to strenuous efforts to be what we are called to be. If Christian people thought more earnestly on what Jesus Christ means them to be to the world, they would not so often counterwork His purpose and shirk their own duties. Crowns are heavy to wear. Gifts are calls to service. If we are chosen to be His ministers, we have solemn responsibilities. If we are to burn incense before Him, our censers need to be bright and free from strange fire. If we are the lights of the world, our business is to shine.

SACRIFICE RENEWED

'Then they went in to Hezekiah the king, and said, We have cleansed all the house of the Lord, and the altar of burnt-offering, with all the vessels thereof, and the shew-bread table, with all the vessels thereof. 19. Moreover, all the vessels, which king Ahaz in his reign did cast away in his transgression, have we prepared and sanctified, and, behold, they are before the altar of the Lord. 20. Then Hezekiah the king rose early, and gathered the rulers of the city, and went up to the house of the Lord. 21. And they brought seven bullocks, and seven rams, and seven lambs, and seven he goats, for a sin-offering for the kingdom, and for the sanctuary, and for Judah. And he commanded the priests, the sons of Aaron, to offer them on the altar of the Lord. 22. So they killed the bullocks, and the priests received the blood, and sprinkled it on the altar: likewise, when they had killed the rams, they sprinkled the blood upon the altar: they killed also the lambs, and they sprinkled the blood upon the altar. 23. And they brought forth the he goats for the sin-offering before the king and the congregation; and they laid their hands upon them. 24. And the priests killed them, and they made reconciliation with their blood upon the altar, to make an atonement for all Israel: for the king commanded that the burnt-offering and the sin-offering should be made for all Israel. 25. And he set the Levites in the house of the Lord with cymbals, with psalteries, and with harps, according to the commandment of David, and of Gad the king's seer, and Nathan the prophet: for so was the commandment of the Lord by His prophets. 26. And the Levites stood with the instruments of David, and the priests with the trumpets. 27. And Hezekiah commanded to offer the burnt-offering upon the altar. And when the burnt-offering began, the song of the Lord began also with the trumpets, and with the instruments ordained by David king of Israel. 28. And all the congregation worshipped, and the singers sang, and the trumpeters sounded: and all this continued until the burnt-offering was finished. 29. And when they had made an end of offering, the king and all that were present with him bowed themselves, and worshipped. 30. Moreover, Hezekiah the king and the princes commanded the Levites to sing praises unto the Lord with the words of David, and of Asaph the seer. And they sang praises with gladness, and they bowed their heads and worshipped. 31. Then Hezekiah answered and said, Now ye have consecrated yourselves unto the Lord, come near, and bring sacrifices and thank-offerings into the house of the Lord. And the congregation brought in sacrifices and thank-offerings; and as many as were of a free heart burnt offerings.—2 CHRON. xxix. 18-31.

AHAZ, Hezekiah's father, had wallowed in idolatry, worshipping any and every god but Jehovah. He had shut up the Temple, defiled the sacred vessels, and 'made him altars in every corner of Jerusalem.' And the result was that he brought the kingdom very near ruin, was not allowed to be buried in the tombs of the kings, and left his son a heavy task to patch up the mischief he had wrought. Hezekiah began at the right end of his task. 'In the first year of his reign, in the first month,' he set about restoring the worship of Jehovah. The relations with Syria and Damascus would come right if the relations with Judah's God were right. 'First things first' was his motto, and perhaps he discerned the true sequence more accurately than some great political pundits do nowadays. So neglected had the Temple been that a strong force of priests and Levites took a fortnight to 'carry forth the filthiness out of the holy place to the brook Kidron,' and to cleanse and ceremonially sanctify the sacred vessels. Then followed at once the re-establishment of the Temple worship, which is narrated in the passage.

The first thing to be noted is that the whole movement back to Jehovah was a one-man movement. It was Hezekiah's doing and his only. No priest is named as prominent in it, and the slowness of the whole order is especially branded in verse 34. No prophet is named; was there any one prompting the king? Perhaps

Isaiah did, though his chapter I., with its scathing repudiation of 'the burnt offerings of rams and the fat of fed beasts,' suggests that he did not think the restoration of sacrifice so important as that the nation should 'cease to do evil and learn to do well.' The people acquiesced in the king's worship of Jehovah, as they had acquiesced in other kings' worship of Baal or Moloch or Hadad. When kings take to being religious reformers, they make swift converts, but their work is as slight as it is speedy, and as short-lived as it is rapid. Manasseh was Hezekiah's successor, and swept away all his work after twenty-nine years, and apparently the mass of his people followed him just as they had followed Hezekiah. Religion must be a matter of personal conviction and individual choice. Imposed from without, or adopted because other people adopt it, it is worthless.

Another point to notice is that Hezekiah's reformation was mainly directed to ritual, and does not seem to have included either theology or ethics. Was he quite right in his estimate of what was the first thing? Isaiah, in the passage already referred to, does not seem to think so. To him, as to all the prophets, foul hands could not bring acceptable sacrifices, and worship was an abomination unless preceded by obedience to the command: 'Put away the evil of your doings from before Mine eyes.' The filth in the hearts of the men of Judah was more 'rank, and smelt to heaven' more offensively, than that in the Temple, which took sixteen days to shovel into Kidron. No doubt ceremonial bulked more largely in the days of the Old Covenant than it does in those of the New, and both the then stage of revelation and the then spiritual stature of the recipients of revelation required that it should do so.

But the true religious reformers, the prophets, were never weary of insisting that, even in those days, moral and spiritual reformation should come first, and that unless it did, ritual worship, though it were nominally offered to Jehovah, was as abhorrent to Him as if it had been avowedly offered to Baal. Not a little so-called Christian worship to-day, judged by the same test, is as truly heathen superstition as if it had been paid to Mumbo-Jumbo.

But when all deductions have been made, the scene depicted in the passage is not only an affecting, but an instructive one. Strangely unlike our notions of worship, and to us almost repulsive, must have been the slaying of three hundred and seventy animals and the offering of them as burnt offerings. Try to picture the rivers of blood, the contortions of the dumb brutes, the priests bedaubed with gore, the smell of the burnt flesh, the blare of the trumpets, the shouts of the worshippers, the clashing cymbals, and realise what a world parts it from 'They went up into the upper chamber where they were abiding ... these all with one accord continued steadfastly in prayer, with the women, and Mary, the mother of Jesus, and with His brethren'! Sacrifice has been the essential feature in all religions before Christ. It has dropped out of worship wherever Christ has been accepted. Why? Because it spoke of a deep, permanent, universal need, and because Christ was recognised as having met the need. People who deny the need, and people who deny that Jesus on the Cross has satisfied it, may be invited to explain these two facts, written large on the history of humanity.

That brings us to the most important aspect of Hezekiah's great sacrifice. It sets forth the stages by which men can approach to God. It is symbolic of spiritual facts, and prophetic of Christ's work and of our way of coming to God through Him. The first requisite for Judah's return to Jehovah, whom they had forsaken, was the presentation of a 'sin offering.' The king and the congregation laid their hands on the heads of the goats, thereby, as it were, transferring their own sinful personality to them. Thus laden with the nation's sins, they were slain, and in their death the nation, as it were, bore the penalty of its sin. Representation and substitution were dramatised in the sacrifice. The blood sprinkled on the altar (which had previously been 'sanctified' by sprinkling of blood, and so made capable of presenting what touched it to Jehovah), made 'atonement for all Israel.' We note in passing the emphasis of 'Israel' here, extending the benefit of the sacrifice to the separated tribes of the Northern Kingdom, in a gush of yearning love and desire that they, too, might be reconciled to Jehovah. And is not this the first step towards any man's reconciliation with God? Is not

> 'My faith would lay her hand
> On that dear head of Thine,'

the true expression of the first requisite for us all? Jesus is the sin-offering for the world. In His death He bears the world's sin. His blood is presented to God, and if we have associated ourselves with Him by faith, that blood sprinkled on the altar covers all our sins.

Then followed in this parabolic ceremonial the burnt offering. And that is the second stage of our return to God, for it expresses the consecration of our forgiven selves, as being consumed by the holy and blessed fire of a self-devotion, kindled by the 'unspeakable gift,' which fire, burning away all foulness, will make us tenfold ourselves. That fire will burn up only our bonds, and we shall walk at liberty in it. And that burnt-offering will always be accompanied with 'the song of Jehovah,' and the joyful sound of the trumpets and 'the instruments of David.' The treasures of Christian poetry have always been inspired by the Cross, and the consequent rapture of self-surrender. Calvary is the true fountain of song.

The last stage in Hezekiah's great sacrifice was 'thank-offerings,' brought by 'as many as were of a willing heart.' And will not the self-devotion, kindled by the fire of love, speak in daily life by practical service, and the whole activities of the redeemed man be a long thank-offering for the Lamb who 'bears away the sins of the world'? And if we do not thus offer our whole lives to God, how shall we profess to have taken the priceless benefit of Christ's death? Hezekiah followed the order laid down in the Law, and it is the only order that leads to the goal. First, the atoning sacrifice of the slain Lamb; next, our identification with Him and it by faith; then the burnt-offering of a surrendered self, with the song of praise sounding ever through it; and last, the life of service, offering all our works to God, and so reaching the perfection of life on earth and antedating the felicities of heaven.

A LOVING CALL TO REUNION

'And Hezekiah sent to all Israel and Judah, and wrote letters also to Ephraim and Manasseh, that they should come to the house of the Lord at Jerusalem, to keep the passover unto the Lord God of Israel. 2. For the king had taken counsel, and his princes, and all the congregation in Jerusalem, to keep the passover in the second month. 3. For they could not keep it at that time, because the priests had not sanctified themselves sufficiently, neither had the people gathered themselves together to Jerusalem. 4. And the thing pleased the king and all the congregation. 5. So they established a decree to make proclamation throughout all Israel, from Beer-sheba even to Dan, that they should come to keep the passover unto the Lord God of Israel at Jerusalem: for they had not done it of a long time in such sort as it was written. 6. So the posts went with the letters from the king and his princes throughout all Israel and Judah, and according to the commandment of the king, saying, Ye children of Israel, turn again unto the Lord God of Abraham, Isaac, and Israel, and he will return to the remnant of you, that are escaped out of the hand of the kings of Assyria. 7. And be not ye like your fathers, and like your brethren, which trespassed against the Lord God of their fathers, who therefore gave them up to desolation, as ye see. 8. Now, be ye not stiffnecked, as your fathers were, but yield yourselves unto the Lord, and enter into His sanctuary, which He hath sanctified for ever: and serve the Lord your God, that the fierceness of His wrath may turn away from you. 9. For if ye turn again unto the Lord, your brethren and your children shall find compassion before them that lead them captive, so that they shall come again into this land: for the Lord your God is gracious and merciful, and will not turn away His face from you, if ye return unto Him. 10. So the posts passed from city to city through the country of Ephraim and Manasseh, even unto Zebulun: but they laughed them to scorn, and mocked them. 11. Nevertheless divers of Asher and Manasseh and of Zebulun humbled themselves, and came to Jerusalem. 12. Also in Judah the hand of God was to give them one heart to do the commandment of the king and of the princes, by the word of the Lord. 13. And there assembled at Jerusalem much people to keep the feast of unleavened bread in the second month, a very great congregation.'—2 CHRON. xxx. 1-13.

THE date of Hezekiah's passover is uncertain, for, while the immediate connection of this narrative with the preceding account of his cleansing the Temple and restoring the sacrificial worship suggests that the passover followed directly on those events, which took place at the beginning of the reign, the language employed in the message to the northern tribes (vers. 6, 7, 9) seems to imply the previous fall of the kingdom of Israel. If so, this passover did not occur till after 721 B.C., the date of the capture of Samaria, six years after Hezekiah's accession.

The sending of messengers from Jerusalem on such

an errand would scarcely have been possible if the northern kingdom had still been independent. Perhaps its fall was thought by Hezekiah to open the door to drawing 'the remnant that were escaped' back to the ancient unity of worship, at all events, if not of polity. No doubt a large number had been left in the northern territory, and Hezekiah may have hoped that calamity had softened their enmity to his kingdom, and perhaps touched them with longings for the old worship. At all events, like a good man, he will stretch out a hand to the alienated brethren, now that evil days have fallen on them. The hour of an enemy's calamity should be our opportunity for seeking to help and proffering reconciliation. We may find that trouble inclines wanderers to come back to God.

The alteration of the time of keeping the passover from the thirteenth day of the first month to the same day of the second was in accordance with the liberty granted in Numbers ix. 10, 11, to persons unclean by contact with a dead body or 'in a journey afar off.' The decision to have the passover was not taken in time to allow of the necessary removal of uncleanness from the priests nor of the assembling of the people, and therefore the permission to defer it for a month was taken advantage of, in order to allow full time for the despatch of the messengers and the journeys of the farthest northern tribes. It is to be observed that Hezekiah took his subjects into counsel, since the step intended was much too great for him to venture on of his own mere motion. So the overtures went out clothed with the authority of the whole kingdom of Judah. It was the voice of a nation that sought to woo back the secessionists.

The messengers were instructed to supplement the

official letters of invitation with earnest entreaties as from the king, of which the gist is given in verses 6-9. With the skill born of intense desire to draw the long-parted kingdoms together, the message touches on ancestral memories, recent bitter experiences, yearnings for the captive kinsfolk, the instinct of self-preservation, and rises at last into the clear light of full faith in, and insight into, God's infinite heart of pardoning pity.

Note the very first words, 'Ye children of Israel,' and consider the effect of this frank recognition of the northern kingdom as part of the undivided Israel. Such recognition might have been misunderstood or spurned when Samaria was gay and prosperous; but when its palaces were desolate, the effect of the old name, recalling happier days, must have been as if the elder brother had come out from the father's house and entreated the prodigal to come back to his place at the fireside. The battle would be more than half won if the appeal that was couched in the very name of Israel was heeded.

Note further how firmly and yet lovingly the sin of the northern kingdom is touched on. The name of Jehovah as the God of Abraham, Isaac, and Israel, recalls the ancient days when the undivided people worshipped Him, and the still more ancient, and, to hearers and speakers alike, more sacred, days when the patriarchs received wondrous tokens that He was their God, and they were His people; while the recurrence of 'Israel' as the name of Jacob adds force to its previous use as the name of all His descendants. The possible rejection of the invitation, on the ground which the men of the north, like the Samaritan woman, might have taken, that they were true to their fathers' worship, is cut away by the reminder that that worship was an innovation, since the fathers of the present generation had been apostate from the God of *their* fathers. The appeal to antiquity often lands men in a bog because it is not carried far enough back. 'The fathers' may lead astray, but if the antiquity to which we appeal is that of which the New Testament is the record, the more conservative we are, the nearer the truth shall we be.

Again, the message touched on a chord that might easily have given a jarring note; namely, the misfortunes of the kingdom. But it was done with so delicate a hand, and so entirely without a trace of rejoicing in a neighbour's calamities, that no susceptibilities could be ruffled, while yet the solemn lesson is unfalteringly pointed. 'He gave them up to desolation, as ye see.' Behind Assyria was Jehovah, and Israel's fall was not wholly explained by the disparity between its strength and the conquerors'. Under and through the play of criminal ambition, cruelty, and earthly politics, the unseen Hand wrought; and the teaching of all the Old Testament history is condensed into that one sad sentence, which points to facts as plain as tragical. In deepest truth it applies to each of us; for, if we trespass against God, we draw down evil on our heads with both hands, and shall find that sin brings the worst desolation—that which sheds gloom over a godless soul.

We note further the deep true insight into God's character and ways expressed in this message. There is a very striking variation in the three designations of Jehovah as 'the God of Abraham, Isaac, and Israel' (ver. 6), 'the god of their [that is, the preceding generation] fathers' (ver. 7), and 'your God' (ver. 8). The relation which had subsisted from of old had not been broken by man's apostasy. Jehovah still was, in a true sense, their God, even if His relation to them only bound Him not to leave them unpunished. So their very sufferings proved them His, for 'What son is he whom the father chasteneth not?' But strong, sunny confidence in God shines from the whole message, and reaches its climax in the closing assurance that He is merciful and gracious. The evil results of rebellion are not omitted, but they are not dwelt on. The true magnet to draw wanderers back to God is the loving proclamation of His love. Unless we are sure that He has a heart tender with all pity, and 'open as day to melting charity,' we shall not turn to Him with our hearts.

The message puts the response which it sought in a variety of ways; namely, turning to Jehovah, not being stiff-necked, yielding selves to Jehovah, entering into His sanctuary. More than outward participation in the passover ceremonial is involved. Submission of will, abandonment of former courses of action, docility of spirit ready to be directed anywhere, the habit of abiding with God by communion—all these, the standing characteristics of the religious life, are at least suggested by the invitations here. We are all summoned thus to yield ourselves to God, and especially to do so by surrendering our wills to Him, and to 'enter into His sanctuary,' by keeping up such communion with Him as that, however and wherever occupied, we shall still 'dwell in the house of the Lord all the days of our lives.'

And the summons to return unto God is addressed to us all even more urgently than to Israel. God Himself invites us by the voice of His providences, by His voice within, and by the voice of Jesus Himself, who is ever saying to each of us, by His death and passion, by His resurrection and ascension, 'Turn ye! turn ye! why will ye die?' and who has more than endorsed Hezekiah's messengers' assurance that 'Jehovah will not turn away His face from' us by His own gracious promise, 'Him that cometh to Me I will in no wise cast out.'

The king's message met a mingled reception. Some mocked, some were moved and accepted. So, alas! is it with the better message, which is either 'a savour of life unto life or of death unto death.' The same fire melts wax and hardens clay. May it be with all of us as it was in Judah—that we 'have one heart, to do the commandment' and to accept the merciful summons to the great passover!

A STRANGE REWARD FOR FAITHFULNESS

'After these things, and the establishment thereof, Sennacherib, king of Assyria, came.'—2 CHRON. XXXII. 1.

THE Revised Version gives a much more accurate and significant rendering of a part of these words. It reads: 'After these things and *this faithfulness*, Sennacherib, king of Assyria, came.' What are 'these things' and 'this faithfulness'? The former are the whole of the events connected with the religious reformation in Judah, which King Hezekiah inaugurated and carried through so brilliantly and successfully. This 'faithfulness' directly refers to a word in a couple of verses before the text: 'Thus did Hezekiah throughout all Judah; and he wrought that which was good and right and *faithfulness* before the Lord his God.' And, after these things, the re-establishment of religion and this 'faithfulness,' though Hezekiah was perfect before God in all ritual observances and in practical righteousness, and though he was seeking the Lord his God with all his heart, here is what came of it:—'After this faithfulness came' not blessings or prosperity, but 'Sennacherib, king of Assyria'! The chronicler not only tells this as singular, but one can feel that he is staggered by it. There is a tone of perplexity and wonder in his voice as he records that *this* was what followed the faithful righteousness and heart-devotion of the best king that ever sat on the throne of Judah. I think that this royal martyr's experience is really a mirror of the experience of devout men in all ages and a revelation of the great law and constant processes of the Divine Providence. And from that point of view I wish to speak now, not only on the words I have read, but on what follows them.

I. We have here the statement of the mystery.

It is the standing puzzle of the Old Testament, how good men come to be troubled, and how bad men come to be prosperous. And although we Christian men and women are a great deal too apt to suppose that we have outlived that rudimentary puzzle of the religious mind, yet I do not think by any means that we have. For we hear men, when the rod falls upon themselves, saying, 'What have I done that I should be smitten thus?' or when their friends suffer, saying, 'What a marvellous thing it is that such a good man as A, B, or C should have so much trouble!' or, when widespread calamities strike a community, standing aghast at the broad and dark shadows that fall upon a nation or a continent, and wondering what the meaning of all this heaped misery is, and why the world is thus allowed to run along its course surrounded by an atmosphere made up of the breath of sighs, and swathed in clouds which are moist with tears.

My text gives us an illustration in the sharpest form of the mystery. 'After these things and this faithfulness, Sennacherib came'—and he always comes in one shape or another. For, to begin with, a good man's goodness does not lift him out of the ordinary associations and contingencies and laws of life. If he has inherited a diseased constitution, his devotion will not make him a healthy man. If he has little common sense, his godliness will not make him prosper in worldly affairs. If he is tied to unfortunate connections, he will have to suffer. If he happens to be in a decaying branch of business, his prayers will not make him prosperous. If he falls in the way of poisonous gas from a sewer, his godliness will not exempt him from an attack of fever. So all round the horizon we see this: that the godly man is involved like any other man in the ordinary contingencies and possible evils of life. Then, have we to say that God has nothing to do with these?

Again, Hezekiah's story teaches us how second causes are God's instruments, and He is at the back of everything. There are two sources of our knowledge of the history of Judah in the time with which we are concerned. One is the Bible, the other is the Assyrian monuments; and it is a most curious contrast to read the two narratives of the same events, agreeing about the facts, but disagreeing utterly in the spirit. Why? Because the one tells the story from the world's point of view, and the other tells it from God's point of view. So when you take the one narrative, it is simply this: 'There was a conspiracy down in the south against the political supremacy of Assyria, and a lot of little confederate kinglets gathered themselves; and Hezekiah, of Judah, was one, along with So-and-So of such-and-such a petty land, and they leaned upon Egypt; and I, Sennacherib, came down among them, and they tumbled to pieces, and that is all.' Then the Bible comes in, and it says that God ordered all those political complications, and that they were all the working out of His purposes, and that 'the axe in His hand,' as Isaiah has it so picturesquely, was this proud king of Assyria, with his boastful mouth and vainglorious words.

Now, that is the principle by which we have to estimate all the events that befall us. There are two ways of looking at them. You may look at them from the under side or from the top side. You may see them as they appear to men who cannot look beyond their noses and only have concern with the visible cranks and shafting, or you may look at them from the engine-room and take account of the invisible power that drives them all. In the one case you will regard it as a mystery that good men should have to suffer so; in the other case, you will say, 'It is the Lord, let Him do'—even when He does it through Sennacherib and his like, 'let Him do what seemeth Him good.'

Then there is another thing to be taken into account —that is, that the better a man is, the more faithful he is and the more closely he cleaves to God, and seeks, like this king, to do, with all his heart, all his work in the service of the House of God and to seek his God, the more sure is he to bring down upon himself certain forms of trouble and trial. The rebellion which, from the Assyrian side of the river, seemed to be a mere political revolt, from the Jordan side of the river seemed to be closely connected with the religious reformation. And it was just because Hezekiah and his people came back to God that they rebelled against the King of Assyria and served him not. If you provoke Sennacherib, Sennacherib will be down upon you very quickly. That is to say, being translated, if you will live like Christian men and women and fling down the gage of battle to the world and to the evil that lies in every one of us, and say, 'No, I have nothing to do with you. My law is not your law, and, God helping me, my practice shall not be your practice,' then you will find out that the power that you have defied has a very long arm and a very tight grasp, and you will have to make up your minds that, in some shape or other, the old law will be fulfilled about you. Through much tribulation we must enter the Kingdom.

II. Now, secondly, my text and its context solve the mystery which it raises.

The chronicler, as I said, wishes us to notice the sequence, strange as it is, and to wonder at it for a moment, in order that we may be prepared the better to take in the grand explanation that follows. And the explanation lies in the facts that ensue.

Did Sennacherib come to destroy? By no means! Here were the results: first, a stirring to wholesome energy and activity. If annoyances and troubles and sorrows, great or small, do nothing else for us, they would be clear and simple gain if they woke us up, for the half of men pass half of their lives half-asleep. And anybody that has ever come through a great sorrow and can remember what deep fountains were opened in his heart that he knew nothing about before, and how powers that were all unsuspected by himself suddenly came to him, and how life, instead of being a trivial succession of nothings, all at once became significant and solemn—any man who can remember that, will feel that if there were nothing else that his troubles did for him than to shake him out of torpor and rouse him to a tension of wholesome activity, so that he cried out:

> 'Call forth thy powers, my soul! and dare
> The conflict of unequal war,'

he would have occasion to bless God for the roughest handling. The tropics are very pleasant for lazy people, but they sap the constitution and make work impossible; and after a man has lived for a while in their perpetual summer, he begins to long for damp and mist and frost and east winds which bring bracing to the system and make him fit to work. God takes us often into very ungenial climates, and the vindication of it is that we may be set to active service. That was the first good thing that Sennacherib's coming did.

The next was that his invasion increased dependence upon God. You will remember the story of the insolent taunts and vulgar vaunting by him and his servants, and the one answer that was given: 'Hezekiah, the king, and Isaiah the son of Amoz the prophet, prayed and cried to God.' Ah! dear brethren, anything that drives us to His breast is blessing. We may call it evil when we speak from the point of view of the foolish senses and the quivering heart, but if it blows us into His arms, any wind, the roughest and the fiercest, is to be welcomed more than lazy calms or gentle zephyrs. If, realising our own weakness and impotence, we are made to hang more completely upon

Him, then let us be thankful for whatever has been the means of such a blessed issue. That was the second good thing that Sennacherib did.

The third good thing that he—not exactly did—but that was done through him, was that experience of God's delivering power was enriched. You remember the miracle of the destruction of the army. I need not dilate upon it. A man who can look back and say, 'Thou hast been with me in six troubles,' need never be afraid of the seventh; and he who has hung upon that strong rope when he has been swinging away down in the darkness and asphyxiating atmosphere of the pit, and has been drawn up into the sunshine again, will trust it for all coming time. If there were no other explanation, the enlarged and deepened experience of the realities of God's Gospel and of God's grace, which are bought only by sorrow, would be a sufficient explanation of any sorrow that any of us have ever had to carry.

> 'Well roars the storm to him who hears
> A deeper voice across the storm.'

There are large tracts of Scripture which have no meaning, no blessedness to us until they have been interpreted to us by losses and sorrows. We never know the worth of the lighthouse until the November darkness and the howling winds come down upon us, and then we appreciate its preciousness.

So, dear friends! the upshot of the whole is just that old teaching, that if we realised what life is for, we should wonder less at the sorrows that are in it. For life is meant to make us partakers of His holiness, not to make us happy. Our happiness is a secondary purpose, not out of view of the Divine love, but it is not the primary one. And the direct intention and mission of sorrow, like the direct intention and mission of joy, are to further that great purpose, that we 'should be partakers of His holiness.' 'Every branch in Me that beareth fruit, He purgeth it, that it may bring forth more fruit.'

III. Lastly, my text suggests a warning against letting prosperity undo adversity's work.

Hezekiah came bravely through his trials. They did exactly what God wanted them to do; they drove him to God, they forced him down upon his knees. When Sennacherib's letter came, he took it to the Temple and spread it before God, and said, 'O Lord! it is Thy business. It is addressed to me, but it is meant for Thee; do Thou answer it.' And so he received the help that he wanted. But he broke down after that. He was 'exalted'; and the allies, his neighbours, that had not lifted a finger to help him when he needed their help, sent him presents which would have been a great deal more seasonable when he was struggling for his life with Sennacherib. What 'came after (God's) faithfulness'? This—'his heart was lifted up, and he rendered not according to the benefit rendered to him.' Therefore the blow had to come down again. A great many people take refuge in archways when it rains, and run out as soon as it holds up, and a great many people take religion as an umbrella, to put down when the sunshine comes. We cross the bridge and forget it, and when the leprosy is out of us we do not care to go back and give thanks. Sometimes too, we begin to think, 'After all, it was we that killed Sennacherib's army, and not the angel.' And so, like dull scholars, we need the lesson repeated once, twice, thrice, 'here a little and there a little, precept upon precept, line upon line.' There is none of us that has so laid to heart our past difficulties and trials that it is safe for God to burn the rod as long as we are in this life.

Dear friends! do not let it be said of us, 'In vain have I smitten thy children. They have received no correction'; but rather let us keep close to Him, and seek to learn the sweet and loving meaning of His sharpest strokes. Then the little book, 'written within and without with lamentation and woe,' which we all in our turn have to absorb and make our own, may be 'bitter in the mouth,' but will be 'sweet as honey' thereafter.

MANASSEH'S SIN AND REPENTANCE

'So Manasseh made Judah and the inhabitants of Jerusalem to err, and to do worse than the heathen, whom the Lord had destroyed before the children of Israel. 10. And the Lord spake to Manasseh, and to his people: but they would not hearken. 11. Wherefore the Lord brought upon them the captains of the host of the king of Assyria, which took Manasseh among the thorns, and bound him with fetters, and carried him to Babylon. 12. And when he was in affliction, he besought the Lord his God, and humbled himself greatly before the God of his fathers, 13. And prayed unto him: and he was intreated of him, and heard his supplication, and brought him again to Jerusalem into his kingdom. Then Manasseh knew that the Lord He was God. 14. Now after this he built a wall without the city of David, on the west side of Gihon, in the valley, even to the entering in at the fish gate, and compassed about Ophel, and raised it up a very great height, and put captains of war in all the fenced cities of Judah. 15. And he took away the strange gods, and the idol out of the house of the Lord, and all the altars that he had built in the mount of the house of the Lord, and in Jerusalem, and cast them out of the city. 16. And he repaired the altar of the Lord, and sacrificed thereon peace offerings and thank offerings, and commanded Judah to serve the Lord God of Israel.'—2 CHRON. xxxiii. 9-16.

THE story of Manasseh's sin and repentance may stand as a typical example. Its historical authenticity is denied on the ground that it appears only in this Book of Chronicles. I must leave others to discuss that matter; my purpose is to bring out the teaching contained in the story.

The first point in it is the stern indictment against Manasseh and his people. The experience which has saddened many a humbler home was repeated in the royal house, where a Hezekiah was followed by a Manasseh, who scorned all that his father had worshipped, and worshipped all that his father had loathed. Happily the father's eyes were closed long before the idolatrous bias of his son could have disclosed itself. Succeeding to the throne at twelve years of age, he could not have begun his evil ways at once, and probably would have been preserved from them if his father had lived long enough to mould his character. A child of twelve, flung on to a throne, was likely to catch the infection of any sin that was in the atmosphere. The narrative specifies two points in which, as he matured in years, and was confirmed in his course of conduct, he went wrong: first, in his idolatry; and second, in his contempt of remonstrances and warnings. As to the former, the preceding context gives a terrible picture. He was smitten with a very delirium of idolatry, and wallowed in any and every sort of false worship. No matter what strange god was presented, there were hospitality, an altar, and an offering for him. Baal, Moloch, 'the host of heaven,' wizards, enchanters, anybody who pretended to have any sort of black art, all were welcome, and the more the better. No doubt, this eager acceptance of a miscellaneous multitude of deities was partly reaction from the monotheism of the former reign, but also it was the natural result of being surrounded by the worshippers of these various gods; and it was an unconscious confession of the insufficiency of each and all of them to fill the void in the heart, and satisfy the needs of the spirit. There are 'gods many, and lords many,' because they are insufficient; 'the Lord our God is one Lord,' because He, in His single Self, is more than all these, and is enough for any and every man.

We may note, too, that at the beginning of the chapter Manasseh is said to have done '*like* unto the abominations of the heathen,' while in verse 9 he is said to have done 'evil *more* than did the nations.' When a worshipper of Jehovah does *like* the heathen, he does *worse* than they. An apostate Christian is more guilty than one who has never 'tasted the good word of God,' and is likely to push his sins to a more flagrant wickedness. 'The corruption of the best is the worst.' We cannot do what the world does without being more deeply guilty than they.

The narrative lays stress on the fact that the king's inclination to idolatry was agreeable to the people. The kings, who fought against it, had to resist the popular current, but at the least encouragement from those in high places the nation was ready to slide back. Rulers who wish to lower the standard of morality or religion have an easy task; but the people who follow their lead are not free from guilt, though they can plead that they only followed. The second count in the indictment is the refusal of king and people to listen to God's remonstrances. 2 Kings, chap. xxi., gives the prophets' warnings at greater length. 'They would not hearken,'—can anything madder and sadder be said of any of us than that? Is it not the very sin of sins, and the climax of suicidal folly, that God should call and men stop their ears? And yet how many of us pay no more regard to His voice, in His providences, in our own consciences, in history, in Scripture, and, most penetrating and beseeching of all, in Christ, than to idle wind whistling through an archway! Our own evil deeds stop our ears, and the stopped ears make further evil deeds more easy.

The second step in this typical story is merciful chastisement, meant to secure a hearing for God's voice. 2 Kings tells the threat, but not the fulfilment; Chronicles tells the fulfilment, but not the threat. We note how emphatically God's hand is recognised behind the political complications which brought the Assyrians to Jerusalem, and how particularly it is stated that the invasion was not headed by Esarhaddon, but by his generals. The place of Manasseh's captivity also is specified, not as Nineveh, as might have been expected, but as Babylon. These details, especially the last, look like genuine history. It is history which carries a lesson. Here is one conspicuous instance of the divine method, which is working to-day as it did then. God's hand is behind the secondary causes of events. Our sorrows and 'misfortunes' are sent to us by Him, not hurled at us by human hands only, or occurring by the working of impersonal laws. They are meant to make us bethink ourselves, and drop evil things from our hands and hearts. It is best to be guided by His eye, and not need 'bit and bridle'; but if we make ourselves stubborn as 'the mule, which has no understanding,' it is second best that we should taste the whip, that it may bring us to run in harness on the road which He wills. If we habitually looked at calamities as His loving chastisement, intended to draw us to Himself, we should not have to stand perplexed so often at what we call the mysteries of His providence.

The next step in the story is the yielding of the sinful heart when smitten. The worst affliction is an affliction wasted, which does us no good. And God has often to lament, 'In vain have I smitten your children; they received no correction.' Sorrow has in itself no power to effect the purpose for which it is sent; but all depends on how we take it. It sometimes makes us hard, bitter, obstinate in clinging to evil. A heart that has been disciplined by it, and still is undisciplined, is like iron hammered on an anvil, and made the more close-grained thereby. But this king took his chastisement wisely. An accepted sorrow is an angel in disguise, and nothing which drives us to God is a calamity. Manasseh praying was freer in his chains than ever he had been in his prosperity. Manasseh humbling himself greatly before God was higher than when, in the pride of his heart, he shut God out from it.

Affliction should clear our sight, that we may see ourselves as we are; and, if we do, there will be an end of high looks, and we shall 'take the lowest room.' Thus humbled, we shall pray as the self-confident and outwardly prosperous cannot do. Sorrow has done its best on us when, like some strong hand on our shoulders, it has brought us to our knees. No affliction has yielded its full blessing to us unless it has thus set us by Manasseh's side.

The next step in the story is the loving answer to the humbled heart, and the restoration to the kingdom. 'He was entreated of him.' No doubt, political circumstances brought about Manasseh's reinstatement, as they had brought about his captivity, but it was God that 'brought him again to his kingdom.' We may not receive again lost good things, but we may be quite sure that God never fails to hear the cry of the humble, and that, if there is one voice that more surely reaches His ear and moves His heart than another, it is the voice of His chastened children, who cry to Him out of the depths, and there have learned their own sin and sore need. He will be entreated of them, and, whether He gives back lost good or not, He will give Himself, in whom all good is comprehended. Manasseh's experience may be repeated in us.

And the best part of it was, not that he received back his kingdom, but that 'then Manasseh knew that the Lord He was God.' The name had been but a name to him, but now it had become a reality. Our traditional, second-hand belief in God is superficial and largely unreal till it is deepened and vivified by experience. If we have cried to Him, and been lightened, then we have a ground of conviction that cannot be shaken. Formerly we could at most say, 'I believe in God,' or, 'I think there is a God,' but now we can say, 'I know,' and no criticism nor contradiction can shake that. Such knowledge is not the knowledge won by the understanding alone, but it is acquaintance with a living Person, like the knowledge which loving souls have of each other; and he who has that knowledge as the issue of his own experience may smile at doubts and questionings, and say with the Apostle of Love, 'We know that we are of God, . . . and we know that the Son of God is come, and hath given us an understanding, that we may know Him that is true.' Then, if we have that knowledge, we shall listen to the same Apostle's commandment, 'Keep yourselves from idols,' even as the issue of Manasseh's knowledge of God was that 'he took away the strange gods, and the idol out of the house of the Lord.'

JOSIAH

'Josiah was eight years old when he began to reign, and he reigned in Jerusalem one and thirty years. 2. And he did that which was right in the sight of the Lord, and walked in the ways of David his father, and declined neither to the right hand, nor to the left. 3. For in the eighth year of his reign, while he was yet young, he began to seek after the God of David his father: and in the twelfth year he began to purge Judah and Jerusalem from the high places, and the groves, and the carved images, and the molten images. 4. And they brake down the altars of Baalim in his presence; and the images, that were on high above them, he cut down; and the groves, and the carved images, and the molten images, he brake in pieces, and made dust of them, and strowed it upon the graves of them that had sacrificed unto them. 5. And he burnt the bones of the priests upon their altars, and cleansed Judah and Jerusalem. 6. And so did he in the cities of Manasseh, and Ephraim, and Simeon, even unto Naphtali, with their mattocks round about. 7. And when he had broken down the altars and the groves, and had beaten the graven images into powder, and cut down all the idols throughout all the land of Israel, he returned to Jerusalem. 8. Now in the eighteenth year of his reign, when he had purged the land, and the house, he sent Shaphan the son of Azaliah, and Maaseiah the governor of the city, and Joah the son of Joahaz the recorder, to repair the house of the Lord his God. 9. And when they came to Hilkiah the high priest, they delivered the money that was brought into the house of God, which the Levites that kept the doors had gathered of the hand of Manasseh and Ephraim, and of all the remnant of Israel, and of all Judah and Benjamin; and they returned to Jerusalem. 10. And they put it in the hand of the workmen that had the oversight of the house of the Lord, and they gave it to the workmen that wrought in the house of the Lord, to repair and amend the house: 11. Even to the artificers and builders gave they it, to buy hewn stone, and timber for couplings, and to floor the houses which the kings of Judah had destroyed. 12. And the men did the work faithfully: and the overseers of them were Jahath and Obadiah, the Levites, of the sons of Merari; and Zechariah and Meshullam, of the sons of the Kohathites, to set it forward; and other of the Levites, all that could skill of instruments of musick. 13. Also they were over the bearers of burdens, and were overseers of all that wrought the work in any manner of service: and of the Levites there were scribes, and officers, and porters.'—2 CHRON. xxxiv. 1-13.

ANOTHER boy king, even younger than his grandfather Manasseh had been at his accession, and another reversal of the father's religion! These vibrations from idolatry to Jehovah-worship, at the pleasure of the king, sadly tell how little the people cared whom they worshipped, and how purely a matter of ceremonies and names both their idolatry and their Jehovah-worship were. The religion of the court was the religion of the nation, only idolatry was more congenial than the service of God. How far the child monarch Josiah had a deeper sense of what that service meant we cannot decide, but the little outline sketch of him in verses

2 and 3 is at least suggestive of his having it, and may well stand as a fair portrait of early godliness.

A child eight years old, who had been lifted on to the throne of a murdered father, must have had a strong will and a love of goodness to have resisted the corrupting influences of royalty in a land full of idols. Here again we see that, great as may be the power of circumstances, they do not determine character; for it is always open to us either to determine whether we yield to them or resist them. The prevailing idolatry influenced the boy, but it influenced him to hate it with all his heart. So out of the nettle danger we may pluck the flower safety. The men who have smitten down some evil institution have generally been brought up so as to feel its full force.

'He did that which was right in the eyes of Jehovah' —that may mean simply that he worshipped Jehovah by outward ceremonies, but it probably means more; namely, that his life was pure and God-pleasing, or, as we should say, clean and moral, free from the foul vices which solicit a young prince. 'He walked in the ways of David his father'—not being one of the 'emancipated' youths who think it manly to throw off the restraints of their fathers' faith and morals. He 'turned not aside to the right hand or to the left'—but marched right onwards on the road that conscience traced out for him, though tempting voices called to him from many a side-alley that seemed to lead to pleasant places. 'While he was yet young, he began to seek after the God of David his father'—at the critical age of sixteen, when Easterns are older than we, in the flush of early manhood, he awoke to deeper experiences and felt the need for a closer touch of God. A career thus begun will generally prelude a life pure, strenuous, and blessed with a clearer and clearer vision of the God who is always found of them that seek Him. Such a childhood, blossoming into such a boyhood, and flowering in such a manhood, is possible to every child among us. It will 'still bring forth fruit in old age.'

The two incidents which the passage narrates, the purging of the land and the repair of the Temple, are told in inverted order in 2 Kings, but the order here is probably the more accurate, as dates are given, whereas in 2 Kings, though the purging is related after the Temple restoration, it is not said to have occurred after. But the order is of small consequence. What is important is the fiery energy of Josiah in the work of destruction of the idols. Here, there, everywhere, he flames and consumes. He darts a flash even into the desolate ruins of the Israelitish kingdom, where the idols had survived their devotees and still bewitched the scanty fragments of Israel that remained. The altars of stone were thrown down, the wooden sun-pillars were cut to pieces, the metal images were broken and ground to powder. A clean sweep was made.

A dash of ferocity mingled with contempt appears in Josiah's scattering the 'dust' of the images on the graves of their worshippers, as if he said: 'There you lie together, pounded idols and dead worshippers, neither able to help the other!' The same feelings prompted digging up the skeletons of priests and burning the bones on the very altars that they had served, thus defiling the altars and executing judgment on the priests. No doubt there were much violence and a strong strain of the 'wrath of man' in all this. Iconoclasts are wont to be 'violent'; and men without convictions, or who are partisans of what the iconoclasts are rooting out, are horrified at their want of 'moderation.' But though violence is always unchristian, indifference to rampant evils is not conspicuously more Christian, and, on the whole, you cannot throttle snakes in a graceful attitude or without using some force to compress the sinuous neck.

The restoration of the Temple comes after the cleansing of the land, in Chronicles, and naturally in the order of events, for the casting out of idols must always precede the building or repairing of the Temple of God. Destructive work is very poor unless it is for the purpose of clearing a space to build the Temple on. Happy the man or the age which is able to do both! Josiah and Joash worked at restoring the Temple in much the same fashion, but Josiah had a priesthood more interested than Joash had.

But we may note one or two points in his restoration. He had put his personal effort into the preparatory extirpation of idols, but he did not need to do so now. He could work this time by deputy. And it is noteworthy that he chose 'laymen' to carry out the restoration. Perhaps he knew how Joash had been balked by the knavery of the priests who were diligent in collecting money, but slow in spending it on the Temple. At all events, he delegated the work to three highly-placed officials, the secretary of state, the governor of Jerusalem, and the official historian.

It appears that for some time a collection had been going on for Temple repairs; probably it had been begun six years before, when the 'purging' of the land began. It had been carried on by the Levites, and had been contributed to even by 'the remnant of Israel' in the northern kingdom, who, in their forlorn weakness, had begun to feel the drawings of ancient brotherhood and the tie of a common worship. This fund was in the keeping of the high priest, and the three commissioners were instructed to require it from him. Here 2 Kings is clearer than our passage, and shows that what the three officials had mainly to do was to get the money from Hilkiah, and to hand it over to the superintendents of the works.

There are two remarkable points in the narrative; one is the observation that 'the men did the work faithfully,' which comes in rather enigmatically here, but in 2 Kings is given as the reason why no accounts were kept. Not an example to be imitated, and the sure way to lead subordinates sooner or later to deal unfaithfully; but a pleasant indication of the spirit animating all concerned.

Surely these men worked 'as ever in the great Taskmaster's eye.' That is what makes us work faithfully, whether we have any earthly overseer or audit or no. Another noteworthy matter is that not only were the superintendents of the work—the 'contractors,' as we might say—Levites, but so were also the inferior superintendents, or, as we might say, 'foremen.'

And not only so, but they were those that 'were skilful with instruments of music.' What were musicians doing there? Did the building rise

> 'with the sound
> Of dulcet symphonies and voices sweet?'

May we not gather from this singular notice the great thought that for all rearing of the true Temple, harps of praise are no less necessary than swords or trowels, and that we shall do no right work for God or man unless we do it as with melody in our hearts? Our lives must be full of music if we are to lay even one stone in the Temple.

JOSIAH AND THE NEWLY FOUND LAW

'And when they brought out the money that was brought into the house of the Lord, Hilkiah the priest found a book of the law of the Lord given by Moses. 15. And Hilkiah answered and said to Shaphan the scribe, I have found the book of the law in the house of the Lord. And Hilkiah delivered the book to Shaphan. 16 And Shaphan carried the book to the king, and brought the king word back again, saying, All that was committed to thy servants, they do it. 17. And they have gathered together the money that was found in the house of the Lord, and have delivered it into the hand of the overseers, and to the hand of the workmen. 18. Then Shaphan the scribe told the king, saying, Hilkiah the priest hath given me a book. And Shaphan read it before the king. 19. And it came to pass, when the king had heard the words of the law, that he rent his clothes. 20. And the king commanded Hilkiah, and Ahikam the son of Shaphan, and Abdon the son of Micah, and Shaphan the scribe, and Asaiah a servant of the king's, saying, 21. Go, enquire of the Lord for me, and for them that are left in Israel and in Judah, concerning the words of the book that is found: for great is the wrath of the Lord that is poured out upon us, because our fathers have not kept the word of the Lord, to do after all that is written in this book. 22. And Hilkiah, and they that the king had appointed, went to Huldah the prophetess, the wife of Shallum the son of Tikvath, the son of Hasrah, keeper of the wardrobe; (now she dwelt in Jerusalem in the college;) and they spake to her to that effect. 23. And she answered them, Thus saith the Lord God of Israel, Tell ye the man that sent you to me. 24. Thus saith the Lord, Behold, I will bring evil upon this place, and upon the inhabitants thereof, even all the curses that are written in the book which they have read before the king of Judah: 25. Because they have forsaken Me, and have burned incense unto other gods, that they might provoke Me to anger with all the works of their hands; therefore My wrath shall be poured out upon this place, and shall not be quenched. 26. And as for the king of Judah, who sent you to enquire of the Lord, so shall ye say unto him, Thus saith the Lord God of Israel concerning the words which thou hast heard; 27. Because thine heart was tender, and thou didst humble thyself before God, when thou heardest His words against this place, and against the inhabitants thereof, and humbledst thyself before Me, and did rendst thy clothes, and weep before Me; I have even heard thee also, saith the Lord. 28. Behold, I will gather thee to thy fathers, and thou shalt be gathered to thy grave in peace, neither shall thine eyes see all the evil that I will bring upon this place, and upon the inhabitants of the same. So they brought the king word again.'—2 CHRON. xxxiv. 14-28.

ABOUT one hundred years separated Hezekiah's restoration from Josiah's. Neither was more than a momentary arrest of the strong tide running in the opposite direction; and Josiah's was too near the edge of the cataract to last, or to avert the plunge. There is nothing more tragical than the working of the law which often sets the children's teeth on edge by reason of the fathers' eating of sour grapes.

I. The first point in this passage is the discovery of the book of the Law.

The book had been lost before it was found. For how long we do not know, but the fact that it had been so carelessly kept is eloquent of the indifference of priests and kings, its appointed guardians. Lawbreakers have a direct interest in getting rid of lawbooks, just as shopkeepers who use short yardsticks and light weights are not anxious the standards should be easily accessible. If we do not make God's law our guide, we shall wish to put it out of sight, that it may not be our accuser. What more sad or certain sign of evil can there be than that we had rather not 'hear what God the Lord will speak'?

The straightforward story of our passage gives a most natural explanation of the find. Hilkiah was likely to have had dark corners cleared out in preparation for repairs and in storing the subscriptions, and many a mislaid thing would turn up. If it be possible that the book of the Law should have been neglected (and the religious corruption of the last hundred years makes that only too certain), its discovery in some dusty recess is very intelligible, and would not have been doubted but for the exigencies of a theory. 'Reading between the lines' is fascinating, but risky; for the reader is very likely unconsciously to do what Hilkiah is said to have done—namely, to invent what he thinks he finds.

Accepting the narrative as it stands, we may see in it a striking instance of the indestructibleness of God's Word. His law is imperishable, and its written embodiment seems as if it, too, had a charmed life. When we consider the perils attending the transmission of ancient manuscripts, the necessary scarcity of copies before the invention of printing, the scattering of the Jewish people, it does appear as if a divine hand had guarded the venerable book. How came this strange people, who never kept their Law, to swim through all their troubles, like Cæsar with his commentaries between his teeth, bearing aloft and dry, the Word which they obeyed so badly? 'Write it ... in a book, that it may be for the time to come for ever and ever.' The permanence of the written Word, the providence that has watched over it, the romantic history of its preservation through ages of neglect, and the imperishable gift to the world of an objective standard of duty, remaining the same from age to age, are all suggested by this reappearance of the forgotten Law.

It may suggest, too, that honest efforts after reformation are usually rewarded by clearer knowledge of God's will. If Hilkiah had not been busy in setting wrong things right, he would not have found the book in its dark hiding-place. We are told that the coincidence of the discovery at the nick of time is suspicious. So it is, if you do not believe in Providence. If you do, the coincidence is but one instance of His sending gifts of the right sort at the right moment. It is not the first time nor the last that the attempt to keep God's law has led to larger knowledge of the law. It is not the first time nor the last that God has sent to His faithful servants an opportune gift. What the world calls accidental coincidence deeper wisdom discerns to be the touch of God's hand.

Again, the discovery reminds us that the true basis of all religious reform is the Word of God. Josiah had begun to restore the Temple, but he did not know till he heard the Law read how great the task was which he had taken in hand. That recovered book gave impulse and direction to his efforts. The nearest parallel is the rediscovery of the Bible in the sixteenth century, or, if we may take one incident as a symbol of the whole, Luther's finding the dusty Latin Bible among the neglected convent books. The only reformation for an effete or secularised church is in its return to the Bible. Faded flowers will lift up their heads when plunged in water. The old Bible, discovered and applied anew, must underlie all real renovation of dead or moribund Christianity.

II. The next point here is the effect of the rediscovered Law. Shaphan was closely connected with Josiah, as his office made him a confidant. It is ordinarily taken for granted that he and the other persons named in this lesson formed a little knot of earnest Jehovah worshippers, fully sympathising with the Reformation, and that among them lay the authorship of the book. But we know nothing about them except what is told here and in the parallel in Kings. One of them, Ahikam, was a friend and protector of Jeremiah, and Shaphan the scribe was the father of another of Jeremiah's friends. They may all have been in accord with the king, or they may not.

At all events, Shaphan took the book to Josiah. We can picture the scene—the deepening awe of both men as the whole extent of the nation's departure from God became clearer and clearer, the tremulous tones of the reader, and the silent, fixed attention of the listener as the solemn threatenings came from Shaphan's reluctant, pallid lips. There was enough in them to touch a harder heart than Josiah's. We cannot suppose that, knowing the history of the past, and being sufficiently enlightened to 'seek after the God of David his father,' he did not know in a general way that sin meant sorrow, and national disobedience national death. But we all have the faculty of blunting the cutting edge of truth, especially if it has been familiar, so that some novelty in the manner of its presentation, or even its repetition without novelty sometimes, may turn commonplace and impotent truth into a mighty instrument to shake and melt.

So it seems to have been with Josiah. Whether new or old, the Word found him as it had never done before. The venerable copy from which Shaphan read, the coincidence of its discovery just then, the dishonour done to it for so long, may all have helped the impression. However it arose, it was made. If a man will give God's Word a fair hearing, and be honest with himself, it will bring him to his knees. No man rightly uses God's law who is not convinced by it of his sin, and impelled to that self-abased sorrow of which the rent royal robes were the passionate expression. Josiah was wise when he did not turn his thoughts to other people's sins, but began with his own, even whilst he included others. The first function of the law is to arouse the knowledge of sin, as Paul profoundly teaches. Without that penitent knowledge religion is superficial, and reformation merely external. Unless we 'abhor ourselves, and repent in dust and ashes,' Scripture has not done its work on us, and all our reading of it is in vain. Nor is there any good reason why familiarity with it should weaken its power. But, alas! it too often does. How many of us would stand in awe of God's judgments if we heard them for the first time, but listen to them unmoved, as to thunder without lightning, merely because we know them so well! That is a reason for attending to them, not for neglecting.

Josiah's sense of sin led him to long for a further

word from God; and so he called these attendants named in verse 20, and sent them to 'enquire of the Lord . . . concerning the words of the book.' What more did he wish to know? The words were plain enough, and their application to Israel and him indubitable. Clearly, he could only wish to know whether there was any possibility of averting the judgments, and, if so, what was the means. The awakened conscience instinctively feels that threatenings cannot be God's last words to it, but must have been given that they might not need to be fulfilled. We do not rightly sorrow for sin unless it quickens in us a desire for a word from God to tell us how to escape. The Law prepares for the Gospel, and is incomplete without it. 'The soul that sinneth, it shall die,' cannot be all which a God of pity and love has to say. A faint promise of life lies in the very fact of threatening death, faint indeed, but sufficient to awaken earnest desire for yet another word from the Lord. We rightly use the solemn revelations of God's law when we are driven by them to cry, 'What must I do to be saved?'

III. So we come to the last point, the double-edged message of the prophetess. Josiah does not seem to have told his messengers where to go; but they knew, and went straight to a very unlikely person, the wife of an obscure man, only known as his father's son. Where was Jeremiah of Anathoth? Perhaps not in the city at the time. There had been prophetesses in Israel before. Miriam, Deborah, the wife of Isaiah, are instances of 'your daughters' prophesying; and this embassy to Huldah is in full accord with the high position which women held in that state, of which the framework was shaped by God Himself. In Christ

Jesus 'there is neither male nor female,' and Judaism approximated much more closely to that ideal than other lands did.

Huldah's message has two parts: one the confirmation of the threatenings of the Law; one the assurance to Josiah of acceptance of his repentance and gracious promise of escape from the coming storm. These two are precisely equivalent to the double aspect of the Gospel, which completes the Law, endorsing its sentence and pointing the way of escape.

Note that the former part addresses Josiah as 'the man that sent you,' but the latter names him. The embassy had probably not disclosed his name, and Huldah at first keeps up the veil, since the personality of the sender had nothing to do with her answer; but when she comes to speak of pardon and God's favour, there must be no vagueness in the destination of the message, and the penitent heart must be tenderly bound up by a word from God straight to itself. The threatenings are general, but each single soul that is sorry for sin may take as its very own the promise of forgiveness. God's great 'Whosoever' is for me as certainly as if my name stood on the page.

The terrible message of the inevitableness of the destruction hanging over Jerusalem is precisely parallel with the burden of all Jeremiah's teaching. It was too late to avert the fall. The external judgments must come now, for the emphasis of the prophecy is in its last words, it 'shall not be quenched.' But that did not mean that repentance was too late to alter the whole character of the punishment, which would be fatherly chastisement if meekly accepted. So, too, Jeremiah taught, when he exhorted submission to the 'Chaldees.' It is never too late to seek mercy, though it may be too late to hope for averting the outward consequences of sin.

As for Josiah, his penitence was accepted, and he was assured that he would be gathered to his fathers. That expression, as is clear from the places where it occurs, is not a synonym for either death or burial, from both of which it is distinguished, but is a dim promise of being united, beyond the grave, with the fathers, who, in some one condition, which we may call a place, are gathered into a restful company, and wander no more as pilgrims and sojourners in this lonely and changeful life.

Josiah died in battle. Was that going to his grave in peace? Surely yes! if, dying, he felt God's presence, and in the darkness saw a great light. He who thus dies, though it be in the thick of battle, and with his heart's blood pouring from an arrow-wound down on the floor of the chariot, dies in peace, and into peace.

THE FALL OF JUDAH

'Zedekiah was one and twenty years old when he began to reign, and reigned eleven years in Jerusalem. 12. And he did that which was evil in the sight of the Lord his God, and humbled not himself before Jeremiah the prophet speaking from the mouth of the Lord. 13. And he also rebelled against king Nebuchadnezzar, who had made him swear by God: but he stiffened his neck, and hardened his heart from turning unto the Lord God of Israel. 14. Moreover all the chief of the priests, and the people, transgressed very much after all the abominations of the heathen; and polluted the house of the Lord which he had hallowed in Jerusalem. 15. And the Lord God of their fathers sent to them by His messengers, rising up betimes, and sending; because He had compassion on His people, and on His dwelling-place: 16. But they mocked the messengers of God, and despised His words, and misused His prophets, until the wrath of the Lord arose against His people, till there was no remedy. 17. Therefore he brought upon them the king of the Chaldees, who slew their young men with the sword in the house of their sanctuary, and had no compassion upon young man or maiden, old man, or him that stooped for age: he gave them all into his hand. 18. And all the vessels of the house of God, great and small, and the treasures of the house of the Lord, and the treasures of the king, and of his princes; all these he brought to Babylon. 19. And they burnt the house of God, and brake down the wall of Jerusalem, and burnt all the palaces thereof with fire, and destroyed all the goodly vessels thereof. 20. And them that had escaped from the sword carried he away to Babylon; where they were servants to him and his sons until the reign of the kingdom of Persia: 21. To fulfil the word of the Lord by the mouth of Jeremiah, until the land had enjoyed her sabbaths: for as long as she lay desolate she kept sabbath, to fulfil threescore and ten years.'—2 CHRON. xxxvi. 11-21.

BIGNESS is not greatness, nor littleness smallness. Nebuchadnezzar's conquest of Judah was, in his eyes, one of the least important of his many victories, but it is the only one of them which survives in the world's memory and keeps his name as a household word. The Jews were a mere handful, and their country a narrow strip of land between the desert and the sea; but little Judæa, like little Greece, has taught the world. The tragedy of its fall has importance quite disproportioned to its apparent magnitude. Our passage brings together Judah's sin and Judah's punishment, and we shall best gather the lessons of its fall by following the order of the text.

Consider the sin. There is nothing more remarkable than the tone in which the chronicler, like all the Old Testament writers, deals with the national sin. Patriotic historians make it a point of pride and duty to gloss over their country's faults, but these singular narrators paint them as strongly as they can. Their love of their country impels them to 'make known to Israel its transgression and to Judah its sin.' There are tears in their eyes, as who can doubt? But there is no faltering in their voices as they speak. A higher feeling than misguided 'patriotism' moves them. Loyalty to Israel's God forces them to deal honestly with Israel's sin. That is the highest kind of love of country, and might well be commended to loud-mouthed 'patriots' in modern lands.

Look at the piled-up clauses of the long indictment of Judah in verses 12 to 16. Slow, passionless, unsparing, the catalogue enumerates the whole black list.

It is like the long-drawn blast of the angel of judgment's trumpet. Any trace of heated emotion would have weakened the impression. The nation's sin was so crimson as to need no heightening of colour. With like judicial calmness, with like completeness, omitting nothing, does 'the book,' which will one day be opened, set down every man's deeds, and he will be 'judged according to the things that are written in this book.' Some of us will find our page sad reading.

But the points brought out in this indictment are instructive. Judah's idolatry and 'trespass after all the abominations of the heathen' is, of course, prominent, but the spirit which led to their idolatry, rather than the idolatry itself, is dwelt on. Zedekiah's doing 'evil in the sight of the Lord' is regarded as aggravated by his not humbling himself before Jeremiah, and the head and front of his offending is that 'he stiffened his neck and hardened his heart from turning unto the Lord.' Similarly, the people's sin reaches its climax in their 'mocking' and 'scoffing' at the prophets and 'despising' God's words by them. So then, an evil life has its roots in an alienated heart, and the source of all sin is an obstinate self-will. That is the sulphur-spring from which nothing but unwholesome streams can flow, and the greatest of all sins is refusing to hear God's voice when He speaks to us.

Further, this indictment brings out the patient love of God seeking, in spite of all their deafness, to find a way to the sinners' ears and hearts. In a bold transference to Him of men's ways, He is said to have 'risen early' to send the prophets. Surely that means earnest effort. The depths of God's heart are disclosed when we are bidden to think of His compassion as the motive for the prophet's messages and threatenings. What a wonderful and heart-melting revelation of God's placableness, wistful hoping against hope, and reluctance to abandon the most indurated sinner, is given in that centuries-long conflict of the patient God with treacherous Israel! That divine charity suffered long and was kind, endured all things and hoped all things.

Consider the punishment. The tragic details of the punishment are enumerated with the same completeness and suppression of emotion as those of the sin. The fact that all these were divine judgments brings the chronicler to the Psalmist's attitude. 'I was dumb, I opened not my mouth because Thou didst it.' Sorrow and pity have their place, but the awed recognition of God's hand outstretched in righteous retribution must come first. Modern sentimentalists, who are so tender-hearted as to be shocked at the Christian teachings of judgment, might learn a lesson here.

The first point to note is that a time arrives when even God can hope for no amendment and is driven to change His methods. His patience is not exhausted, but man's obstinacy makes another treatment inevitable. God lavished benefits and pleadings for long years in vain, till He saw that there was 'no remedy.' Only then did He, as if reluctantly forced, do 'His work, His strange work.' Behold, therefore, the 'goodness and severity' of God, goodness in His long delay, severity in the final blow, and learn that His purpose is the same though His methods are opposite.

To the chronicler God is the true Actor in human affairs. Nebuchadnezzar thought of his conquest as won by his own arm. Secular historians treat the fall of Zedekiah as simply the result of the political conditions of the time, and sometimes seem to think that it could not be a divine judgment because it was brought about by natural causes. But this old chronicler sees deeper, and to him, as to us, if we are wise, 'the history of the world is the judgment of the world.' The Nebuchadnezzars are God's axes with which He hews down fruitless trees. They are responsible for their acts, but they are His instruments, and it is His hand that wields them.

The iron band that binds sin and suffering is disclosed in Judah's fall. We cannot allege that the same close connection between godlessness and national disaster is exemplified now as it was in Israel. Nor can we contend that for individuals suffering is always the fruit of sin. But it is still true that 'righteousness exalteth a nation,' and that 'by the soul only are the nations great,' in the true sense of the word. To depart from God is always 'a bitter and an evil thing' for communities and individuals, however sweet draughts of outward prosperity may for a time mask the bitterness. Not armies nor fleets, not ships, colonies and commerce, not millionaires and trusts, not politicians and diplomatists, but the fear of the Lord and the keeping of His commandments, are the true life of a nation. If Christian men lived up to the ideal set them by Jesus, 'Ye are the salt of the land,' and sought more earnestly and wisely to leaven their nation, they would be doing more than any others to guarantee its perpetual prosperity.

The closing words of this chapter, not included in the passage, are significant. They are the first words of the Book of Ezra. Whoever put them here perhaps wished to show a far-off dawn following the stormy sunset. He opens a 'door of hope' in 'the valley of trouble.' It is an Old Testament version of 'God hath not cast away His people whom He foreknew.' It throws a beam of light on the black last page of the chronicle, and reveals that God's chastisement was in love, that it was meant for discipline, not for destruction, that it was educational, and that the rod was burned when the lesson had been learned. It was learned, for the Captivity cured the nation of hankering after idolatry, and whatever defects it brought back from Babylon, it brought back a passionate abhorrence of all the gods of the nations.

EZRA

THE EVE OF THE RESTORATION

'Now in the first year of Cyrus king of Persia, that the word of the Lord by the mouth of Jeremiah might be fulfilled, the Lord stirred up the spirit of Cyrus king of Persia, that he made a proclamation throughout all his kingdom, and put it also in writing, saying, 2. Thus saith Cyrus king of Persia, The Lord God of heaven hath given me all the kingdoms of the earth: and He hath charged me to build Him an house at Jerusalem, which is in Judah. 3. Who is there among you of all His people? his God be with him, and let him go up to Jerusalem, which is in Judah, and build the house of the Lord God of Israel (He is the God), which is in Jerusalem. 4. And whosoever remaineth in any place where he sojourneth, let the men of his place help him with silver, and with gold, and with goods, and with beasts, besides the freewill offering for the house of God that is in Jerusalem. 5. Then rose up the chief of the fathers of Judah and Benjamin, and the priests, and the Levites, with all them whose spirit God had raised, to go up to build the house of the Lord which is in Jerusalem. 6. And all they that were about them strengthened their hands with vessels of silver, with gold, with goods, and with beasts, and with precious things, besides all that was willingly offered. 7. Also Cyrus the king brought forth the vessels of the house of the Lord, which Nebuchadnezzar had brought forth out of Jerusalem, and had put them in the house of his gods; 8. Even those did Cyrus king of Persia bring forth by the hand of Mithredath the treasurer, and numbered them unto Sheshbazzar, the prince of Judah. 9. And this is the number of them: thirty chargers of gold, a thousand chargers of silver, nine and twenty knives, 10. Thirty basons of gold, silver basons of a second sort four hundred and ten, and other vessels a thousand. 11. All the vessels of gold and of silver were five thousand and four hundred. All these did Sheshbazzar bring up with them of the captivity that were brought up from Babylon unto Jerusalem.'
—Ezra i. 1-11.

Cyrus captured Babylon 538 B.C., and the 'first year' here is the first after that event. The predicted seventy years' captivity had nearly run out, having in part done their work on the exiles. Colours burned in on china are permanent; and the furnace of bondage had, at least, effected this, that it fixed monotheism for ever in the inmost substance of the Jewish people. But the bulk of them seem to have had little of either religious or patriotic enthusiasm, and preferred Babylonia to Judea. We are here told of the beginning of the return of a portion of the exiles—forty-two thousand, in round numbers.

'The Lord stirred up the spirit of Cyrus.' That unveils the deepest cause of what fell into place, to the superficial observers, as one among many political events of similar complexion. We find among the inscriptions a cylinder written by order of Cyrus, which shows that he reversed the Babylonian policy of deporting conquered nations. 'All their peoples,' says he, in reference to a number of nations of whom he found members in exile in Babylonia, 'I assembled and restored to their lands and the gods . . . whom Nabonidos . . . had brought into Babylon, I settled in peace in their sanctuaries' (Sayce, *Fresh Light from the Ancient Monuments*, p. 148). It was, then, part of a wider movement, which sent back Zerubbabel and his people to Jerusalem, and began the rebuilding of the Temple. No doubt, Cyrus had seen that the old plan simply brought an element of possible rebellion into the midst of the country, and acted on grounds of political prudence.

But our passage digs deeper to find the true cause. Cyrus was God's instrument, and the statesman's insight was the result of God's illumination. The divine causality moves men, when they move themselves. It was not only in the history of the chosen people that God's purpose is wrought out by more or less conscious and willing instruments. The principle laid down by the writer of this book is of universal application, and the true 'philosophy of history' must recognise as underlying all other so-called causes and forces the one uncaused Cause, of whose purposes kings and politicians are the executants, even while they freely act according to their own judgments, and, it may be, in utter unconsciousness of Him. It concerns our tranquillity and hopefulness, in the contemplation of the bewildering maze and often heart-breaking tragedy of mundane affairs, to hold fast by the conviction that God's unseen Hand moves the pieces on the board, and presides over all the complications. The difference between 'sacred' and 'profane' history is not that one is under His direct control, and the other is not. What was true of Cyrus and his policy is as true of England. Would that politicians and all men recognised the fact as clearly as this historian did!

I. Cyrus's proclamation sounds as if he were a Jehovah-worshipper, but it is to be feared that his religion was of a very accommodating kind. It used to be said that, as a Persian, he was a monotheist, and would consequently be in sympathy with the Jews; but the same cylinder already quoted shatters that idea, and shows him to have been a polytheist, ready to worship the gods of Babylon. He there ascribes his conquest to 'Merodach, the great lord,' and distinctly calls himself that god's 'worshipper.' Like other polytheists, he had room in his pantheon for the gods of other nations, and admitted into it the deities of the conquered peoples.

The use of the name 'Jehovah' would, no doubt, be most simply accounted for by the supposition that Cyrus recognised the sole divinity of the God of Israel; but that solution conflicts with all that is known of him, and with his characterisation in Isaiah xlv. as 'not knowing' Jehovah. More probably, his confession of Jehovah as the God of heaven was consistent in his mind with a similar confession as to Bel-Merodach or the supreme god of any other of the conquered nations. There is, however no improbability in the supposition that the prophecies concerning him in Isaiah xlv. may have been brought to his knowledge, and be referred to in the proclamation as the 'charge' given to him to build Jehovah's Temple. But we must not exaggerate the depth or exclusiveness of his belief in the God of the Jews.

Cyrus's profession of faith, then, is an example of official and skin-deep religion, of which public and individual life afford plentiful instances in all ages and faiths. If we are to take their own word for it, most great conquerors have been very religious men, and have asked a blessing over many a bloody feast. All religions are equally true to cynical politicians, who are ready to join in worshipping 'Jehovah, Jove, or Lord,' as may suit their policy. Nor is it only in high places that such loosely worn professions are found. Perhaps there is no region of life in which insincerity, which is often quite unconscious, is so rife as in regard to religious belief. But unless my religion is everything, it is nothing. 'All in all, or not at all,' is the requirement of the great Lover of souls. What a winnowing of chaff from wheat there would be, if that test could visibly separate the mass which is gathered on His threshing-floor, the Church!

Cyrus's belief in Jehovah illustrates the attitude which was natural to a polytheist, and is so difficult for us to enter into. A vague belief in One Supreme, above all other gods, and variously named by different nations, is buried beneath mountains of myths about lesser gods, but sometimes comes to light in many pagan minds. This blind creed, if creed it can be called, is joined with the recognition of deities belonging to each nation, whose worship is to be co-extensive with the race of which they are patrons, and who may be absorbed into the pantheon of a conqueror, just as a vanquished king may be allowed an honourable captivity at the victor's capital. Thus Cyrus could in a sense worship Jehovah, the God of Israel, without thereby being rebellious to Merodach.

There are people, even among so-called Christians, who try the same immoral and impossible division of what must in its very nature be wholly given to One Supreme. To 'serve God and mammon' is demonstrably an absurd attempt. The love and trust and obedience which are worthy of Him must be wholehearted, whole-souled, whole-willed. It is as impossible to love God with part of one's self as it is for a husband to love his wife with half his heart, and another woman with the rest. To divide love is to slay it. Cyrus had some kind of belief in Jehovah; but his own words, so wonderfully recovered in the inscription already referred to, proved that he had not listened to the command, 'Him only shalt thou serve.' That command grips us as closely as it did the Jews, and is as truly broken by thousands calling themselves Christians as by any idolaters.

The substance of the proclamation is a permission to return to any one who wished to do so, a sanction of the rebuilding of the Temple, and an order to the native inhabitants to render help in money, goods, and beasts. A further contribution towards the building was suggested as 'a free-will offering.' The return, then, was not to be at the expense of the king, nor was any tax laid on for it; but neighbourly goodwill, born of seventy years of association, was invoked, and, as we find, not in vain. God had given the people favour in the eyes of those who had carried them captive.

II. The long years of residence in Babylonia had weakened the homesickness which the first generation of captives had, no doubt, painfully experienced, and but a small part of them cared to avail themselves of the opportunity of return. One reason is frankly given by Josephus: 'Many remained in Babylon, not wishing to leave their possessions behind them.' 'The heads of the fathers' houses [who may have exercised some sort of government among the captives], the priests and Levites,' made the bulk of the emigrants; but in each class it was only those 'whose spirit God had stirred up' (as he had done Cyrus') that were devout or patriotic enough to face the wrench of removal and the difficulties of repeopling a wasted land. There was nothing to tempt any others, and the brave little band had need of all their fortitude. But no heart in which the flame of devotion burned, or in which were felt the drawings of that passionate love of the city and soil where God dwelt (which in the best days of the nation was inseparable from devotion), could remain behind. The departing contingent, then, were the best part of the whole; and the lingerers were held back by love of ease, faint-heartedness, love of wealth, and the like ignoble motives.

How many of us have had great opportunities offered for service, which we have let slip in like manner! To have doors opened which we are too lazy, too cowardly, too much afraid of self-denial, to enter, is the tragedy and the crime of many a life. It is easier to live among the low levels of the plain of Babylon, than to take to the dangers and privations of the weary tramp across the desert. The ruins of Jerusalem are a much less comfortable abode than the well-furnished houses which have to be left. Prudence says, 'Be content where you are, and let other people take the trouble of such mad schemes as rebuilding the Temple.' A thousand excuses sing in our ears, and we let the moment in which alone some noble resolve is possible slide past us, and the rest of life is empty of another such. Neglected opportunities, unobeyed calls to high deeds, we all have in our lives. The saddest of all words is, 'It might have been.' How much wiser, happier, nobler, were the daring souls that rose to the occasion, and flung ease and wealth and companionship behind them, because they heard the divine command couched in the royal permission, and humbly answered, 'Here am I; send me'!

III. The third point in the passage is singular—the inventory of the Temple vessels returned by Cyrus. As to its particulars, we need only note that Sheshbazzar is the same as Zerubbabel; that the exact translation of some of the names of the vessels is doubtful; and that the numbers given under each head do not correspond with the sum total, the discrepancy indicating error somewhere in the numbers.

But is not this dry enumeration a strange item to come in the forefront of the narrative of such an event? We might have expected some kind of production of the enthusiasm of the returning exiles, some account of how they were sent on their journey, something which we should have felt worthier of the occasion than a list of bowls and nine-and-twenty knives. But it is of a piece with the whole of the first part of this Book of Ezra, which is mostly taken up with a similar catalogue of the members of the expedition. The list here indicates the pride and joy with which the long hidden and often desecrated vessels were received. We can see the priests and Levites gazing at them as they were brought forth, their hearts, and perhaps their eyes, filling with sacred memories. The Lord had 'turned again the captivity of Zion,' and these sacred vessels lay there, glittering before them, to assure them that they were not as 'them that dream.' Small things become great when they are the witnesses of a great thing.

We must remember, too, how strong a hold the externals of worship had on the devout Jew. His faith was much more tied to form than ours ought to be, and the restoration of the sacrificial implements as a pledge of the re-establishment of the Temple worship would seem the beginning of a new epoch of closer relation to Jehovah. It is almost within the lifetime of living men that all Scotland was thrilled with emotion by the discovery, in a neglected chamber, of a chest in which lay, forgotten, the crown and sceptre of the Stuarts. A like wave of feeling passed over the exiles as they had given back to their custody these Temple vessels. Sacreder ones are given into our hands, to carry across a more dangerous desert. Let us hear the charge, 'Be ye clean, that bear the vessels of the Lord,' and see that we carry them, untarnished and unlost, to 'the house of the Lord which is in Jerusalem.'

ALTAR AND TEMPLE

'And when the seventh month was come, and the children of Israel were in the cities, the people gathered themselves together as one man to Jerusalem. 2. Then stood up Jeshua the son of Jozadak, and his brethren the priests, and Zerubbabel the son of Shealtiel, and his brethren, and builded the altar of the God of Israel, to offer burnt offerings thereon, as it is written in the law of Moses the man of God. 3. And they set the altar upon his bases; for fear was upon them because of the people of those countries: and they offered burnt offerings thereon unto the Lord, even burnt offerings morning and evening. 4. They kept also the feast of tabernacles, as it is written, and offered the daily burnt offerings by number, according to the custom, as the duty of every day required; 5. And afterward offered the continual burnt offering, both of the new moons, and of all the set feasts of the Lord that were consecrated, and of every one that willingly offered a freewill offering unto the Lord. 6. From the first day of the seventh month began they to offer burnt offerings unto the Lord. But the foundation of the Temple of the Lord was not yet laid. 7. They gave money also unto the masons, and to the carpenters; and meat, and drink, and oil, unto them of Zidon, and to them of Tyre, to bring cedar trees from Lebanon to the sea of Joppa, according to the grant that they had of Cyrus king of Persia. 8. Now in the second year of their coming unto the house of God at Jerusalem, in the second month, began Zerubbabel the son of Shealtiel, and Jeshua the son of Jozadak, and the remnant of their brethren the priests and the Levites, and all they that were come out of the captivity unto Jerusalem; and appointed the Levites, from twenty years old and upward, to set forward the work of the house of the Lord. 9. Then stood Jeshua with his sons and his brethren, Kadmiel and his sons, the sons of Judah, together, to set forward the workmen in the house of God: the sons of Henadad, with their sons and their brethren the Levites. 10. And when the builders laid the foundation of the Temple of the Lord, they set the priests in their apparel with trumpets, and the Levites, the sons of Asaph, with cymbals, to praise the Lord, after the ordinance of David king of Israel. 11. And they sang together by course in praising and giving thanks unto the Lord; because He is good, for His mercy endureth for ever toward Israel. And all the people shouted with a great shout, when they praised the Lord, because the foundation of the house of the Lord was laid. 12. But many of the priests and Levites and chief of the fathers, who were ancient men, that had seen the first house, when the foundation of this house was laid before their eyes, wept with a loud voice; and many shouted aloud for joy: 13. So that the people could not discern the noise of the shout of joy from the noise of the weeping of the people: for the people shouted with a loud shout, and the noise was heard afar off.'—EZRA iii. 1-13.

WHAT an opportunity of 'picturesque' writing the author of this book has missed by his silence about the incidents of the march across the dreary levels from Babylon to the verge of Syria! But the very silence is eloquent. It reveals the purpose of the book, which is to tell of the re-establishment of the Temple and its worship. No doubt the tone of the whole is somewhat prosaic, and indicative of an age in which the externals of worship bulked largely; but still the central point of the narrative was really the centre-point of the events. The austere simplicity of biblical history shows the real points of importance better than more artistic elaboration would do.

This passage has two main incidents—the renewal of the sacrifices, and the beginning of rebuilding the Temple.

The date given in verse 1 is significant. The first day of the seventh month was the commencement of the great festival of tabernacles, the most joyous feast of the year, crowded with reminiscences from the remote antiquity of the Exodus, and from the dedication of Solomon's Temple. How long had passed since Cyrus' decree had been issued we do not know, nor whether his 'first year' was reckoned by the same chronology as the Jewish year, of which we here arrive at the seventh month. But the journey across the desert must have taken some months, and the previous preparations could not have been suddenly got through, so that there can have been but a short time between the arrival in Judea and the gathering together 'as one man to Jerusalem.'

There was barely interval enough for the returning exiles to take possession of their ancestral fields before they were called to leave them unguarded and hasten to the desolate city. Surely their glad and unanimous obedience to the summons, or, as it may even have been, their spontaneous assemblage unsummoned, is no small token of their ardour of devotion, even if they were somewhat slavishly tied to externals. It would take a good deal to draw a band of new settlers in our days to leave their lots and set to putting up a church before they had built themselves houses.

The leaders of the band of returned exiles demand a brief notice. They are Jeshua, or Joshua, and Zerubbabel. In verse 2 the ecclesiastical dignitary comes first, but in verse 8 the civil. Similarly in Ezra ii. 2, Zerubbabel precedes Jeshua. In Haggai, the priest is pre-eminent; in Zechariah the prince. The truth seems to be that each was supreme in his own department, and that they understood each other cordially, or, Zechariah says, 'the counsel of peace' was 'between them both.' It is sometimes bad for the people when priests and rulers lay their heads together; but it is even worse when they pull different ways, and subjects are torn in two by conflicting obligations.

Jeshua was the grandson of Seraiah, the unfortunate high-priest whose eyes Nebuchadnezzar put out after the fall of Jerusalem. His son Jozadak succeeded to the dignity, though there could be no sacrifices in Babylon, and after him his son Jeshua. He cannot have been a young man at the date of the return; but age had not dimmed his enthusiasm, and the high-priest was where he ought to have been, in the forefront of the returning exiles. His name recalls the other Joshua, likewise a leader from captivity and the desert; and, if we appreciate the significance attached to names in Scripture, we shall scarcely suppose it accidental that these two, who had similar work to do, bore the same name as the solitary third, of whom they were pale shadows, the greater Joshua, who brings His people from bondage into His own land of peace, and builds the Temple.

Zerubbabel ('Sown in Babylon') belonged to a collateral branch of the royal family. The direct Davidic line through Solomon died with the wretched Zedekiah and Jeconiah, but the descendants of another son of David's, Nathan, still survived. Their representative was one Salathiel, who, on the failure of the direct line, was regarded as the 'son of Jeconiah' (1 Chron. iii. 17). He seems to have had no son, and Zerubbabel, who was really his nephew (1 Chron. iii. 19), was legally adopted as his son. In this makeshift fashion, some shadow of the ancient royalty still presided over the restored people. We see Zerubbabel better in Haggai and Zechariah than in Ezra, and can discern the outline of a strong, bold, prompt nature. He had a hard task, and he did it like a man. Patient, yet vigorous, glowing with enthusiasm, yet clear-eyed, self-forgetful, and brave, he has had scant justice done him, and ought to be a very much more familiar and honoured figure than he is. 'Who art thou, O great mountain? Before Zerubbabel thou shalt become a plain.' Great mountains only become plains before men of strong wills and fixed faith.

There is something very pathetic in the picture of the assembled people groping amid the ruins on the Temple hill, to find 'the bases,' the half-obliterated outlines, of the foundations of the old altar of burnt offerings. What memories of Araunah's threshing-floor, and of the hovering angel of destruction, and of the glories of Solomon's dedication, and of the long centuries during which the column of smoke had gone up continually from that spot, and of the tragical day when the fire was quenched, and of the fifty years of extinction, must have filled their hearts! What a conflict of gladness and sorrow must have troubled their spirits as the flame again shot upwards from the hearth of God, cold for so long!

But the reason for their so quickly rearing the altar is noteworthy. It was because 'fear was upon them because of the people of the countries.' The state of the Holy Land at the return must be clearly comprehended. Samaria and the central district were in the hands of bitter enemies. Across Jordan in the east, down on the Philistine plain in the west, and in the south where Edom bore sway, eager enemies sulkily watched the small beginnings of a movement which they were interested in thwarting. There was only the territory of Judah and Benjamin left free for the exiles, and they had reason for their fears; for their neighbours knew that if restitution was to be the order of the day, they would have to disgorge a good deal. What was the defence against such foes which these frightened men thought most impregnable? That altar!

No doubt, much superstition mingled with their religion. Haggai leaves us under no illusions as to their moral and spiritual condition. They were no patterns of devoutness or of morality. But still, what they did carries an eternal truth; and they were reverting to the original terms of Israel's tenure of their land when they acted on the conviction that their worship of Jehovah according to His commandment was their surest way of finding shelter from all their enemies. There are differences plain enough between their condition and ours; but it is as true for us as ever it was for them, that our safety is in God, and that, if we want to find shelter from impending dangers, we shall be wiser to betake ourselves to the altar and sit suppliant there than to make defences for ourselves. The ruined Jerusalem was better guarded by that altar than if its fallen walls had been rebuilt.

The whole ritual was restored, as the narrative tells with obvious satisfaction in the enumeration. To us this punctilious attention to the minutiæ of sacrificial worship sounds trivial. But we equally err if we try to bring such externalities into the worship of the Christian Church, and if we are blind to their worth at an earlier stage.

There cannot be a temple without an altar, but there may be an altar without a temple. God meets men at the place of sacrifice, even though there be no house for His name. The order of events here teaches us what is essential for communion with God. It is the altar. Sacrifice laid there is accepted, whether it stand on a bare hill-top, or have round it the courts of the Lord's house.

The second part of the passage narrates the laying of the foundations of the Temple. There had been contracts entered into with masons and carpenters, and arrangements made with the Phœnicians for timber, as soon as the exiles had returned; but of course some time elapsed before the stone and timber were sufficient to make a beginning with. Note in verse 7 the reference to Cyrus' grant as enabling the people to get these stores together. Whether the whole preparations, or only the transport of cedar wood, is intended to be traced to the influence of that decree, there seems to be a tacit contrast, in the writer's mind, with the glorious days when no heathen king had to be consulted, and Hiram and Solomon worked together like brothers. Now, so fallen are we, that Tyre and Sidon will not look at us unless we bring Cyrus' rescript in our hands!

If the 'years' in verses 1 and 8 are calculated from the same beginning, some seven months were spent in preparation, and then the foundation was laid. Two things are noted—the humble attempt at making some kind of a display on the occasion, and the conflict of feeling in the onlookers. They had managed to get some copies of the prescribed vestments; and the narrator emphasises the fact that the priests were 'in their apparel,' and that the Levites had cymbals, so that some approach to the pomp of Solomon's dedication was possible. They did their best to adhere to the ancient prescriptions, and it was no mere narrow love of ritual that influenced them. However we may breathe a freer air of worship, we cannot but sympathise with that earnest attempt to do everything 'according to the order of David king of Israel.' Not only punctiliousness as to ritual, but the magnetism of glorious memories, prescribed the reproduction of that past. Rites long proscribed become very sacred, and the downtrodden successors of mighty men will cling with firm grasp to what the greater fathers did.

The ancient strain which still rings from Christian lips, and bids fair to be as eternal as the mercies which it hymns, rose with strange pathos from the lips of the crowd on the desolate Temple mountain, ringed about by the waste solitudes of the city: 'For He is good, for His mercy endureth for ever toward Israel.' It needed some faith to sing that song then, even with the glow of return upon them. What of all the weary years? What of the empty homesteads, and the surrounding enemies, and the brethren still in Babylon? No doubt some at least of the rejoicing multitude had learned what the captivity was meant to teach, and had come to bless God, both for the long years of exile, which had burned away much dross, and for the incomplete work of restoration, surrounded though they were with foes, and little as was their strength to fight. The trustful heart finds occasion for unmingled praise in the most mingled cup of joy and sorrow.

There can have been very few in that crowd who had seen the former Temple, and their memories of its splendour must have been very dim. But partly remembrance and partly hearsay made the contrast of the past glories and the present poverty painful. Hence that pathetic and profoundly significant incident of the blended shouts of the young and tears of the old. One can fancy that each sound jarred on the ears of those who uttered the other. But each was wholly natural to the years of the two classes. Sad memories gather, like evening mists, round aged lives, and the temptation of the old is unduly to exalt the past, and unduly to depreciate the present. Welcoming shouts for the new befit young lips, and they care little about the ruins that have to be carted off the ground for the foundations of the temple which they are to have a hand in building. However imperfect, it is better to them than the old house where the fathers worshipped.

But each class should try to understand the other's feelings. The friends of the old should not give a churlish welcome to the new, nor those of the new forget the old. It is hard to blend the two, either in individual life or in a wider sphere of thought or act. The seniors think the juniors revolutionary and irreverent; the juniors think the seniors fossils. It is possible to unite the shout of joy and the weeping. Unless a spirit of reverent regard for the past presides over the progressive movements of this or any day, they will not lay a solid foundation for the temple of the future. We want the old and the young to work side by side, if the work is to last and the sanctuary is to be ample enough to embrace all shades of character and tendencies of thought. If either the grey beards of Solomon's court or the hot heads of Rehoboam's get the reins in their hands, they will upset the chariot. That mingled sound of weeping and joy from the Temple hill tells a more excellent way.

BUILDING IN TROUBLOUS TIMES

'Now when the adversaries of Judah and Benjamin heard that the children of the captivity builded the temple unto the Lord God of Israel; 2. Then they came to Zerubbabel, and to the chief of the fathers, and said unto them, Let us build with you: for we seek your God, as ye do; and we do sacrifice unto Him since the days of Esar-haddon king of Assur, which brought us up hither. 3. But Zerubbabel, and Jeshua, and the rest of the chief of the fathers of Israel, said unto them, Ye have nothing to do with us to build an house unto our God; but we ourselves together will build unto the Lord God of Israel, as king Cyrus the king of Persia hath commanded us. 4. Then the people of the land weakened the hands of the people of Judah, and troubled them in building, 5. And hired counsellors against them, to frustrate their purpose, all the days of Cyrus king of Persia, even until the reign of Darius king of Persia.'—EZRA iv. 1-5.

OPPOSITION began as soon as the foundations were laid, as is usually the case with all great attempts to build God's house. It came from the Samaritans, the mingled people who were partly descendants of the ancient remnant of the northern kingdom, left behind after the removal by deportation of the bulk of its population, and partly the descendants of successive layers of immigrants, planted in the empty territory by successive Assyrian and Babylonian kings. Esar-haddon was the first who had sent colonists, about one hundred and thirty years before the return. The writer calls the Samaritans 'the adversaries,' though they began by offers of friendship and alliance. The name implies that these offers were perfidious, and a move in the struggle.

One can easily understand that the Samaritans looked with suspicion on the new arrivals, the ancient possessors of the land, coming under the auspices of the new dynasty, and likely to interfere with their position if not reduced to inferiority or neutralised somehow. The proposal to unite in building the Temple was a political move; for, in old-world ideas, co-operation in Temple-building was incorporation in national unity. The calculation, no doubt, was that if the returning exiles could be united with the much more numerous Samaritans, they would soon be absorbed in them. The only chance for the smaller body was to keep itself apart, and to run the risk of its isolation.

The insincere request was based on an untruth, for the Samaritans did not worship Jehovah as the Jews, but along with their own gods (2 Kings xvii. 25-41). To divide His dominion with others was to dethrone Him altogether. It therefore became an act of faithfulness to Jehovah to reject the entangling alliance. To have accepted it would have been tantamount to frustrating the very purpose of the return, and consenting to be muzzled about the sin of idolatry. But the chief lesson which exile had burned in on the Jewish mind was a loathing of idolatry, which is in remarkable contrast to the inclination to it that had marked their previous history. So one answer only was possible, and it was given with unwelcome plainness of speech, which might have been more courteous, and not less firm. It flatly denied any common ground; it claimed exclusive relation to 'our God,' which meant, 'not yours'; it underscored the claim by reiterating that Jehovah was the 'God of Israel'; it put forward the decree of Cyrus, as leaving no option but to confine the builders to the people whom it had empowered to build.

Now, it is easy to represent this as a piece of impolitic narrowness, and to say that its surly bigotry was rightly punished by the evils that it brought down on the returning exiles. The temper of much flaccid Christianity at present delights to expand in a lazy and foolish 'liberality,' which will welcome anybody to come and take a hand at the building, and accepts any profession of unity in worship. But there is no surer way of taking the earnestness out of Christian work and workers than drafting into it a mass of non-Christians, whatever their motives may be. Cold water poured into a boiling pot will soon stop its bubbling, and bring down its temperature. The churches are clogged and impeded, and their whole tone lowered and chilled, by a mass of worldly men and women. Nothing is gained, and much is in danger of being lost, by obliterating the lines between the church and the world. The Jew who thought little of the difference between the Samaritan worship with its polytheism, and his own monotheism, was in peril of dropping to the Samaritan level. The Samaritan who was accepted as a true worshipper of Jehovah, though he had a bevy of other gods in addition, would have been confirmed in his belief that the differences were unimportant. So both would have been harmed by what called itself 'liberality,' and was in reality indifference.

No doubt, Zerubbabel had counted the cost of faithfulness, and he soon had to pay it. The would-be friends threw off the mask, and, as they could not hinder by pretending to help, took a plainer way to stop progress. All the weapons that Eastern subtlety and intrigue could use were persistently employed to 'weaken the hands' of the builders, and the most potent of all methods, bribery to Persian officials, was freely used. The opponents triumphed, and the little community began to taste the bitterness of high hopes disappointed and noble enterprises frustrated. How differently things had turned out from the expectations with which the company had set forth from Babylon! The rough awakening to realities disillusions us all when we come to turn dreams into facts. The beginning of laying the Temple foundations is put in 536 B.C.; the first year of Darius was 522. How soon after the commencement of the work the Samaritan tricks succeeded we do not know, but it must have been some time before the death of Cyrus in 529. For weary years then the sanguine band had to wait idly, and no doubt enthusiasm died out: they had enough to do in keeping themselves alive, and in holding their own amidst enemies. They needed, as we all do, patience, and a willingness to wait for God's own time to fulfil His own promise.

THE NEW TEMPLE AND ITS WORSHIP

'And the elders of the Jews builded, and they prospered through the prophesying of Haggai the prophet and Zechariah the son of Iddo: and they builded, and finished it, according to the commandment of the God of Israel, and according to the commandment of Cyrus, and Darius, and Artaxerxes king of Persia. 15. And this house was finished on the third day of the month Adar, which was in the sixth year of the reign of Darius the king. 16. And the children of Israel, the priests, and the Levites, and the rest of the children of the captivity, kept the dedication of this house of God with joy, 17. And offered at the dedication of this house of God an hundred bullocks, two hundred rams, four hundred lambs; and for a sin offering for all Israel, twelve he-goats, according to the number of the tribes of Israel. 18. And they set the priests in their divisions, and the Levites in their courses, for the service of God, which is at Jerusalem; as it is written in the book of Moses. 19. And the children of the captivity kept the passover upon the fourteenth day of the first month. 20. For the priests and the Levites were purified together, all of them were pure, and killed the passover for all the children of the captivity, and for their brethren the priests, and for themselves. 21. And the children of Israel, which were come again out of captivity, and all such as had separated themselves unto them from the filthiness of the heathen of the land, to seek the Lord God of Israel, did eat, 22. And kept the feast of unleavened bread seven days with joy: for the Lord had made them joyful, and turned the heart of the king of Assyria unto them, to strengthen their hands in the work of the house of God, the God of Israel.'
—EZRA. vi. 14-22.

THERE are three events recorded in this passage,—the completion of the Temple, its dedication, and the keeping of the passover some weeks thereafter. Four years intervene between the resumption of building and its successful finish, much of which time had been occupied by the interference of the Persian governor, which compelled a reference to Darius, and resulted in his confirmation of Cyrus' charter. The king's stringent orders silenced opposition, and seem to have been loyally, however unwillingly, obeyed. About twenty-three years passed between the return of the exiles and the completion of the Temple.

I. The prosperous close of the long task (vers. 14, 15). The narrative enumerates three points in reference to the completion of the Temple which are very significant, and, taken together, set forth the stimulus and law and helps of work for God.

It is expressive of deep truth that first in order is named, as the cause of success, 'the prophesying of Haggai and Zechariah.' 'Practical men,' no doubt, then as always, set little store by the two prophets' fiery words, and thought that a couple of masons would have done more for the building than they did. The contempt for 'ideas' is the mark of shallow and vulgar minds. Nothing is more practical than principles and motives which underlie and inform work, and these two prophets did more for building the Temple by their words than an army of labourers with their hands. 'There are diversities of operations,' and it is not given to every man to handle a trowel; but no good work will be prosperously accomplished unless there be engaged in it prophets who rouse and rebuke and hearten, and toilers who by their words are encouraged and saved from forgetting the sacred motives and great ends of their work in the monotony and multiplicity of details.

Still more important is the next point mentioned. The work was done 'according to the commandment of the God of Israel.' There is peculiar beauty and pathos in that name, which is common in Ezra. It speaks of the sense of unity in the nation, though but a fragment of it had come back. There was still an Israel, after all the dreary years, and in spite of present separation. God was still its God, though He had hidden His face for so long. An inextinguishable faith, wistful but assured, in His unalterable promise, throbs in that name, so little warranted by a superficial view of circumstances, but so amply vindicated by a deeper insight. His 'commandment' is at once the warrant and the standard for the work of building. In His service we are to be sure that He bids, and then to carry out His will whoever opposes.

We are to make certain that our building is 'according to the pattern showed in the mount,' and, if so, to stick to it in every point. There is no room for more than one architect in rearing the temple. The working drawings must come from Him. We are only His workmen. And though we may know no more of the general plan of the structure than the day-labourer who carries a hod does, we must be sure that we have His orders for our little bit of work, and then we may be at rest even while we toil. They who build according to His commandment build for eternity, and their work shall stand the trial by fire. That motive turns what without it were but 'wood, hay, stubble,' into 'gold and silver and precious stones.'

The last point is that the work was done according to the commandment of the heathen kings. We need not discuss the chronological difficulty arising from the mention of Artaxerxes here. The only king of that name who can be meant reigned fifty years after the events here narrated. The mention of him here has been explained by 'the consideration that he contributed to the maintenance, though not to the building, of the Temple.' Whatever is the solution, the intention of the mention of the names of the friendly monarchs is plain. 'The king's heart is in the hand of the Lord as the watercourses; He turneth it whithersoever He will.' The wonderful providence, surpassing all hopes, which gave the people 'favour in the eyes of them that carried them captive,' animates the writer's thankfulness, while he recounts that miracle that the commandment of God was re-echoed by such lips. The repetition of the word in both clauses underscores, as it were, the remarkable concurrence.

II. The dedication of the Temple (vers. 16-18). How long the dedication was after the completion is not specified. The month Adar was the last of the Jewish year, and corresponded nearly with our March. Probably the ceremonial of dedication followed immediately on the completion of the building. Probably few, if any, of the aged men, who had wept at the founding, survived to see the completion of the Temple. A new generation had no such sad contrasts of present lowliness and former glory to shade their gladness. So many dangers surmounted, so many long years of toil interrupted and hope deferred, gave keener edge to joy in the fair result of them all.

We may cherish the expectation that our long tasks, and often disappointments, will have like ending if they have been met and done in like spirit, having been stimulated by prophets and commanded by God. It is not wholesome nor grateful to depreciate present blessings by contrasting them with vanished good. Let us take what God gives to-day, and not embitter it by remembering yesterday with vain regret. There is a remembrance of the former more splendid Temple in the name of the new one, which is thrice repeated in the passage,—'this house.' But that phrase expresses gratitude quite as much as, or more than, regret. The former house is gone, but there is still 'this house,' and it is as truly God's as the other was. Let us grasp the blessings we have, and be sure that in them is continued the substance of those we have lost.

The offerings were poor, if compared with Solomon's 'two and twenty thousand oxen, and an hundred and twenty thousand sheep' (1 Kings viii. 63), and no doubt the despisers of the 'day of small things,' whom Zechariah had rebuked, would be at their depreciating work again. But 'if there be first a willing mind, it is accepted according to that a man hath, and not according to that he hath not.' The thankfulness of the offerers, not the number of their bullocks and rams, made the sacrifice well pleasing. But it would not have been so if the exiles' resources had been equal to the great King's. How many cattle had they in their stalls at home, not how many they brought to the Temple, was the important question. The man who says, 'Oh! God accepts small offerings,' and gives a mite while he keeps talents, might as well keep his mite too; for certainly God will not have it.

A significant part of the offerings was the 'twelve he-goats, according to the number of the tribes of Israel.' These spoke of the same confidence as we have already noticed as being expressed by the designation of 'the God of Israel.' Possibly scattered members of all the tribes had come back, and so there was a kind of skeleton framework of the nation present at the dedication; but, whether that be so or not, that handful of people was not Israel. Thousands of their brethren still lingered in exile, and the hope of their return must have been faint. Yet God's promise remained, and Israel was immortal. The tribes were still twelve, and the sacrifices were still theirs. A thrill of emotion must have touched many hearts as the twelve goats were led up to the altar. So an Englishman feels as he looks at the crosses on the Union Jack.

But there was more than patriotism in that sacrifice. It witnessed to unshaken faith. And there was still more expressed in it than the offerers dreamed; for it prophesied of that transformation of the national into the spiritual Israel, in virtue of which the promises remain true, and are inherited by the Church of Christ in all lands.

The re-establishment of the Temple worship with the appointment of priests and Levites, according to the ancient ordinance, naturally followed on the dedication.

III. The celebration of the Passover (vers. 19-22). It took place on the fourteenth day of the first month, and probably, therefore, very soon after the dedication. They 'kept the feast, . . . for the priests and Levites were purified together.' The zeal of the sacerdotal class in attending to the prescriptions for ceremonial purity made it possible that the feast should be observed. How much of real devotion, and how much of mere eagerness to secure their official position, mingled with this zeal, cannot be determined. Probably there was a touch of both. Scrupulous observance of ritual is easy religion, especially if one's position is improved by it. But the connection pointed out by the writer is capable of wide applications. The true purity and earnestness of preachers and teachers of all degrees has much to do with their hearers' and scholars' participation in the blessings of the Gospel. If priests are not pure, they cannot kill the passover. Earnest teachers make earnest scholars. Foul hands cannot dispense the bread of life.

There is a slight deviation from the law in the ritual as here stated, since it was prescribed that each householder should kill the passover lamb for his house. But from the time of Hezekiah the Levites seem to have done it for the congregation (2 Chron. xxx. 17), and afterwards for the priests also (2 Chron. xxxv. 11, 14).

Verse 21 tells that not only the returned exiles, but also 'all such as had separated themselves unto them from the filthiness of the heathen of the land, to seek the Lord God of Israel,' ate the passover. It may be questioned whether these latter were Israelites, the descendants of the residue who had not been deported, but who had fallen into idolatry during the exile, or heathens of the mixed populations who had been settled in the vacant country. The emphasis put on their turning to Israel and Israel's God seems to favour the latter supposition. But in any case, the fact presents us with an illustration of the proper effect of the presence anywhere of a company of God's true worshippers. If we purify ourselves, and keep the feast of the true passover with joy as well as purity, we shall not want for outsiders who will separate themselves from the more subtle and not less dangerous idolatries of modern life, to seek the Lord God of Israel. If His Israel is what it ought to be, it will attract. A bit of scrap-iron in contact with a magnet is a magnet. They who live in touch with Him who said, 'I will draw all men unto Me' will share His attractive power in the measure of their union with Him.

The week after the passover feast was, according to the ritual, observed as the feast of unleavened bread. The narrative touches lightly on the ceremonial, and dwells in conclusion on the joy of the worshippers and its cause. They do well to be glad whom God makes glad. All other joy bears in it the seeds of death. It is, in one aspect, the end of God's dealings, that we should be glad in Him. Wise men will not regard that as a less noble end than making us pure; in fact, the two are united. The 'blessed God' is glad in our gladness when it is His gladness.

Notice the exulting wonder with which God's miracle of mercy is reported in its source and its glorious result. The heart of the king was turned to them, and no power but God's could have done that. The issue of that divine intervention was the completed Temple, in which once more the God of that Israel which He had so marvellously restored dwelt in the midst of His people.

GOD THE JOY-BRINGER

'They kept the feast ... seven days with joy; for the Lord had made them joyful.'—EZRA vi. 22.

TWENTY years of hard work and many disappointments and dangers had at last, for the Israelites returning from the captivity, been crowned by the completion of the Temple. It was a poor affair as compared with the magnificent house that had stood upon Zion; and so some of them 'despised the day of small things.' They were ringed about by enemies;

they were feeble in themselves; there was a great deal to darken their prospects and to sadden their hearts; and yet, when memories of the ancient days came back, and once more they saw the sacrificial smoke rising from the long cold and ruined altar, they rejoiced in God, and they kept the passover amid the ruins, as my text tells us, for the 'seven days' of the statutory period 'with joy,' because, in spite of all, 'the Lord had made them joyful.'

I think if we take this simple saying we get two or three thoughts, not altogether irrelevant to universal experience, about the true and the counterfeit gladnesses possible to us all.

I. Look at that great and wonderful thought—God the joy-maker.

We do not often realise how glad God is when we are glad, and how worthy an object of much that He does is simply the prosperity and the blessedness of human hearts. The poorest creature that lives has a right to ask from God the satisfaction of its instincts, and every man has a claim on God—because he is God's creature—to make him glad. God honours all cheques legitimately drawn on Him, and answers all claims, and regards Himself as occupied in a manner entirely congruous with His magnificence and His infinitude, when He stoops to put some kind of vibrating gladness into the wings of a gnat that dances for an hour in the sunshine, and into the heart of a man that lives his time for only a very little longer.

God is the Joy-maker. There are far more magnificent and sublime thoughts about Him than that; but I do not know that there is any that ought to come nearer to our hearts, and to silence more of our grumblings and of our distrust, than the belief that the gladness of His children is an end contemplated by Him in all that He does. Whether we think it of small importance or no, He does not think it so, that all mankind should rejoice in Himself. And this is a marvellous revelation to break out of the very heart of that comparatively hard system of ancient Judaism. 'The Lord hath made them joyful.'

Turning away from the immediate connection of these words, let me remind you of the great outlines of the divine provision for gladdening men's hearts. I was going to say that God had only one way of making us glad; and perhaps that is in the deepest sense true. That way is by putting Himself into us. He gives us Himself to make us glad; for nothing else will do it—or, at least, though there may be many subordinate sources of joy, if there be in the innermost shrine of our spirits an empty place, where the Shekinah ought to shine, no other joys will suffice to settle and to rejoice the soul. The secret of all true human well-being is close communion with God; and when He looks at the poorest of us, desiring to make us blessed, He can but say, 'I will give Myself to that poor man; to that ignorant creature; to that wayward and prodigal child; to that harlot in her corruption; to that worldling in his narrow godlessness; I will give Myself, if they will have Me.' And thus, and only thus, does He make us truly, perfectly, and for ever glad.

Besides that, or rather as a sequel and consequence of that, there come such other God-given blessings as these to which my text refers. What were the outward reasons for the restored exiles' gladness? 'The Lord had made them joyful, and turned the heart of the king . . . unto them to strengthen their hands in the work of the house of God, the God of Israel.'

So, then, He pours into men's lives by His providences the secondary and lower gifts which men, according to changing circumstances, need; and He also satisfies the permanent physical necessities of all orders of beings to whom He has given life. He gives Himself for the spirit; He gives whatever is contributory to any kind of gladness; and if we are wise we shall trace all to Him. He is the Joy-giver; and that man has not yet understood either the sanctity of life or the full sweetness of its sweetest things unless he sees, written over every one of them, the name of God, their giver. Your common mercies are His love tokens, and they all come to us, just as the gifts of parents to their children do, with this on the fly-leaf, 'With a father's love.' Whatever comes to God's child with that inscription, surely it ought to kindle a thrill of gladness. That 'the king of Assyria's heart is turned'; shall we thank the king of Assyria? Yes and No! For it was God who 'turned' it. Oh! to carry the quiet confidence of that thought into all our daily life, and see His name written upon everything that contributes to make us blessed. God is the true Source and Maker of every joy.

And by the side of that we must put this other thought—there are sources of joy with which He has nothing to do. There are people who are joyful—and there are some of them listening now—not because God made them joyful, but because 'the world, the devil, and the flesh' have given them ghastly caricatures of the true gladness. And these rival sources of blessedness, the existence of which my text suggests, are the enemies of all that is good and noble in us and in our joys. God made these men joyful, and so their gladness was wholesome.

II. Note the consequent obligation and wisdom of taking our God-given joys.

'They kept the feast with joy, for the Lord had made them joyful.' Then it is our obligation to accept and use what it is His blessedness to give. Be sure you take Him. When He is waiting to pour all His love into your heart, and all His sweetness into your sensitive spirit, to calm your anxieties, to deepen your blessedness, to strengthen everything that is good in you, to be to you a stay in the midst of crumbling prosperity, and a Light in the midst of gathering darkness, be sure that you take the joy that waits your acceptance. Do not let it be said that, when the Lord Christ has come down from heaven, and lived upon earth, and gone back to heaven, and sent His Spirit to dwell in you, you lock the door against the entrance of the joy-bringing Messenger, and are sad and restless and discontented because you have shut out the God who desires to abide in your hearts.

'They kept the feast with joy, because the Lord had made them joyful.' Oh! how many Christian men and women there are, who in the midst of the abundant and wonderful provision for continual cheerfulness and buoyancy of spirit given to them in the promises of the Gospel, in the gifts of Christ, in the indwelling of the Divine Spirit, do yet go through life creeping and sad, burdened and anxious, perplexed and at their wits' end, just because they will not have the God who yearns to come to them, or at least will not have Him in anything like the fullness and the completeness in which He desires to bestow Himself. If God gives, surely we are bound to receive. It is an obligation upon Christian men and women, which they do not sufficiently realise, to be glad, and it is a commandment needing to be reiterated. 'Rejoice in the Lord always; and again I say, rejoice.' Would that Christian experience in this generation was more alive to the obligation and the blessedness of perpetual joy arising from perpetual communion with Him.

Further, another obligation is to recognise Him in all common mercies, because He is at the back of them all. Let them always proclaim Him to us. Oh! if we did not go through the world blinded to the real Power that underlies all its motions, we should feel that everything was vocal to us of the loving-kindness of our Father in heaven. Link Him, dear friend! with everything that makes your heart glad; with everything pleasant that comes to you. There is nothing good or sweet but it flows from Him. There is no common delight of flesh or sense, of sight or taste or smell, no little enjoyment that makes the moment pass more brightly, no drop of oil that eases the friction of the wheels of life, but it may be elevated into greatness and nobleness, and will then first be understood in its true significance, if it is connected with Him. God does not desire to be put away high up on a pedestal above our lives, as if He regulated the great things and the trifles regulated themselves; but He seeks to come, as air into the lungs, into every particle of the mass of life, and to fill it all with His own purifying presence.

Recognise Him in common joys. If, when we sit down to partake of them, we would say to ourselves, 'The Lord has made us joyful,' all our home delights, all our social pleasures, all our intellectual and all our sensuous ones—rest and food and drink and all other goods for the body—they would all be felt to be great, as they indeed are. Enjoyed in Him, the smallest is great; without Him, the greatest is small. 'The Lord made them joyful'; and what is large enough for Him to give ought not to be too small for us to receive with recognition of His hand.

Another piece of wholesome counsel in this matter is—Be sure that you use the joys which God does give. Many good people seem to think that it is somehow devout and becoming to pitch most of their songs in a minor key, and to be habitually talking about trials and disappointments, and 'a desert land,' and 'Brief life is here our portion,' and so on, and so on. There are two ways in which you can look at the world and at everything that befalls you. There is enough in everybody's life to make him sad if he sulkily selects these things to dwell upon. There is enough in everybody's life to make him continually glad if he wisely picks out these to think about. It depends altogether on the angle at which you look at your life what you see in it. For instance, you know how children do when they get a bit of a willow wand into their possession. They cut off rings of bark, and get the switch alternately white and black, white and black, and so on right away to the tip. Whether will you look at the white rings or the black ones? They are both there. But if you rightly look at the black you will find out that there is white below it, and it only needs a very little stripping off of a film to make it into white too. Or, to put it into simpler words, no Christian man has the right to regard anything that God's Providence brings to him as such unmingled evil that it ought to make him sad. We are bound to 'rejoice in the Lord always.'

I know how hard it is, but sure am I that it is possible for a man, if he keeps near Jesus Christ, to reproduce Paul's paradox of being 'sorrowful yet always rejoicing,' and even in the midst of darkness and losses and sorrows and blighted hopes and disappointed aims to rejoice in the Lord, and to 'keep the feast with gladness, because the Lord has made him joyful.' Nor do we discharge our duty, unless side by side with the sorrow which is legitimate, which is blessed, strengthening, purifying, calming, moderating, there is also 'joy unspeakable and full of glory.'

Again, be sure that you limit your delights to God-made joys. Too many of us have what parts of our nature recognise as satisfaction, and are glad to have, apart from Him. There is nothing sadder than the joys that come into a life, and do not come from God. Oh! let us see to it that we do not fill our cisterns with poisonous sewage when God is waiting to fill them with the pure 'river of the water of life.' Do not let us draw our blessedness from the world and its evils. Does my joy help me to come near to God? Does it interfere with my communion with Him? Does it aid me in the consecration of myself? Does my conscience go with it when my conscience is most awake? Do I recognise Him as the Giver of the thing that is so blessed? If we can say Yes! to these questions, we can venture to believe that our blessedness comes from God, and leads to God, however homely, however sensuous and material may be its immediate occasion. But if not, then the less we have to do with such sham gladness the better. 'Even in laughter the heart is sorrowful, and the end of that mirth is heaviness.' The alternative presented for the choice of each of us is whether we will have surface joy and a centre of dark discontent, or surface sorrow and a centre of calm blessedness. The film of stagnant water on a pond full of rottenness simulates the glories of the rainbow, in which pure sunshine falls upon the pure drops, but it is only painted corruption after all, a sign of rotting; and if a man puts his lips to it it will kill him. Such is the joy which is apart from God. It is the 'crackling of thorns under a pot'—the more fiercely they burn the sooner they are ashes. And, on the other hand, 'these things have I spoken unto you that My joy might remain in you, and that your joy might be full.'

It is not 'for seven days' that we 'keep the feast' if God has 'made us joyful,' but for all the rest of the days of time, and for the endless years of the calm gladnesses of the heavens.

HEROIC FAITH

'I was ashamed to require of the king a band of soldiers and horsemen to help us against the enemy in the way: because we had spoken unto the king, saying, The hand of our God is upon them all for good that seek Him.... 23. So we fasted and besought our God for this.... 31. The hand of our God was upon us, and He delivered us from the hand of the enemy, and of such as lay in wait by the way. 32. And we came to Jerusalem.'—EZRA viii. 22, 23, 31, 32.

THE memory of Ezra the scribe has scarcely had fairplay among Bible-reading people. True, neither his character nor the incidents of his life reach the height of interest or of grandeur belonging to the earlier men and their times. He is no hero, or prophet; only a scribe; and there is a certain narrowness as well as a prosaic turn about his mind, and altogether one feels that he is a smaller man than the Elijahs and Davids of the older days. But the homely garb of the scribe covered a very brave devout heart, and the story of his life deserves to be more familiar to us than it is.

This scrap from the account of his preparations for the march from Babylon to Jerusalem gives us a glimpse of a high-toned faith, and a noble strain of feeling. He and his company had a long weary journey of four months before them. They had had little experience of arms and warfare, or of hardships and desert marches, in their Babylonian homes. Their caravan was made unwieldy and feeble by the presence of a large proportion of women and children. They had much valuable property with them. The stony desert, which stretches unbroken from the Euphrates to the uplands on the east of Jordan, was infested then as now by wild bands of marauders, who might easily swoop down on the encumbered march of Ezra and his men, and make a clean sweep of all which they had. And he knew that he had but to ask and have an escort from the king that would ensure their safety till they saw Jerusalem. Artaxerxes' surname, 'the long-handed,' may have described a physical peculiarity, but it also expressed the reach of his power; his arm could reach these wandering plunderers, and if Ezra and his troop were visibly under his protection, they could march secure. So it was not a small exercise of trust in a higher Hand that is told us here so simply. It took some strength of principle to abstain from asking what it would have been so natural to ask, so easy to get, so comfortable to have. But, as he says, he remembered how confidently he has spoken of God's defence, and he feels that he must be true to his professed creed, even if it deprives him of the king's guards. He halts his followers for three days at the last station before the desert, and there, with fasting and prayer, they put themselves in God's hand; and then the band, with their wives and little ones, and their substance,—a heavily-loaded and feeble caravan,—fling themselves into the dangers of the long, dreary, robber-haunted march. Did not the scribe's robe cover as brave a heart as ever beat beneath a breastplate?

That symbolic phrase, 'the hand of our God,' as expressive of the divine protection, occurs with remarkable frequency in the books of Ezra and Nehemiah, and though not peculiar to them, is yet strikingly characteristic of them. It has a certain beauty and force of its own. The hand is of course the seat of active power. It is on or over a man like some great shield held aloft above him, below which there is safe hiding. So that great Hand bends itself over us, and we are secure beneath its hollow. As a child sometimes carries a tender-winged butterfly in the globe of its two hands that the bloom on the wings may not be ruffled by fluttering, so He carries our feeble, unarmoured souls enclosed in the covert of His Almighty hand. 'Who hath measured the waters in the hollow of His hand?' 'Who hath gathered the wind in His fists?' In that curved palm where all the seas lie as a very little thing, we are held; the grasp that keeps back the tempests from their wild rush, keeps us, too, from being smitten by their blast. As a father may lay his own large muscular hand on his child's tiny fingers to help him, or as 'Elisha put his hands on the king's hands,' that the contact might strengthen him to shoot the 'arrow of the Lord's deliverance,' so the hand of our God is upon us to impart power as well as protection; and our 'bow abides in strength,' when 'the arms of our hands are made strong by the hands of the mighty God of Jacob.' That was Ezra's faith, and that should be ours.

Note Ezra's sensitive shrinking from anything like inconsistency between his creed and his practice. It was easy to talk about God's protection when he was safe behind the walls of Babylon; but now the pinch had come. There was a real danger before him and his unwarlike followers. No doubt, too, there were plenty of people who would have been delighted to catch him tripping; and he felt that his cheeks would have tingled with shame if they had been able to say, 'Ah! that is what all his fine professions come to, is it? He wants a convoy, does he? We thought as much. It is always so with these people who talk in that style. They are just like the rest of us when the pinch comes.' So, with a high and keen sense of what was required by his avowed principles, he will have no guards for the road. *There* was a man whose religion was at any rate not a fair-weather religion. It did not go off in fine speeches about trusting to the protection of God, spoken from behind the skirts of the king, or from the middle of a phalanx of his soldiers. He clearly meant what he said, and believed every word of it as a prose fact, which was solid enough to build conduct on.

I am afraid a great many of us would rather have tried to reconcile our asking for a band of horsemen with our professed trust in God's hand; and there would have been plenty of excuses very ready about using means as well as exercising faith, and not being called upon to abandon advantages, and not pushing a good principle to Quixotic lengths, and so on, and so on. But whatever truth there is in such considerations, at any rate we may well learn the lesson of this story—to be true to our professed principles; to beware of making our religion a matter of words; to live, when the time for putting them into practice comes, by the maxims which we have been forward to proclaim when there was no risk in applying them; and to try sometimes to look at our lives with the eyes of people who do not share our faith, that we may bring our actions up to the mark of what they expect of us. If 'the Church' would oftener think of what 'the world' looks for from it, it would seldomer have cause to be ashamed of the terrible gap between it words and its deeds.

Especially in regard to this matter of trust in an unseen Hand, and reliance on visible helps, we all need to be very rigid in our self-inspection. Faith in the good hand of God upon us for good should often lead to the abandonment, and always to the subordination, of material aids. It is a question of detail, which each man must settle for himself as each occasion arises, whether in any given case abandonment or subordination is our duty. This is not the place to enter on so large and difficult a question. But, at all events, let us remember, and try to work into our own lives, that principle which the easy-going Christianity of this day has honeycombed with so many exceptions, that it scarcely has any whole surface left at all; that the absolute surrender and forsaking of external helps and goods is sometimes essential to the preservation and due expression of reliance on God.

There is very little fear of any of us pushing that principle to Quixotic lengths. The danger is all the other way. So it is worth while to notice that we have here an instance of a man's being carried by a certain lofty enthusiasm further than the mere law of duty would take him. There would have been no harm in Ezra's asking an escort, seeing that his whole enterprise was made possible by the king's support. He would not have been 'leaning on an arm of flesh' by availing himself of the royal troops, any more than when he used the royal firman. But a true man often feels that he cannot do the things which he might without sin do. 'All things are lawful for me, but all things are not expedient,' said Paul. The same Apostle eagerly contended that he had a perfect right to money support from the Gentile Churches; and then, in the next breath, flamed up into, 'I have used none of these things, for it were better for me to die, than that any man should make my glorying void.' A sensitive spirit, or one profoundly stirred by religious emotion, will, like the apostle whose feet were moved by love, far outrun the slower soul, whose steps are only impelled by the thought of duty. Better that the cup should run over than that it should not be full. Where we delight to do His will, there will often be more than a scrupulously regulated enough; and where there is not sometimes that 'more,' there will never be enough.

> 'Give all thou canst; high Heaven rejects the lore
> Of nicely calculated less or more.'

What shall we say of people who profess that God is their portion, and are as eager in the scramble for money as anybody? What kind of a commentary will sharp-sighted, sharp-tongued observers have a right to make on us, whose creed is so unlike theirs, while our lives are identical? Do you believe, friends! that 'the hand of our God is upon all them for good that seek Him'? Then, do you not think that racing after the prizes of this world, with flushed cheeks and labouring breath, or longing, with a gnawing hunger of heart, for any earthly good, or lamenting over the removal of creatural defences and joys, as if heaven were empty because some one's place here is, or as if God were dead because dear ones die, may well be a shame to us, and a taunt on the lips of our enemies? Let us learn again the lesson from this old story,—that if our faith in God is not the veriest sham, it demands and will produce, the abandonment sometimes and the subordination always, of external helps and material good.

Notice, too, Ezra's preparation for receiving the divine help. There, by the river Ahava, he halts his company like a prudent leader, to repair omissions, and put the last touches to their organisation before facing the wilderness. But he has another purpose also. 'I proclaimed a fast there, to seek of God a right way for us.' There was no foolhardiness in his courage; he was well aware of all the possible dangers on the road; and whilst he is confident of the divine protection, he knows that, in his own quiet, matter-of-fact words, it is given 'to all them that *seek* Him.' So his faith not only impels him to the renunciation of the Babylonian guard, but to earnest supplication for the defence in which he is so confident. He is sure it will be given—so sure, that he will have no other shield; and yet he fasts and prays that he and his company may receive it. He prays because he is sure that he will receive it, and does receive it because he prays and is sure.

So for us, the condition and preparation on and by which we are sheltered by that great Hand, is the faith that asks, and the asking of faith. We must forsake the earthly props, but we must also believingly desire to be upheld by the heavenly arms. We make God responsible for our safety when we abandon other defence, and commit ourselves to Him. With eyes open to our dangers, and full consciousness of our own unarmed and unwarlike weakness, let us solemnly commend ourselves to Him, rolling all our burden on His strong arms, knowing that He is able to keep that which we have committed to Him. He will accept the trust, and set His guards about us. As the song of the returning exiles, which may have been sung by the river Ahava, has it: 'My help cometh from the Lord. The Lord is thy keeper. The Lord is thy shade upon thy right hand.'

So our story ends with the triumphant vindication of this Quixotic faith. A flash of joyful feeling breaks through the simple narrative, as it tells how the words spoken before the king came true in the experience of the weaponless pilgrims: 'The hand of our God *was* upon us, and He delivered us from the hand of the enemy, and of such as lay in wait by the way; and we came to Jerusalem.' It was no rash venture that we made. He was all that we hoped and asked. Through all the weary march He led us. From the wild, desert-born robbers, that watched us from afar, ready to come down on us, from ambushes and hidden perils, He kept us, because we had none other help, and all our hope was in Him. The ventures of faith are ever rewarded. We cannot set our expectations from God too high. What we dare scarcely hope now we shall one day remember. When we come to tell the completed story of our lives, we shall have to record the fulfilment of all God's promises, and the accomplishment of all our prayers that were built on these. Here let us cry, 'Be

Thy hand upon us.' Here let us trust, Thy hand will be upon us. Then we shall have to say, 'The hand of our God was upon us,' and as we look from the watch-towers of the city, on the desert that stretches to its very walls, and remember all the way by which He led us, we shall rejoice over His vindication of our poor faith, and praise Him that 'not one thing hath failed of all the things which the Lord our God spake concerning us.'

THE CHARGE OF THE PILGRIM PRIESTS

'Watch ye, and keep them, until ye weigh them ... at Jerusalem, in the chambers of the house of the Lord.'—EZRA viii. 29.

THE little band of Jews, seventeen hundred in number, returning from Babylon, had just started on that long pilgrimage, and made a brief halt in order to get everything in order for their transit across the desert; when their leader Ezra, taking count of his men, discovers that amongst them there are none of the priests or Levites. He then takes measures to reinforce his little army with a contingent of these, and entrusts to their special care a very valuable treasure in gold, and silver, and sacred vessels, which had been given to them for use in the house of the Lord. The words which I have taken as text are a portion of the charge which he gave to those twelve priestly guardians of the precious things, that were to be used in worship when they got back to the Temple. 'Watch and keep them, until ye weigh them in the chambers of the house of the Lord.'

So I think I may venture, without being unduly fanciful, to take these words as a type of the injunctions which are given to us Christian people; and to see in them a striking and picturesque representation of the duties that devolve upon us in the course of our journey across the desert to the Temple-Home above.

And to begin with, let me remind you, for a moment or two, what the precious treasure is which is thus entrusted to our keeping and care. We can scarcely, in such a connection and with such a metaphor, forget the words of our Lord about a certain king that went to receive his kingdom, and to return; who called together his servants, and gave to each of them according to their several ability, with the injunction to trade upon that until he came. The same metaphor which our Master employed lies in this story before us—in the one case, sacrificial vessels and sacred treasures; in the other case, the talents out of the rich possessions of the departing king.

Nor can we forget either the other phase of the same figure which the Apostle employs when he says to his 'own son' and substitute, Timothy: 'That good thing which was committed unto thee, keep by the Holy Ghost which dwelleth in us,' nor that other word to the same Timothy, which says: 'O Timothy! keep that which was committed to thy trust, and avoid profane and vain babblings, and oppositions of science, falsely so called.' In these quotations, the treasure, and the rich deposit, is the faith once delivered to the saints; the solemn message of love and peace in Jesus Christ, which was entrusted, first of all to those preachers, but as truly to every one of Christ's disciples.

So, then, the metaphor is capable of two applications. The first is to the rich treasure and solemn trust of our own nature, of our own souls; the faculties and capacities, precious beyond all count, rich beyond all else that a man has ever received. Nothing that you have is half so much as that which you are. The possession of a soul that knows and loves, and can obey; that trusts and desires; that can yearn and reach out to Jesus Christ, and to God in Christ; of a conscience that can yield to His command; and faculties of comprehending and understanding what comes to them from Jesus Christ—that is more than any other possession, treasure, or trust. That which you and I carry with us—the infinite possibilities of these awful spirits of ours—the tremendous faculties which are given to every human soul, and which, like a candle plunged into oxygen, are meant to burn far more brightly under the stimulus of Christian faith and the possession of God's truth, are the rich deposit committed to our charge. You priests of the living God, you men and women, you say that you are Christ's, and therefore are consecrated to a nobler priesthood than any other—to you is given this solemn charge: 'That good thing which is committed unto thee, keep by the Holy Ghost that dwelleth in you.' The precious treasure of your own natures, your own hearts, your own understandings, wills, consciences, desires—keep these, until they are weighed in the house of the Lord in Jerusalem.

And in like manner, taking the other aspect of the metaphor—we have given to us, in order that we may do something with it, that great deposit and treasure of truth, which is all embodied and incarnated in Jesus Christ our Lord. It is bestowed upon us that we may use it for ourselves, and in order that we may carry it triumphantly all through the world. Possession involves responsibility always. The word of salvation is given to us. If we go tampering with it, by erroneous apprehension, by unfair usage, by failing to apply it to our own daily life; then it will fade and disappear from our grasp. It is given to us in order that we may keep it safe, and carry it high up, across the desert, as becomes the priests of the most high God.

The treasure is first—our own selves—with all that we are and may be, under the stimulating and quickening influence of His grace and Spirit. The treasure is next —His great word of salvation, once delivered unto the saints, and to be handed on, without diminution or alteration in its fair perspective and manifold harmonies, to the generations that are to come. So, think of yourselves as the priests of God, journeying through the wilderness, with the treasures of the Temple and the vessels of the sacrifice for your special deposit and charge.

Further, I touch on the command, the guardianship that is here set forth. 'Watch ye, and keep them.' That is to say, I suppose, according to the ordinary idiom of the Old Testament, 'Watch, in order that you may keep.' Or to translate it into other words: The treasure which is given into our hands requires, for its safe preservation, unceasing vigilance. Take the picture of my text: These Jews were four months, according to the narrative, in travelling from their first station upon their journey to Jerusalem across the desert. There were enemies lying in wait for them by the way. With noble self-restraint and grand chivalry, the leader of the little band says: 'I was ashamed to require of the king a band of soldiers and horsemen, to help us against the enemy in the way; because we had spoken unto the king, saying,

The hand of our God is upon all them for good that seek Him; but His power and His wrath is against all that forsake Him.' And so they would not go to him, cap in hand, and ask him to give them a guard to take care of them; but 'We fasted and besought our God for this; and He was intreated of us.'

Thus the little company, without arms, without protection, with nothing but a prayer and a trust to make them strong, flung themselves into the pathless desert with all those precious things in their possession; and all the precaution which Ezra took was to lay hold of the priests in the little party, and to say: 'Here! all through the march do you stick by these precious things. Whoever sleeps, do you watch. Whoever is careless, be you vigilant. Take these for your charge, and remember I weigh them here before we start, and they will be all weighed again when we get there. So be alert.'

And is not that exactly what Christ says to us? 'Watch; keep them; be vigilant, that ye may keep; and keep them, because they will be weighed and registered when you arrive there.'

I cannot do more than touch upon two or three of the ways in which this charge may be worked out, in its application for ourselves, beginning with that first one which is implied in the words of the text—*unslumbering vigilance*; then *trust*, like the trust which is glorified in the context, depending only on 'the good hand of our God upon us'; then *purity*, because, as Ezra said, 'Ye are holy unto the Lord. The vessels are holy also'; and therefore ye are the fit persons to guard them. And besides these, there is, in our keeping our trust, a method which does not apply to the incident before us; namely, *use*, in order to their preservation.

x

That is to say, first of all, no slumber; not a moment's relaxation; or some of those who lie in wait for us on the way will be down upon us, and some of the precious things will go. While all the rest of the wearied camp slept, the guardians of the treasure had to outwatch the stars. While others might straggle on the march, lingering here or there, or resting on some patch of green, they had to close up round their precious charge; others might let their eyes wander from the path, they had ever to look to their charge. For them the journey had a double burden, and unslumbering vigilance was their constant duty.

We likewise have unslumberingly and ceaselessly to watch over that which is committed to our charge. For, depend upon it, if for an instant we turn away our heads, the thievish birds that flutter over us will be down upon the precious seed that is in our basket, or that we have sown in the furrows, and it will be gone. Watch, that ye may keep.

And then, still further, see how in this story before us there are brought out very picturesquely, and very simply, deeper lessons still. It is not enough that a man shall be for ever keeping his eye upon his own character and his own faculties, and seeking sedulously to cultivate and improve them, as he that must give an account. There must be another look than that. Ezra said, in effect, 'Not all the cohorts of Babylon can help us; and we do not want them. We have one strong hand that will keep us safe'; and so he, and his men, with all this mass of wealth, so tempting to the wild robbers that haunted the road, flung themselves into the desert, knowing that all along it there were, as he says, 'such as lay in wait for them.' His confidence was: 'God will bring us all safe out to the end there; and we shall carry every glittering piece of the precious things that we brought out of Babylon right into the Temple of Jerusalem.' Yet he says, 'Watch ye and keep them.'

What does that come to in reference to our religious experience? Why this: 'Work out your own salvation with fear and trembling; for it is God that worketh in you, both to will and to do of His own good pleasure.' You do not need these external helps. Fling yourself wholly upon His keeping hand, and also watch and keep yourselves. 'I know in whom I have believed, and that He is able to keep that which I have committed unto Him against that day,' is the complement of the other words, 'That good thing which was committed unto thee, keep by the Holy Ghost.'

So guardianship is, first, unceasing vigilance; and then it is lowly trust. And besides that, it is *punctilious purity*. 'I said unto them, Ye are holy unto the Lord; the vessels are holy unto the Lord. Watch ye, and keep them.'

It was fitting that priests should carry the things that belonged to the Temple. No other hands but consecrated hands had a right to touch them. To none other guardianship but the guardianship of the possessors of a symbolic and ceremonial purity, could the vessels of a symbolic and ceremonial worship be entrusted; and to none others but the possessors of real and spiritual holiness can the treasures of the true Temple, of an inward and spiritual worship, be entrusted. 'Be ye clean that bear the vessels of the Lord,' said Isaiah using a kindred metaphor. The only way to keep our treasure undiminished and untarnished, is to keep ourselves pure and clean.

And, lastly, we have to exercise a guardianship which

not only means unslumbering vigilance, lowly trust, punctilious purity, but also requires the constant *use* of the treasure.

'Watch ye, and keep them.' Although the vessels which those priests bore through the desert were used for no service during all the weary march, they weighed just the same when they got to the end as at the beginning; though, no doubt, even their fine gold had become dim and tarnished through disuse. But if we do not use the vessels that are entrusted to our care, *they* will *not* weigh the same. The man that wrapped up his talent in the napkin, and said, 'Lo, there thou hast that is thine,' was too sanguine. There was never an unused talent rolled up in a handkerchief yet, but when it was taken out and put into the scales it was lighter than when it was committed to the keeping of the earth. Gifts that are used fructify. Capacities that are strained to the uttermost increase. Service strengthens the power for service; and just as the reward for work is more work, the way for making ourselves fit for bigger things is to do the things that are lying by us. The blacksmith's arm, the sailor's eye, the organs of any piece of handicraft, as we all know, are strengthened by exercise; and so it is in this higher region.

And so, dear brethren, take these four words—vigilance, trust, purity, exercise. 'Watch ye, and keep them, until they are weighed in the chambers of the House of the Lord.'

And, lastly, think of that weighing in the House of the Lord. Cannot you see the picture of the little band when they finally reach the goal of their pilgrimage; and three days after they arrived, as the narrative tells us, went up into the Temple, and there, by number and by weight, rendered up their charge, and were clear of their responsibility? 'And the first came and said, Lord, thy pound hath gained ten pounds. And he said, Well, thou good servant, because thou hast been faithful in a very little, have thou authority over ten cities.'

Oh! how that thought of the day when they would empty out the rich treasure upon the marble pavement, and clash the golden vessels into the scales, must have filled their hearts with vigilance during all the weary watches, when desert stars looked down upon the slumbering encampment, and they paced wakeful all the night. And how the thought, too, must have filled their hearts with joy, when they tried to picture to themselves the sigh of satisfaction, and the sense of relief with which, after all the perils, their 'feet would stand within thy gates, O Jerusalem,' and they would be able to say, 'That which thou hast given us, we have kept, and nothing of it is lost.'

A lifetime would be a small expenditure to secure that; and though it cannot be that you and I will meet the trial and the weighing of that great day without many failures and much loss, yet we may say: 'I know in whom I have believed, and that He is able to keep my deposit—whether it be in the sense of that which I have committed unto Him, or in the sense of that which He has committed unto me—against that day.' We may hope that, by His gracious help and His pitying acceptance, even such careless stewards and negligent watchers as we are, may lay ourselves down in peace at the last, saying, 'I have kept the faith,' and may be awakened by the word, 'Well done! good and faithful servant.'

THE BOOK OF NEHEMIAH

A REFORMER'S SCHOOLING

'The words of Nehemiah the son of Hachaliah. And it came to pass in the month Chisleu, in the twentieth year, as I was in Shushan the palace, 2. That Hanani, one of my brethren, came, he and certain men of Judah; and I asked them concerning the Jews that had escaped, which were left of the captivity, and concerning Jerusalem. 3. And they said unto me, The remnant that are left of the captivity there in the province are in great affliction and reproach: the wall of Jerusalem also is broken down, and the gates thereof are burned with fire. 4. And it came to pass, when I heard these words, that I sat down and wept, and mourned certain days, and fasted, and prayed before the God of heaven, 5. And said, I beseech Thee, O Lord God of heaven, the great and terrible God, that keepeth covenant and mercy for them that love Him and observe His commandments: 6. Let Thine ear now be attentive, and Thine eyes open, that Thou mayest hear the prayer of Thy servant, which I pray before Thee now, day and night, for the children of Israel Thy servants, and confess the sins of the children of Israel, which we have sinned against Thee: both I and my father's house have sinned. 7. We have dealt very corruptly against Thee, and have not kept the commandments, nor the statutes, nor the judgments, which Thou commandedst Thy servant Moses. 8. Remember, I beseech Thee, the word that Thou commandedst Thy servant Moses, saying, If ye transgress, I will scatter you abroad among the nations: 9. But if ye turn unto Me, and keep My commandments, and do them; though there were of you cast out unto the uttermost part of the heaven, yet will I gather them from thence, and will bring them unto the place that I have chosen to set My name there. 10. Now these are Thy servants and Thy people, whom Thou hast redeemed by Thy great power, and by Thy strong hand. 11. O Lord, I beseech Thee, let now Thine ear be attentive to the prayer of Thy servant, and to the prayer of Thy servants, who desire to fear Thy name: and prosper, I pray Thee, Thy servant this day, and grant him mercy in the sight of this man. For I was the king's cupbearer.'—NEH. i. 1-11.

THE date of the completion of the Temple is 516 B.C.; that of Nehemiah's arrival 445 B.C. The colony of returned exiles seems to have made little progress during that long period. Its members settled down, and much of their enthusiasm cooled, as we see from the reforms which Ezra had to inaugurate fourteen years before Nehemiah. The majority of men, even if touched by spiritual fervour, find it hard

A REFORMER'S SCHOOLING

to keep on the high levels for long. Breathing is easier lower down. As is often the case, a brighter flame of zeal burned in the bosoms of sympathisers at a distance than in those of the actual workers, whose contact with hard realities and petty details disenchanted them. Thus the impulse to nobler action came, not from one of the colony, but from a Jew in the court of the Persian king.

This passage tells us how God prepared a man for a great work, and how the man prepared himself.

I. Sad tidings and their effect on a devout servant of God (vs. 1-4). The time and place are precisely given. 'The month Chisleu' corresponds to the end of November and beginning of December. 'The twentieth year' is that of Artaxerxes (Neh. ii. 1). 'Shushan,' or Susa, was the royal winter residence, and 'the palace' was 'a distinct quarter of the city, occupying an artificial eminence.' Note the absence of the name of the king. Nehemiah is so familiar with his greatness that he takes for granted that every reader can fill the gaps. But, though the omission shows how large a space the court occupied in his thoughts, a true Jewish heart beat below the courtier's robe. That flexibility which enabled them to stand as trusted servants of the kings of many lands, and yet that inflexible adherence to, and undying love of, Israel, has always been a national characteristic. We can think of this youthful cup-bearer as yearning for one glimpse of the 'mountains round about Jerusalem' while he filled his post in Shushan.

His longings were kindled into resolve by intercourse with a little party of Jews from Judæa, among whom was his own brother. They had been to see how things went there, and the fact that one of them was a member of Nehemiah's family seems to imply that the same sentiments belonged to the whole household. Eager questions brought out sorrowful answers. The condition of the 'remnant' was one of 'great affliction and reproach,' and the ground of the reproach was probably (Neh. ii. 17; iv. 2-4) the still ruined fortifications.

It has been supposed that the breaking down of the walls and burning of the gates, mentioned in verse 3, were recent, and subsequent to the events recorded in Ezra; but it is more probable that the project for rebuilding the defences, which had been stopped by superior orders (Ezra iv. 12-16), had not been resumed, and that the melancholy ruins were those which had met the eyes of Zerubbabel nearly a hundred years before. Communication between Shushan and Jerusalem cannot have been so infrequent that the facts now borne in on Nehemiah might not have been known before. But the impression made by facts depends largely on their narrator, and not a little on the mood of the hearer. It was one thing to hear general statements, and another to sit with one's brother, and see through his eyes the dismal failure of the 'remnant' to carry out the purpose of their return. So the story, whether fresh or repeated with fresh force, made a deep dint in the young cupbearer's heart, and changed his life's outlook. God prepares His servants for their work by laying on their souls a sorrowful realisation of the miseries which other men regard, and they themselves have often regarded, very lightly. The men who have been raised up to do great work for God and men, have always to begin by greatly and sadly feeling the weight of the sins and sorrows which they are destined to remove. No man will do worthy work at rebuilding the walls who has not wept over the ruins.

So Nehemiah prepared himself for his work by brooding over the tidings with tears, by fasting and by prayer. There is no other way of preparation. Without the sad sense of men's sorrows, there will be no earnestness in alleviating them, nor self-sacrificing devotion; and without much prayer there will be little consciousness of weakness or dependence on divine help.

Note the grand and apparently immediate resolution to throw up brilliant prospects and face a life of danger and suffering and toil. Nehemiah was evidently a favourite with the king, and had the ball at his foot. But the ruins on Zion were more attractive to him than the splendours of Shushan, and he willingly flung away his chances of a great career to take his share of 'affliction and reproach.' He has never had justice done him in popular estimation. He is not one of the well-known biblical examples of heroic self-abandonment; but he did just what Moses did, and the eulogium of the Epistle to the Hebrews fits him as well as the lawgiver; for he too chose 'rather to suffer with the people of God than to enjoy pleasures for a season.' So must we all, in our several ways, do, if we would have a share in building the walls of the city of God.

II. The prayer (vs. 5-11). The course of thought in this prayer is very instructive. It begins with solemnly laying before God His own great name, as the mightiest plea with Him, and the strongest encouragement to the suppliant. That commencement is no mere proper invocation, conventionally regarded as the right way of beginning, but it expresses the petitioner's effort to lay hold on God's character as the ground of his hope of answer. The terms employed remarkably blend what Nehemiah had learned from Persian religion and what from a better source. He calls upon Jehovah, the great name which was the special possession of Israel. He also uses the characteristic Persian designation of 'the God of heaven,' and identifies the bearer of that name, not with the god to whom it was originally applied, but with Israel's Jehovah. He takes the crown from the head of the false deity, and lays it at the feet of the God of his fathers. Whatsoever names for the Supreme Excellence any tongues have coined, they all belong to our God, in so far as they are true and noble. The modern 'science of comparative religion' yields many treasures which should be laid up in Jehovah's Temple.

But the rest of the designations are taken from the Old Testament, as was fitting. The prayer throughout is full of allusions and quotations, and shows how this cupbearer of Artaxerxes had fed his young soul on God's word, and drawn thence the true nourishment of high and holy thoughts and strenuous resolutions and self-sacrificing deeds. Prayers which are cast in the mould of God's own revelation of Himself will not fail of answer. True prayer catches up the promises that flutter down to us, and flings them up again like arrows.

The prayer here is all built, then, on that name of Jehovah, and on what the name involves, chiefly on the thought of God as keeping covenant and mercy. He has bound Himself in solemn, irrefragable compact, to a certain line of action. Men 'know where to have Him,' if we may venture on the familiar expression. He has given us a chart of His course, and He will adhere to it. Therefore we can go to Him with our prayers, so long as we keep these within the ample space of His covenant, and ourselves within its terms, by loving obedience.

The petition that God's ears might be sharpened and His eyes open to the prayer is cast in a familiar mould. It boldly transfers to Him not only the semblance of man's form, but also the likeness of His processes of action. Hearing the cry for help precedes active intervention in the case of men's help, and the strong imagery of the prayer conceives of similar sequence in God. But the figure is transparent, and the 'anthropomorphism' so plain that no mistakes can arise in its interpretation.

Note, too, the light touch with which the suppliant's relation to God ('Thy servant') and his long-continued cry ('day and night') are but just brought in for a moment as pleas for a gracious hearing. The prayer is 'for Thy servants the children of Israel,' in which designation, as the next clauses show, the relation established by God, and not the conduct of men, is pleaded as a reason for an answer.

The mention of that relation brings at once to Nehemiah's mind the terrible unfaithfulness to it which had marked, and still continued to mark, the whole nation. So lowly confession follows (vs. 6, 7). Unprofitable servants they had indeed been. The more loftily we think of our privileges, the more clearly should we discern our sins. Nothing leads a true heart to such self-ashamed penitence as reflection on God's mercy. If a man thinks that God has taken him for a servant, the thought should bow him with conscious unworthiness, not lift him in self-satisfaction. Nehemiah's confession not only sprung from the thought of Israel's vocation, so poorly fulfilled, but it also laid the groundwork for his further petitions. It is useless to ask God to help us to repair the wastes if we do not cast out the sins which have made them. The beginning of all true healing of sorrow is confession of sins. Many promising schemes for the alleviation of national and other distresses have come to nothing because, unlike Nehemiah's, they did not begin with prayer, or prayed for help without acknowledging sin.

And the man who is to do work for God and to get God to bless his work must not be content with acknowledging other people's sins, but must always say, 'We have sinned,' and not seldom say, 'I have sinned.' That penitent consciousness of evil is indispensable to all who would make their fellows happier. God works with bruised reeds. The sense of individual transgression gives wonderful tenderness, patience amid gainsaying, submission in failure, dependence on God in difficulty, and lowliness in success. Without it we shall do little for ourselves or for anybody else.

The prayer next reminds God of His own words (vs. 8, 9), freely quoted and combined from several passages (Lev. xxvi. 33-45; Deut. iv. 25-31, etc.). The application of these passages to the then condition of things is at first sight somewhat loose, since part of the people were already restored; and the purport of the prayer is not the restoration of the remainder, but the deliverance of those already in the land from their distresses. Still, the promise gives encouragement to the prayer and is powerful with God, inasmuch as it could not be said to have been fulfilled by so incomplete a restoration as that at present realised. What God does must be perfectly done; and His great word

A REFORMER'S SCHOOLING

is not exhausted so long as any fuller accomplishment of it can be imagined.

The reminder of the promise is clinched (v. 10) by the same appeal as formerly to the relation to Himself into which God had been pleased to bring the nation, with an added reference to former deeds, such as the Exodus, in which His strong hand had delivered them. We are always sure of an answer if we ask God not to contradict Himself. Since He has begun He will make an end. It will never be said of Him that He 'began to build and was not able to finish.' His past is a mirror in which we can read His future. The return from Babylon is implied in the Exodus.

A reiteration of earlier words follows, with the addition that Nehemiah now binds, as it were, his single prayer in a bundle with those of the like-minded in Israel. He gathers single ears into a sheaf, which he brings as a 'wave-offering.' And then, in one humble little sentence at the end, he puts his only personal request. The modesty of the man is lovely. His prayer has been all for the people. Remarkably enough, there is no definite petition in it. He never once says right out what he so earnestly desires, and the absence of specific requests might be laid hold of by sceptical critics as an argument against the genuineness of the prayer. But it is rather a subtle trait, on which no forger would have been likely to hit. Sometimes silence is the very result of entire occupation of mind with a thought. He says nothing about the particular nature of his request, just because he is so full of it. But he does ask for favour in the eyes of 'this man,' and that he may be prospered 'this day.'

So this was his morning prayer on that eventful day, which was to settle his life's work. The 'certain days of solitary meditation on his nation's griefs had led to a resolution. He says nothing about his long brooding, his slow decision, his conflicts with lower projects of personal ambition. He 'burns his own smoke,' as we all should learn to do. But he asks that the capricious and potent will of the king may be inclined to grant his request. If our morning supplication is 'Prosper Thy servant this day,' and our purposes are for God's glory, we need not fear facing anybody. However powerful Artaxerxes was, he was but 'this man,' not God. The phrase does not indicate contempt or undervaluing of the solid reality of his absolute power over Nehemiah, but simply expresses the conviction that the king, too, was a subject of God's, and that his heart was in the hand of Jehovah, to mould as He would. The consciousness of dependence on God and the habit of communion with Him give a man a clear sight of the limitations of earthly dignities, and a modest boldness which is equally remote from rudeness and servility.

Thus prepared for whatever might be the issue of that eventful day, the young cupbearer rose from his knees, drew a long breath, and went to his work. Well for us if we go to ours, whether it be a day of crisis or of commonplace, in like fashion! Then we shall have like defence and like calmness of heart.

THE CHURCH AND SOCIAL EVILS

'It came to pass, when I heard these words, that I sat down and wept, and mourned certain days, and fasted, and prayed before the God of heaven.'—NEH. i. 4.

NINETY years had passed since the returning exiles had arrived at Jerusalem. They had encountered many difficulties which had marred their progress and cooled their enthusiasm. The Temple, indeed, was rebuilt, but Jerusalem lay in ruins, and its walls remained as they had been left, by Nebuchadnezzar's siege, some century and a half before. A little party of pious pilgrims had gone from Persia to the city, and had come back to Shushan with a sad story of weakness and despondency, affliction and hostility. One of the travellers had a brother, a youth named Nehemiah, who was a cup-bearer in the court of the Persian king. Living in a palace, and surrounded with luxury, his heart was with his brethren; and the ruins of Jerusalem were dearer to him than the pomp of Shushan.

My text tells how the young cupbearer was affected by the tidings, and how he wept and prayed before God. The accurate dates given in this book show that this period of brooding contemplation of the miseries of his brethren lasted for four months. Then he took a great resolution, flung up brilliant prospects, identified himself with the afflicted colony, and asked for leave to go and share, and, if it might be, to redress, the sorrows which had made so deep a dint upon his heart.

Now, I think that this vivid description, drawn by himself, of the emotions excited in Nehemiah by his countrymen's sorrows, which influenced his whole future, contains some very plain lessons for Christian people, the observance of which is every day becoming more imperative by reason of the drift of public opinion, and the new prominence which is being given to so-called 'social questions.' I wish to gather up one or two of these lessons for you now.

I. First, then, note the plain Christian duty of **sympathetic contemplation of surrounding sorrows.**

Nehemiah might have made a great many very good excuses for treating lightly the tidings that his brother had brought him. He might have said: 'Jerusalem is a long way off. I have my own work to do; it is no part of my business to rebuild the walls of Jerusalem. I am the King's cupbearer. They went with their eyes open, and experience has shown that the people who knew when they were well off, and stayed where they were, were a great deal wiser.' These were not his excuses. He let the tidings fill his heart, and burn there.

Now, the first condition of sympathy is knowledge; and the second is attending to what we do know. Nehemiah had probably known, in a kind of vague way, for many a day how things were going in Palestine. Communications between it and Persia were not so difficult but that there would come plenty of Government despatches; and a man at headquarters who had the ear of the monarch, was not likely to be ignorant of what was going on in that part of his dominions. But there is all the difference between hearing vague general reports, and sitting and hearing your own brother tell you what he had seen with his own eyes. So the impression which had existed before was all inoperative until it was kindled by attention to the facts which all the time had been, in some degree, known.

Now, how many of us are there that know—and don't know—what is going on round about us in the slums and back courts of this city? How many of us are there who are habitually ignorant of what we actually know, because we never, as we say, 'give heed' to it. 'I did not think of that,' is a very poor excuse about matters concerning which there is knowledge, whether there is thought or not. And so I want to press upon all you Christian people the plain duty of knowing what you do know, and of giving an ample place in your thoughts to the stark staring facts around us.

Why! loads of people at present seem to think that the miseries, and hideous vices, and sodden immorality, and utter heathenism, which are found down amongst the foundations of every civic community are as indispensable to progress as the noise of the wheels of a train is to its advancement, or as the bilge-water in a wooden ship is to keep its seams tight. So we prate about 'civilisation,' which means turning men into cities. If agglomerating people into these great communities, which makes so awful a feature of modern life, be necessarily attended by such abominations as we live amongst and never think about, then, better that there had never been civilisation in such a sense at all. Every consideration of communion with and conformity to Jesus Christ, of loyalty to His words, of a true sense of brotherhood and of lower things—such as self-interest—every consideration demands that Christian people shall take to their hearts, in a fashion that the churches have never done yet, 'the condition of England question,' and shall ask, 'Lord! what wouldst Thou have me to do?'

I do not care to enter upon controversy raised by recent utterances, the motive of which may be worthy of admiration, though the expression cannot be acquitted of the charge of exaggeration, to the effect that the Christian churches as a whole have been careless of the condition of the people. It is not true in its absolute sense. I suppose that, taking the country over, the majority of the members of, at all events the Nonconformist churches and congregations, are in receipt of weekly wages or belong to the upper ranks of the working-classes, and that the lever which has lifted them to these upper ranks has been God's Gospel. I suppose it will be admitted that the past indifference with which we are charged belonged to the whole community, and that the new sense of responsibility which has marked, and blessedly marked, recent years, is largely owing to political and other causes which have lately come into operation. I suppose it will not be denied that, to a very large extent, any efforts which have been made in the past for the social, intellectual, and moral, and religious elevation of the people have had their impulse, and to a large extent their support, both pecuniary and active, from Christian churches and individuals. All that is perfectly true and, I believe, undeniable. But it is also true that there remains an enormous, shameful, dead mass of inertness in our churches, and that, unless we can break up that, the omens are bad, bad for society, worse for the church. If cholera is raging in the slums, the suburbs will not escape. If the hovels are infected, the mansions will have to pay their tribute to the disease. If we do not recognise the brotherhood of the suffering and the sinful, in any other fashion—'Then,' as a great teacher told us a generation ago now, and nobody paid any attention to him, 'then they will begin and show you that they are your brethren by killing some of you.' And so self-preservation conjoins with loftier motives to make this sympathetic observation of the surrounding sorrows the plainest of Christian duties.

II. Secondly, such a realisation of the dark facts is indispensable to all true work for alleviating them.

There is no way of helping men but by bearing what

they bear. No man will ever lighten a sorrow of which he has not himself felt the pressure. Jesus Christ's Cross, to which we are ever appealing as the ground of our redemption and the anchor of our hope, is these, thank God! But it is more than these. It is the pattern for our lives, and it lays down, with stringent accuracy and completeness, the enduring conditions of helping the sinful and the sorrowful. The 'saviours of society' have still, in lower fashion, to be crucified. Jesus Christ would never have been 'the Lamb of God that bore away the sins of the world' unless He Himself had 'taken our infirmities and borne our sicknesses.' No work of any real use will be done except by those whose hearts have bled with the feeling of the miseries which they set themselves to cure.

Oh! we all want a far fuller realisation of that sympathetic spirit of the pitying Christ, if we are ever to be of any use in the world, or to help the miseries of any of our brethren. Such a sorrowful and participating contemplation of men's sorrows springing from men's sins will give tenderness to our words, will give patience, will soften our whole bearing. Help that is flung to people, as you might fling a bone to a dog, hurts those whom it tries to help, and patronising help is help that does little good, and lecturing help does little more. You must take blind beggars by the hand if you are going to make them see; and you must not be afraid to lay your white, clean fingers upon the feculent masses of corruption in the leper's glistening whiteness if you are going to make him whole. Go down in order to lift, and remember that without sympathy there is no sufficient help, and without communion with Christ there is no sufficient sympathy.

III. Thirdly, such realisation of surrounding sorrows should drive to communion with God.

Nehemiah wept and mourned, and that was well. But between his weeping and mourning and his practical work there had to be still another link of connection. 'He wept and mourned,' and because he was sad he turned to God, 'and I fasted and prayed certain days.' There he got at once comfort for his sorrows, his sympathies, and deepening of his sympathies, and thence he drew inspiration that made him a hero and a martyr. So all true service for the world must begin with close communion with God.

There was a book published several years since which made a great noise in its little day, and called itself *The Service of Man*, which service it proposed to substitute for the effete conception of worship as the service of God. The service of man is, then, best done when it is the service of God. I suppose nowadays it is 'old-fashioned' and 'narrow,' which is the sin of sins at present, but I for my part have very little faith in the persistence and wide operation of any philanthropic motives except the highest—namely, compassion caught from Jesus Christ. I do not believe that you will get men, year in and year out, to devote themselves in any considerable numbers to the service of man unless you appeal to this highest of motives. You may enlist a little corps—and God forbid that I should deny such a plain fact—of selecter spirits to do purely secular alleviative work, with an entire ignoring of Christian motives, but you will never get the army of workers that is needed to grapple with the facts of our present condition, unless you touch the very deepest springs of conduct, and these are to be found in communion with God. All the rest is surface drainage. Get down to the love of God, and the love of men therefrom, and you have got an Artesian well which will bubble up unfailingly.

And I have not much faith in remedies which ignore religion, and are brought, without communion with God, as sufficient for the disease. I do not want to say one word that might seem to depreciate what are good and valid and noble efforts in their several spheres. There is no need for antagonism—rather, Christian men are bound by every consideration to help to the utmost of their power, even in the incomplete attempts that are made to grapple with social problems. There is room enough for us all. But sure I am that until grapes and waterbeds cure smallpox, and a spoonful of cold water puts out Vesuvius, you will not cure the evils of the body politic by any lesser means than the application of the Gospel of Jesus Christ.

We hear a great deal to-day about a 'social gospel,' and I am glad of the conception, and of the favour which it receives. Only let us remember that the Gospel is social *second*, and individual *first*. And that if you get the love of God and obedience to Jesus Christ into a man's heart it will be like putting gas into a balloon, it will go up, and the man will get out of the slums fast enough; and he will not be a slave to the vices of the world much longer, and you will have done more for him and for the wide circle that he may influence than by any other means. I do not want to depreciate any helpers, but I say it is the work of the Christian church to carry to the world the only thing that will make men deeply and abidingly happy, because it will make them good.

IV. And so, lastly, such sympathy should be the parent of a noble, self-sacrificing life. Look at the man in our text. He had the ball at his feet. He had the *entrée* of a court, and the ear of a king. Brilliant prospects were opening before him, but his brethren's sufferings drew him, and with a noble resolution of self-sacrifice, he shut himself out from the former and went into the wilderness. He is one of the Scripture characters that never have had due honour—a hero, a saint, a martyr, a reformer. He did, though in a smaller sphere, the very same thing that the writer of the Epistle to the Hebrews magnified with his splendid eloquence, in reference to the great Lawgiver, 'And chose rather to suffer affliction with the people of God,' and to turn his back upon the dazzlements of a court, than to 'enjoy the pleasures of sin for a season,' whilst his brethren were suffering.

Now, dear friends! the letter of the example may be put aside; the spirit of it must be observed. If Christians are to do the work that they can do, and that Christ has put them into this world that they may do, there must be self-sacrifice with it. There is no shirking that obligation, and there is no discharging our duty without it. You and I, in our several ways, are as much under the sway of that absolute law, that 'if a corn of wheat fall into the ground and die, it brings forth fruit,' as ever was Jesus Christ or His Apostles. I have nothing to say about the manner of the sacrifice. It is no part of my business to prescribe to you details of duty. It is my business to insist on the principles which must regulate these, and of these principles in application to Christian service there is none more stringent than—'I will not offer unto my God burnt-offering of that which doth cost me nothing.'

I am sure that, under God, the great remedy for

social evils lies mainly here, that the bulk of professing Christians shall recognise and discharge their responsibilities. It is not ministers, city missionaries, Bible-women, or any other paid people that can do the work. It is by Christian men and by Christian women, and, if I might use a very vulgar distinction which has a meaning in the present connection, very specially by Christian ladies, taking their part in the work amongst the degraded and the outcasts, that our sorest difficulties and problems will be solved. If a church does not face these, well, all I can say is, its light will go out; and the sooner the better. 'If thou forbear to deliver them that are appointed to death, and say, Behold! I knew it not, shall not He that weigheth the hearts consider it, and shall He not render to every man according to his work?' And, on the other hand, there are no blessings more rich, select, sweet, and abiding, than are to be found in sharing the sorrow of the Man of Sorrows, and carrying the message of His pity and His redemption to an outcast world. 'If thou draw out thy soul to the hungry, and satisfy the afflicted soul, the Lord shall satisfy thy soul; and thou shalt be as a watered garden, and as a spring of water whose waters fail not.'

'OVER AGAINST HIS HOUSE'

'The priests repaired every one over against his house.'—NEH. iii. 28.

THE condition of our great cities has lately been forced upon public attention, and all kinds of men have been offering their panaceas. I am not about to enter upon that discussion, but I am glad to seize the opportunity of saying one or two things which I think very much need to be said to individual Christian people about their duty in the matter. 'Every man over against his house' is the principle I desire to commend to you as going a long way to solve the problem of how to sweeten the foul life of our modern cities.

The story from which my text is taken does not need to detain us long. Nehemiah and his little band of exiles have come back to a ruined Jerusalem. Their first care is to provide for their safety, and the first step is to know the exact extent of their defencelessness. So we have the account of Nehemiah's midnight ride amongst the ruins of the broken walls. And then we read of the co-operation of all classes in the work of reconstruction. 'Many hands made light work.' Men and women, priests and nobles, goldsmiths, apothecaries, merchants, all seized trowel or spade, and wheeled and piled. One man puts up a long length of wall, another can only manage a little bit; another undertakes the locks, bolts, and bars for the gates. Roughly and hastily the work is done. The result, of course, is very unlike the stately structures of Solomon's or of Herod's time, but it is enough for shelter. We can imagine the sigh of relief with which the workers looked upon the completed circle of their rude fortifications.

The principle of division of labour in our text is repeated several times in this list of the builders. It was a natural one; a man would work all the better when he saw his own roof mutely appealing to be defended, and thought of the dear ones that were there. But I take these words mainly as suggesting some thoughts applicable to the duties of Christian people in view of the spiritual wants of our great cities.

I. I need not do more than say a word or two about the ruins which need repair. If I dwell rather upon the dark side than on the bright side of city life I shall not be understood, as forgetting that the very causes which intensify the evil of a great city quicken the good—the friction of multitudes and the impetus thereby given to all kinds of mental activity. Here amongst us there is much that is admirable and noble —much public spirit, much wise and benevolent expenditure of thought and toil for the general good, much conjoint action by men of different parties, earnest antagonism and earnest co-operation, and a free, bracing intellectual atmosphere, which stimulates activity. All that is true, though, on the other hand, it is not good to live always within hearing of the clatter of machinery and the strife of tongues; and the wisdom that is born of solitary meditation and quiet thought is less frequently met with in cities than is the cleverness that is born of intercourse with men, and newspaper reading.

But there is a tragic other side to all that, which mostly we make up our minds to say little about and to forget. The indifference which has made that ignorance possible, and has in its turn been fed by the ignorance, is in some respects a more shocking phenomenon than the vicious life which it has allowed to rot and to reek unheeded.

Most of us have got so familiarised with the evils that stare us in the face every time we go out upon the pavements, that we have come to think of them as being inseparable from our modern life, like the noise of a carriage wheel from its rotation. And is it so then? Is it indeed inevitable that within a stone's throw of our churches and chapels there should be thousands of men and women that have never been inside a place of worship since they were christened; and have no more religion than a horse? Must it be that the shining structure of our modern society, like an old Mexican temple, must be built upon a layer of living men, flung in for a foundation? Can it not be helped that there should be streets in our cities into which it is unfit for a decent woman to go by day alone, and unsafe for a brave man to venture after nightfall? Must men and women huddle together in dens where decency is as impossible as it is for swine in a sty? Is it an indispensable part of our material progress and wonderful civilisation that vice and crime and utter irreligion and hopeless squalor should go with it? Can all that bilge water really not be pumped out of the ship? If it be so, then I venture to say that, to a very large extent, progress is a delusion, and that the simple life of agricultural communities is better than this unwholesome aggregation of men.

The beginning of Nehemiah's work of repair was that sad midnight ride round the ruined walls. So there is a solemn obligation laid on Christian people to acquaint themselves with the awful facts, and then to meditate on them, till sacred, Christ-like compassion, pressing against the flood-gates of the heart, flings them open, and lets out a stream of helpful pity and saving deeds.

II. So much for my first point. My second is—the ruin is to be repaired mainly by the old Gospel of Jesus

Christ. Far be it from me to pit remedies against each other. The causes are complicated, and the cure must be as manifold as the causes. For my own part I believe that, in regard to the condition of the lowest of our outcast population, drink and lust have done it almost all, and that for all but an infinitesimal portion of it, intemperance is directly or indirectly the cause. That has to be fought by the distinct preaching of abstinence, and by the invoking of legislative restrictions upon the traffic. Wretched homes have to be dealt with by sanitary reform, which may require municipal and parliamentary action. Domestic discomfort has to be dealt with by teaching wives the principles of domestic economy. The gracious influence of art and music, pictures and window-gardening, and the like, will lend their aid to soften and refine. Coffee taverns, baths and wash-houses, workmen's clubs, and many other agencies are doing real and good work. I for one say, 'God speed to them all,' and willingly help them so far as I can.

But, as a Christian man, I believe that I know a thing that if lodged in a man's heart will do pretty nearly all which they aspire to do; and whilst I rejoice in the multiplied agencies for social elevation, I believe that I shall best serve my generation, and I believe that ninety-nine out of a hundred of you will do so too, by trying to get men to love and fear Jesus Christ the Saviour. If you can get His love into a man's heart, that will produce new tastes and new inclinations, which will reform, and sweeten, and purify faster than anything else does.

They tell us that Nonconformist ministers are never seen in the slums; well, that is a libel! But I should like to ask why it is that the Roman Catholic priest is seen there more than the Nonconformist minister? Because the one man's congregation is there, and the other man's is not—which, being translated into other words, is this: the religion of Jesus Christ mostly keeps people out of the slums, and certainly it will take a man out of them if once it gets into his heart, more certainly and quickly than anything else will.

So, dear friends! if we have in our hearts and in our hands this great message of God's love, we have in our possession the germ out of which all things that are lovely and of good report will grow. It will purify, elevate, and sweeten society, because it will make individuals pure and strong, and homes holy and happy. We do not need to draw comparisons between this and other means of reparation, and still less to feel any antagonism to them or the benevolent men who work them; but we should fix it in our minds that the principles of Christ's Gospel adhered to by individuals, and therefore by communities, would have rendered such a condition of things impossible, and that the true repair of the ruin wrought by evil and ignorance, in the single soul, in the family, the city, the nation, the world, is to be found in building anew on the One Foundation which God has laid, even Jesus Christ, the Living Stone, whose pure life passes into all that are grounded and founded on Him.

III. Lastly, this remedy is to be applied by the individual action of Christian men and women on the people nearest them.

'The priests repaired every one over against his house.' We are always tempted, in the face of large disasters, to look for heroic and large remedies, and to invoke corporate action of some sort, which is a great deal easier for most of us than the personal effort that is required. When a great scandal and danger like this of the condition of the lower layers of our civic population is presented before men, for one man that says, 'What can *I* do?' there are twenty who say, 'Somebody should do something. Government should do something. The Corporation should do something. This, that, or the other aggregate of men should do something.' And the individual calmly and comfortably slips his neck out of the collar and leaves it on the shoulders of these abstractions.

As I have said, there are plenty of things that need to be done by these somebodies. But what they do (they will be a long time in doing it), when they do get to work will only touch the fringe of the question, and the substance and the centre of it *you* can set to work upon this very day if you like, and not wait for anybody either to set you the example or to show you the way.

If you want to do people good you can; but you must pay the price for it. That price is personal sacrifice and effort. The example of Jesus Christ is the all-instructive one in the case. People talk about Him being their Pattern, but they often forget that whatever more there was in Christ's Cross and Passion there was this in it:—the exemplification for all time of the one law by which any reformation can be wrought on men—that a sympathising man shall give himself to do it, and that by personal influence alone men will be drawn and won from out of the darkness and filth. A loving heart and a sympathetic word, the exhibition of a Christian life and conduct, the fact of going down into the midst of evil and trying to lift men out of it, are the old-fashioned and only magnets by which men are drawn to purer and higher life. That is God's way of saving the world—by the action of single souls on single souls. Masses of men can neither save nor be saved. Not in groups, but one by one, particle by particle, soul by soul, Christ draws men to Himself, and He does His work in the world through single souls on fire with His love, and tender with pity learned of Him.

So, dear friends! do not think that any organisation, any corporate activity, any substitution of vicarious service, will solve the problem. It will not. There is only one way of doing it, the old way that we must tread if we are going to do anything for God and our fellows: 'The priests repaired every one over against his house.'

Let me briefly point out some very plain and obvious things which bear upon this matter of individual action. Let me remind you that if you are a Christian man you have in your possession the thing which will cure the world's woe, and possession involves responsibility. What would you think of a man that had a specific for some pestilence that was raging in a city, and was contented to keep it for his own use, or at most for his family's use, when his brethren were dying by the thousand, and their corpses polluting the air? And what shall we say of men and women who call themselves Christians, who have some faith in that great Lord and His mighty sacrifice; who know that the men they meet with every day of their lives are dying for want of it, and who yet themselves do absolutely nothing to spread His name, and to heal men's hurts? What shall we say? God forbid that we should say they are not Christians! but God forbid that anybody should flatter them with the notion that they are anything but most inconsistent Christians!

Still further, need I remind you that if we have found anything in Jesus Christ which has been peace and rest for ourselves, Christ has thereby called us to this work? He has found and saved us, not only for our own personal good. That, of course, is the prime purpose of our salvation, but not its exclusive purpose. He has saved us, too, in order that the Word may be spread through us to those beyond. 'The Kingdom of Heaven is like leaven, which a woman took and hid in three measures of meal until the whole was leavened,' and every little bit of the dough, as it received into itself the leaven, and was transformed, became a medium for transmitting the transformation to the next particle beyond it and so the whole was at last permeated by the power. We get the grace for ourselves that we may pass it on; and as the Apostle says: 'God hath shined into our hearts that we might give the light of the knowledge of the glory of God in the face of Jesus Christ.'

And you *can* do it, you Christian men and women, every one of you, and preach Him to somebody. The possession of His love gives the commission; ay! and it gives the power. There is nothing so mighty as the confession of personal experience. Do not you think that when that first of Christian converts, and first of Christian preachers went to his brother, all full of what he had discovered, his simple saying, 'We have found the Messias,' was a better sermon than a far more elaborate proclamation would have been? My brother! if you have found Him, you can say so; and if you can say so, and your character and your life confirm the words of your lips, you will have done more to spread His name than much eloquence and many an orator. All can preach who can say, 'We have found the Christ.'

The last word I have to say is this: there is no other body that can do it but you. They say:—'What an awful thing it is that there are no churches or chapels in these outcast districts!' If there were they would be what the churches and chapels are now—half empty. Bricks and mortar built up into ecclesiastical forms are not the way to evangelise this or any other country. It is a very easy thing to build churches and chapels. It is not such an easy thing—I believe it is an impossible thing (and that the sooner the Christian church gives up the attempt the better)—to get the godless classes into any church or chapel. Conducted on the principles upon which churches and chapels must needs at present be conducted, they are for another class altogether; and we had better recognise it, because then we shall feel that no multiplication of buildings like this in which we now are, for instance, is any direct contribution to the evangelisation of the waste spots of the country, except in so far as from a centre like this there ought to go out much influence which will originate direct missionary action in places and fashions adapted to the outlying community.

Professional work is not what we want. Any man, be he minister, clergyman, Bible-reader, city missionary, who goes among our godless population with the suspicion of pay about him is the weaker for that. What is needed besides is that ladies and gentlemen that are a little higher up in the social scale than these poor creatures, should go to them themselves; and excavate and work. Preach, if you like, in the technical sense; have meetings, I suppose, necessarily; but the personal contact is the thing, the familiar talk, the simple exhibition of a loving Christian heart, and the unconventional proclamation in free conversation of the broad message of the love of God in Jesus Christ. Why, if all the people in this chapel who can do that would do it, and keep on doing it, who can tell what an influence would come from some hundreds of new workers for Christ? And why should the existence of a church in which the workers are as numerous as the Christians be an Utopian dream? It is simply the dream that perhaps a church might be conceived to exist, all the members of which had found out their plainest, most imperative duty, and were really trying to do it.

No carelessness, no indolence, no plea of timidity or business shift the obligation from your shoulders if you are a Christian. It is your business, and no paid agents can represent you. You cannot buy yourselves substitutes in Christ's army, as they used to do in the militia, by a guinea subscription. We are thankful for the money, because there are kinds of work to be done that unpaid effort will not do. But men ask for your money; Jesus Christ asks for yourself, for your work, and will not let you off as having done your duty because you have paid your subscription. No doubt there are some of you who, from various circumstances, cannot yourselves do work amongst the masses of the outcast population. Well, but you have got people by your side whom you can help. The question which I wish to ask of my Christian brethren and sisters now is this: Is there a man, woman, or child living to whom you ever spoke a word about Jesus Christ? Is there? If not, do not you think it is time that you began?

There are people in your houses, people that sit by you in your counting-house, on your college benches, who work by your side in mill or factory or warehouse, who cross your path in a hundred ways, and God has given them to you that you may bring them to Him. Do you set yourself, dear brother, to work and try to bring them. Oh! if you lived nearer Jesus Christ you would catch the sacred fire from Him; and like a bit of cold iron lying beside a magnet, touching Him, you would yourselves become magnetic and draw men out of their evil and up to God.

Let me commend to you the old pattern: 'The priests repaired every one over against his house'; and beseech you to take the trowel and spade, or anything that comes handiest, and build, in the bit nearest you, some living stones on the true Foundation.

DISCOURAGEMENTS AND COURAGE

'Nevertheless we made our prayer unto our God, and set a watch against them day and night, because of them. 10. And Judah said, The strength of the bearers of burdens is decayed, and there is much rubbish; so that we are not able to build the wall. 11. And our adversaries said, They shall not know, neither see, till we come in the midst among them, and slay them, and cause the work to cease. 12. And it came to pass, that when the Jews which dwelt by them came, they said unto us ten times, From all places whence ye shall return unto us they will be upon you. 13. Therefore set I in the lower places behind the wall, and on the higher places, I even set the people after their families with their swords, their spears, and their bows. 14. And I looked and rose up, and said unto the nobles, and to the rulers, and to the rest of the people, Be not ye afraid of them: remember the Lord, which is great and terrible, and fight for your brethren, your sons, and your daughters, your wives, and your houses. 15. And it came to pass, when our enemies heard that it was known unto us, and God had brought their counsel to nought, that we returned all of us to the wall, every one unto his work. 16. And it came to pass from that time forth, that the half of my servants wrought in the work, and the other half of them held both the spears, the shields, and the bows, and the habergeons; and the rulers were behind all the house of Judah. 17. They which builded on the wall, and they that bare burdens, with those that laded, every one with one of his hands wrought in the work, and with the other hand held a weapon. 18. For the builders, every one had his sword girded by his side, and so builded. And he that sounded the trumpet was by me. 19. And I said unto the nobles, and to the rulers, and to the rest of the people, The work is great and large, and we are separated upon the wall, one far from another. 20. In what place therefore ye hear the sound of the trumpet, resort ye thither unto us: our God shall fight for us. 21. So we laboured in the work: and half of them held the spears from the rising of the morning till the stars appeared.'—NEH. iv. 9-21.

COMMON hatred has a wonderful power of uniting former foes. Samaritans, wild Arabs of the desert, Ammonites, and inhabitants of Ashdod in the Philistine plain would have been brought together for no noble work, but mischief and malice fused them for a time into one. God's work is attacked from all sides. Herod and Pilate can shake hands over their joint antagonism.

This passage paints vividly the discouragements which are apt to dog all good work, and the courage which refuses to be discouraged, and conquers by bold persistence. The first verse (v. 9) may stand as a summary of the whole, though it refers to the preceding, not to the following, verses. The true way to meet opposition is twofold—prayer and prudent watchfulness. 'Pray to God, and keep your powder dry,' is not a bad compendium of the duty of a Christian soldier. The union of appeal to God with the full use of common sense, watchfulness, and prudence, would dissipate many hindrances to successful service.

I. In verses 10-12 Nehemiah tells, in his simple way, of the difficulties from three several quarters which threatened to stop his work. He had trouble from the workmen, from the enemies, and from the mass of Jews not resident in Jerusalem. The enthusiasm of the builders had cooled, and the magnitude of their task began to frighten them. Verse 6 tells us that the wall was completed 'unto the half of it'; that is, to one-half the height, and half-way through is just the critical time in all protracted work. The fervour of beginning has passed; the animation from seeing the end at hand has not sprung up. There is a dreary stretch in the centre, where it takes much faith and self-command to plod on unfainting. Half-way to Australia from England is the region of sickening calms. It is easier to work in the fresh morning or in the cool evening than at midday. So in every great movement there are short-winded people who sit down and pant very soon, and their prudence croaks out undeniable facts. No doubt strength does become exhausted; no doubt there is 'much rubbish' (literally 'dust'). What then? The conclusion drawn is not so unquestionable as the premises. 'We cannot build the wall.' Why not? Have you not built half of it? And was not the first half more embarrassed by rubbish than the second will be?

It is a great piece of Christian duty to recognise difficulties, and not be cowed by them. The true inference from the facts would have been, 'so that we must put all our strength into the work, and trust in our God to help us.' We may not be responsible for discouragements suggesting themselves, but we are responsible for letting them become dissuasives. Our one question should be, Has God appointed the work? If so, it has to be done, however little our strength, and however mountainous the accumulations of rubbish.

The second part in the trio was taken by the enemies —Sanballat and Tobiah and the rest. They laid their plans for a sudden swoop down on Jerusalem, and calculated that, if they could surprise the builders at their work, they would have no weapons to show fight with, and so would be easily despatched. Killing the builders was but a means; the desired end is significantly put last (v. 11), as being the stopping of the abhorred work. But killing the workmen does not cause the work to cease when it is God's work, as the history of the Church in all ages shows. Conspirators should hold their tongues. It was not a hopeful way of beginning an attack, of which the essence was secrecy and suddenness, to talk about it. 'A bird of the air carries the matter.'

The third voice is that of the Jews in other parts of the land, and especially those living on the borders of Samaria, next door to Sanballat. Verse 12 is probably best taken as in the Revised Version, which makes 'Ye must return to us' the imperative and often-repeated summons from these to the contingents from their respective places of abode, who had gone up to Jerusalem to help in building. Alarms of invasion made the scattered villagers wish to have all their men capable of bearing arms back again to defend their own homes. It was a most natural demand, but in this case, as so often, audacity is truest prudence; and in all high causes there come times when men have to trust their homes and dear ones to God's protection. The necessity is heartrending, and we may well pray that we may not be exposed to it; but if it clearly arises, a devout man can have no doubt of his duty. How many American citizens had to face it in the great Civil War! And how character is ennobled by even so severe a sacrifice!

II. The calm heroism of Nehemiah and his wise action in the emergency are told in verses 13-15. He made a demonstration in force, which at once showed that the scheme of a surprise was blown to pieces. It is difficult to make out the exact localities in which he planted his men. 'The lower places behind the wall' probably means the points at which the new fortifications were lowest, which would be the most exposed to assault; and the 'higher places' (Auth. Ver.), or 'open places' (Rev. Ver.), describes the same places from another point of view. They afforded room for posting troops because they were without buildings. At any rate, the walls were manned, and the enemy would have to deal, not with unarmed labourers, but with prepared soldiers. The work was stopped, and trowel and spade exchanged for sword and spear. 'And I looked,' says Nehemiah. His careful eye travelled over the lines, and, seeing all in order, he cheered the little army with ringing words. He had prayed (Neh. i. 5) to 'the great and terrible God,' and now he bids his men remember Him, and thence draw strength and courage. The only real antagonist of fear is faith. If we can grasp God, we shall not dread Sanballat and his crew. Unless we do, the world is full of dangers which it is not folly to fear.

Note, too, that the people are animated for the fight by reminding them of the dear ones whose lives and honour hung on the issue. Nothing is said about fighting for God and His Temple and city, but the motives adduced are not less sacred. Family love is God's best of earthly gifts, and, though it is sometimes duty to 'forget thine own people, and thy father's house,' as we have just seen, nothing short of these highest obligations can supersede the sweet one of straining every nerve for the well-being of dear ones in the hallowed circle of home.

So the plan of a sudden rush came to nothing. It does not appear that the enemy was in sight; but the news of the demonstration soon reached them, and was effectual. Prompt preparation against possible dangers is often the means of turning them aside. Watchfulness is indispensable to vigour of Christian character and efficiency of work. Suspicion is hateful and weakening; but a man who tries to serve God in such a world as this had need to be like the living creatures in the Revelation, having 'eyes all over.' 'Blessed is the man that [in that sense] feareth always.'

The upshot of the alarm is very beautifully told: 'We returned all of us to the wall, every one unto his work.' No time was wasted in jubilation. The work was the main thing, and the moment the interruption was ended, back to it they all went. It is a fine illustration of persistent discharge of duty, and of that most valuable quality, the ability and inclination to keep up the main purpose of a life continuous through interruptions, like a stream of sweet water running through a bog.

III. The remainder of the passage tells us of the standing arrangements made in consequence of the alarm (vs. 16-21). First we hear what Nehemiah did with his own special 'servants,' whether these were slaves who had accompanied him from Shushan (as Stanley supposes), or his body-guard as a Persian official. He divided them into two parts—one to work, one to watch. But he did not carry out this plan with the mass of the people, probably because it would have too largely diminished the number of builders. So he armed them all. The labourers who carried stones, mortar, and the like, could do their work after a fashion with one hand, and so they had a weapon in the other. If they worked in pairs, that would be all the easier. The actual builders needed both hands, and so they had swords stuck in their girdles.

No doubt such arrangements hindered progress, but they were necessary. The lesson often drawn from them is no doubt true, that God's workers must be prepared for warfare as well as building. There have been epochs in which that necessity was realised in a very sad manner; and the Church on earth will always have to be the Church militant. But it is well to remember that building is the end, and fighting is but the means. The trowel, not the sword, is the natural instrument. Controversy is second best—a necessity, no doubt, but an unwelcome one, and only permissible as a subsidiary help to doing the true work, rearing the walls of the city of God.

'He that soundeth the trumpet was by me.' The gallant leader was everywhere, animating by his presence. He meant to be in the thick of the fight, if it should come. And so he kept the trumpeter by his side, and gave orders that when he sounded all should hurry to the place; for there the enemy would be, and Nehemiah would be where they were. 'The work is great and large, and we are separated ... one far from another.' How naturally the words lend themselves to the old lesson so often drawn from them! God's servants are widely parted, by distance, by time, and, alas! by less justifiable causes. Unless they draw together they will be overwhelmed, taken in detail, and crushed. They must rally to help each other against the common foe.

Thank God! the longing for manifest Christian unity is deeper to-day than ever it was. But much remains to be done before it is adequately fulfilled in the recognition of the common bond of brotherhood, which binds us all in one family, if we have one Father. English and American Christians are bound to seek the tightening of the bonds between them and to set themselves against politicians who may seek to keep apart those who both in the flesh and in the spirit are brothers. All Christians have one great Captain; and He will be in the forefront of every battle. His clear trumpet-call should gather all His servants to His side.

The closing verse tells again how Nehemiah's immediate dependants divided work and watching, and adds to the picture the continuousness of their toil from the first grey of morning till darkness showed the stars and ended another day of toil. Happy they who thus 'from morn till noon, from noon till dewy eve,' labour in the work of the Lord! For them, every new morning will dawn with new strength, and every evening be calm with the consciousness of 'something attempted, something done.'

AN ANCIENT NONCONFORMIST

'... So did not I, because of the fear of God.'—NEH. v. 15.

I DO not suppose that the ordinary Bible-reader knows very much about Nehemiah. He is one of the neglected great men of Scripture. He was no prophet, he had no glowing words, he had no lofty visions, he had no special commission, he did not live in the heroic age. There was a certain harshness and dryness; a tendency towards what, when it was more fully developed, became Pharisaism, in the man, which somewhat covers the essential nobleness of his character. But he was brave, cautious, circumspect, disinterested; and he had Jerusalem in his heart.

The words that I have read are a little fragment of his autobiography which deal with a prosaic enough matter, but carry in them large principles. When he was appointed governor of the little colony of returned exiles in Palestine, he found that his predecessors, like Turkish pashas and Chinese mandarins to-day, had been in the habit of 'squeezing' the people of their Government, and that they had requisitioned sufficient supplies of provisions to keep the governor's table well spread. It was the custom. Nobody would have wondered if Nehemiah had conformed to it; but he felt that he must have his hands clean. Why did he not do what everybody else had done in like circumstances? His answer is beautifully simple: 'Because of the fear of God.' His religion went down into the little duties of common life, and imposed upon him a standard far above the maxims that were prevalent round about him. And so, if you will take these words, and disengage them from the small matter concerning which they were originally spoken, I think you will find in them thoughts as to the attitude which we should take to prevalent practices, the motive which should impel us to a sturdy non-compliance, and the power which will enable us to walk on a solitary road. 'So did not I, because of the fear of God.' Now, then, these are my three points:—

I. The attitude to prevalent practices.

Nehemiah would not conform. And unless you can say 'No!' and do it very often, your life will be shattered from the beginning. That non-compliance with customary maxims and practices is the beginning, or, at least, one of the foundation-stones, of all nobleness and strength, of all blessedness and power. Of course it is utterly impossible for a man to denude himself of the influences that are brought to bear upon him by the circumstances in which he lives, and the trend of opinion, and the maxims and practices of the world, in the corner, and at the time, in which his lot is cast. But, on the other hand, be sure of this, that unless you are in a very deep and not at all a technical sense of the word, 'Nonconformists,' you will come to no good. None! It is so easy to do as others do, partly because of laziness, partly because of cowardice, partly because of the instinctive imitation which is in us all. Men are gregarious. One great teacher has drawn an illustration from a flock of sheep, and says that if we hold up a stick, and the first of the flock jumps over it, and then if we take away the stick, all the rest of the flock will jump when they come to the point where the first did so. A great many of us adopt our creeds and opinions, and shape our lives for no better reason than because people round us are thinking in a certain direction, and living in a certain way. It saves a great deal of trouble, and it gratifies a certain strange instinct that is in us all, and it avoids dangers and conflicts that we should, when we are at Rome, do as the Romans do. 'So did not I, because of the fear of God.'

Now, brethren! I ask you to take this plain principle of the necessity of non-compliance (which I suppose I do not need to do much to establish, because, theoretically, we most of us admit it), and apply it all round the circumference of your lives. Apply it to your opinions. There is no tyranny like the tyranny of a majority in a democratic country like ours. It is quite as harsh as the tyranny of the old-fashioned despots. Unless you resolve steadfastly to see with your own eyes, to use your own brains, to stand on your own feet, to be a voice and not an echo, you will be helplessly enslaved by the fashion of the hour, and the opinions that prevail.

'What everybody says'—perhaps—'is true.' What most people say, at any given time, is very likely to be false. Truth has always lived with minorities, so do not let the current of widespread opinion sweep you away, but try to have a mind of your own, and not to be brow-beaten or overborne because the majority of the people round about you are giving utterance, and it may be unmeasured utterance, to any opinions.

Now, there is one direction in which I wish to urge that especially—and now I speak mainly to the young men in my congregation—and that is, in regard to the attitude that so many amongst us are taking to Christian truth. If you have honestly thought out the subject to the best of your ability, and have come to conclusions diverse from those which men like me hold dearer than their lives, that is another matter. But I know that very widely there is spread to-day the fashion of unbelief. So many influential men, leaders of opinion, teachers and preachers, are giving up the old-fashioned Evangelical faith, that it takes a strong man to say that he sticks by it. It is a poor reason to give for your attitude, that unbelief is in the air, and nobody believes those old doctrines now. That may be. There are currents of opinion that are transitory, and that is one of them, depend upon it. But at all events do not be fooled out of your faith, as some of you are tending to be, for no better reason than because other people have given it up. An iceberg lowers the temperature all round it, and the iceberg of unbelief is amongst us to-day, and it has chilled a great many people who could not tell why they have lost the fervour of their faith.

On the other hand, let me remind you that a mere traditional religion, which is only orthodox because other people are so, and has not verified its beliefs by personal experience, is quite as deleterious as an imitative unbelief. Doubtless, I speak to some who plume themselves on 'never having been affected by these currents of popular opinion,' but whose unblemished and unquestioned orthodoxy has no more vitality in it than the other people's heterodoxy. The one man has said, 'What is everywhere always, and by all believed, I believe'; and the other man has said, 'What the select spirits of this day disbelieve, I disbelieve,' and the belief of one and the unbelief of the other are equally worthless, and really identical.

But it is not only, nor mainly, in reference to opinion that I would urge upon you this nonconformity with prevalent practices as the measure of most that is noble in us. I dare not talk to you as if I knew much about the details of Manchester commercial life, but I can say this much, that it is no excuse for shady practices in your trade to say, 'It is the custom of the trade, and everybody does it.' Nehemiah might have said: 'There never was a governor yet but took his forty shekels a day's worth'—about £1,800 of our money—'of provisions from these poor people, and I am not going to give it up because of a scruple. It is the custom, and because it is the custom I can do it.' I am not going into details. It is commonly understood that preachers know nothing about business; that may be true, or it may not. But this, I am sure, is a word in season for some of my friends this evening —do not hide behind the trade. Come out into the open, and deal with the questions of morality involved in your commercial life, as you will have to deal with them hereafter, by yourself. Never mind about other people. 'Oh,' but you say, 'that involves loss.' Very likely! Nehemiah was a poorer man because he fed all these one hundred and fifty Jews at his table, but he did not mind that. It may involve loss, but you will keep God, and that is gain.

Turn this searchlight in another direction. I see a number of young people in my congregation at this moment, young men who are perhaps just beginning their career in this city, and who possibly have been startled when they heard the kind of talk that was going on at the next desk, or from the man that sits beside them on the benches at College. Do not be tempted to follow that multitude to do evil. Unless you are prepared to say 'No!' to a great deal that will be pushed into your face in this great city, as sure as you are living you will make shipwreck of your lives. Do you think that in the forty years and more that I have stood here I have not seen successive generations of young men come into Manchester? I could people many of these pews with the faces of such, who came here buoyant, full of hope, full of high resolves, and with a mother's benediction hanging over their heads, and who got into a bad set, and had not the strength to say 'No,' and they went down and down and down, and then presently somebody asked, 'Where is so-and-so?' 'Oh! his health broke down, and he has gone home to die.' 'His bones are full of the iniquity of his youth'—and he made shipwreck of prospects and of life, because he did not pull himself together when the temptation came, and say, 'So did not I, because of the fear of God.'

II. Now let me ask you to turn with me to the second thought that my text suggests to me; that is,

The motive that impels to this sturdy non-compliance.

Nehemiah puts it in Old Testament phraseology, 'the fear of God'; the New Testament equivalent is 'the love of Christ.' And if you want to take the power and the life out of both phrases, in order to find a modern conventional equivalent, you will say 'religion.' I prefer the old-fashioned language. 'The love of Christ' impels to this non-compliance. Now, my point is this, that Jesus Christ requires from each of us that we shall abstain, restrict ourselves, refuse to do a great many things that are being done round us.

I need not remind you of how continually He spoke about taking up the cross. I need not do more than just remind you of His parable of the two ways, but ask you, whilst you think of it, to note that all the characteristics of each of the ways which He sets forth are given by Him as reasons for refusing the one and walking in the other. For example, 'Enter ye in at the strait gate, for strait is the gate'—that is a reason for going in; 'and narrow is the way'—that is a reason for going in; 'and few there be that find it'—that is a reason for going in. 'Wide is the gate'—that is a reason for stopping out; 'and broad is the way'—that is a reason for stopping out; 'and many there be that go in thereat'—that is a reason for stopping out. Is not that what I said, that the minority is generally right and the majority wrong? Just because there are so many people on the path, suspect it, and expect that the path with fewer travellers is probably the better and the higher.

But to pass from that, what did Jesus Christ mean

by His continual contrast between His disciples and the world? What did He mean by 'the world'? This fair universe, with all its possibilities of help and blessing, and all its educational influences? By no means. He meant by 'the world' the aggregate of things and men considered as separate from God. And when He applied the term to men only, He meant by it very much what we mean when we talk about society. Society is not organised on Christian principles; we all know that, and until it is, if a man is going to be a Christian he must not conform to the world. 'Know ye not that whosoever is a friend of the world is an enemy of God.'

I would press upon you, dear friends! that our Christianity is nothing unless it leads us to a standard, and a course of conduct in conformity with that standard, which will be in diametrical opposition to a great deal of what is patted on the back, and petted and praised by society. Now, there is an easy-going kind of Christianity which does not recognise that, and which is in great favour with many people to-day, and is called 'liberality' and 'breadth,' and 'conciliating and commending Christianity to outsiders,' and I know not what besides. Well, Christ's words seem to me to come down like a hammer upon that sort of thing. Depend upon it, 'the world'—I mean by that the aggregate of godless men organised as they are in society—does not think much of these trimmers. It may dislike an out-and-out Christian, but it knows him when it sees him, and it has a kind of hostile respect for him which the other people will never get. You remember the story of the man that was seeking for a coachman, and whose question to each applicant was, 'How near can you drive to the edge of a precipice?'

He took the man who said: 'I would keep away from it as far as I could.' And the so-called Christian people that seem to be bent on showing how much their lives can be made to assimilate to the lives of men that have no sympathy with their creeds, are like the rash Jehus that tried to go as near the edge as they could. But the consistent Christian will keep as far away from it as he can. There are some of us who seem as if we were most anxious to show that we, whose creed is absolutely inconsistent with the world's practices, can live lives which are all but identical with these practices. Jesus Christ says, through the lips of His Apostle, what He often said in other language by His own lips when He was here on earth: 'Be ye not conformed to the world.'

Surely such a command as that, just because it involves difficulty, self-restraint, self-denial, and sometimes self-crucifixion, ought to appeal, and does appeal, to all that is noble in humanity, in a fashion that that smooth, easy-going gospel of living on the level of the people round us never can do. For remember that Christ's commandment not to be conformed to the world is the consequence of His commandment to be conformed to Himself. 'Thus did not I' comes second; 'This one thing I do' comes first. You will misunderstand the whole genius of the Gospel if you suppose that, as a law of life, it is perpetually pulling men short up, and saying: Don't, don't, don't! There is a Christianity of that sort which is mainly prohibition and restriction, but it is not Christ's Christianity. He begins by enjoining: 'This do in remembrance of Me,' and the man that has accepted that commandment must necessarily say, as he looks out on the world, and its practices: 'So did not I, because of the fear of God.'

III. And now one last word—my text not only suggests the motive which impels to this non-compliance, but also the power which enables us to exercise it.

'The fear of God,' or, taking the New Testament equivalent, 'the love of Christ,' makes it possible for a man, with all his weakness and dependence on surroundings, with all his instinctive desire to be like the folk that are near him, to take that brave attitude, and to refuse to be one of the crowd that runs after evil and lies. I have no time to dwell upon this aspect of my subject, as I should be glad to have done. Let me sum up in a sentence or two what I would have said. Christ will enable you to take this necessary attitude because, in Himself He gives you the Example which it is always safe to follow. The instinct of imitation is planted in us for a good end, and because it is in us, examples of nobility appeal to us. And because it is in us Jesus Christ has lived the life that it is possible for, and therefore incumbent on, us to live. It is safe to imitate Him, and it is easy not to do as men do, if once our main idea is to do as Christ did.

He makes it possible for us, because He gives the strongest possible motive for the life that He prescribes. As the Apostle puts it, 'Ye are bought with a price, be not the servants of men.' There is nothing that will so deliver us from the tyranny of majorities, and of what we call general opinion and ordinary custom, as to feel that we belong to Him because He died for us. Men become very insignificant when Christ speaks, and the charter of our freedom from them lies in our redemption by the blood of Jesus Christ.

Jesus Christ being our Redeemer is our Judge, and

moment by moment He is estimating our conduct, and judging our actions as they are done. 'With me it is a very small matter to be judged of you or of man's judgment. He that judgeth me is the Lord.' Never mind what the people round you say; you do not take your orders from them, and you do not answer to them. Like some official abroad, appointed by the Crown, you do not report to the local authorities; you report to headquarters, and what He thinks about you is the only important thing. So 'the fear of man which bringeth a snare' dwindles down into very minute dimensions when we think of the Pattern, the Redeemer and the Judge to whom we give account.

And so, dear friends! if we will only open our hearts, by quiet humble faith, for the coming of Jesus Christ into our lives, then we shall be able to resist, to refuse compliance, to stand firm, though alone. The servant of Christ is the master of all men. 'All things are yours, whether Paul, or Apollos, or Cephas—all are yours, and ye are Christ's.'

READING THE LAW WITH TEARS AND JOY

And all the people gathered themselves together as one man into the street that was before the water gate; and they spake unto Ezra the scribe to bring the book of the law of Moses, which the Lord had commanded to Israel. 2. And Ezra the priest brought the law before the congregation both of men and women, and all that could hear with understanding, upon the first day of the seventh month. 3. And he read therein before the street that was before the water gate, from the morning until midday, before the men and the women, and those that could understand; and the ears of all the people were attentive unto the book of the law. 4. And Ezra the scribe stood upon a pulpit of wood, which they had made for the purpose; and beside him stood Mattithiah, and Shema, and Anaiah, and Urijah, and Hilkiah, and Maaseiah, on his right hand; and on his left hand Pedaiah, and Mishael, and Malchiah, and Hashum, and Hashbadana, Zechariah, and Meshullam. 5. And Ezra opened the book in the sight of all the people; (for he was above all the people); and when he opened it, all the people stood up: 6. And Ezra blessed the Lord, the great God. And all the people answered, Amen, Amen, with lifting up their hands: and they bowed their heads, and worshipped the Lord with their faces to the ground. 7. Also Jeshua, and Bani, and Sherebiah, Jamin, Akkub, Shabbethai, Hodijah, Maaseiah, Kelita, Azariah, Jozabad, Hanan, Pelaiah, and the Levites, caused the people to understand the law: and the people stood in their place. 8. So they read in the book in the law of God distinctly, and gave the sense, and caused them to understand the reading. 9. And Nehemiah, which is the Tirshatha, and Ezra the priest the scribe, and the Levites that taught the people, said unto all the people, This day is holy unto the Lord your God; mourn not, nor weep. For all the people wept, when they heard the words of the law. 10. Then he said unto them, Go your way, eat the fat, and drink the sweet, and send portions unto them for whom nothing is prepared: for this day is holy unto our Lord: neither be ye sorry; for the joy of the Lord is your strength. 11. So the Levites stilled all the people, saying, Hold your peace, for the day is holy; neither be ye grieved. 12. And all the people went their way to eat, and to drink, and to send portions, and to make great mirth, because they had understood the words that were declared unto them.'—NEH. viii. 1-12.

THE wall was finished on the twenty-fifth day of the month Elul, which was the sixth month. The events recorded in this passage took place on the first day of the seventh month. The year is not given, but the natural inference is that it was the same as that of the finishing of the wall; namely, the twentieth of Artaxerxes. If so, the completion of the fortifications to which Nehemiah had set himself, was immediately followed by this reading of the law, in which Ezra takes the lead. The two men stand in a similar relative position to that of Zerubbabel and Joshua, the one representing the civil and the other the religious authority.

According to Ezra vii. 9, Ezra had gone to Jerusalem about thirteen years before Nehemiah, and had had a weary time of fighting against the corruptions which had crept in among the returned captives. The arrival of Nehemiah would be hailed as bringing fresh, young enthusiasm, none the less welcome and powerful because it had the king's authority entrusted to it. Evidently the two men thoroughly understood one another, and pulled together heartily. We heard nothing about Ezra while the wall was being built. But now he is the principal figure, and Nehemiah is barely mentioned. The reasons for Ezra's taking the prominent part in the reading of the law are given in the two titles by which he is designated in two successive verses (vers. 1, 2). He was 'the scribe' and also 'the priest,' and in both capacities was the natural person for such a work.

The seventh month was the festival month of the year, its first day being that of the Feast of trumpets, and the great Feast of tabernacles as well as the solemn day of atonement occurring in it. Possibly, the prospect of the coming of the times for these celebrations may have led to the people's wish to hear the law, that they might duly observe the appointed ceremonial. At all events, the first thing to note is that it was in consequence of the people's wish that the law was read in their hearing. Neither Ezra nor Nehemiah originated the gathering together. They obeyed a popular impulse which they had not created. We must not, indeed, give the multitude credit for much more than the wish to have their ceremonial right. But there was at least that wish, and possibly something deeper and more spiritual. The walls were completed; but the true defence of Israel was in God, and the condition of His defending was Israel's obedience to His law. The people were, in some measure, beginning to realise that condition with new clearness, in consequence of the new fervour which Nehemiah had brought.

It is singular that, during his thirteen years of residence, Ezra is not recorded to have promulgated the law, though it lay at the basis of the drastic reforms which he was able to carry through. Probably he had not been silent, but the solemn public recitation of the law was felt to be appropriate on occasion of completing the wall. Whether the people had heard it before, or, as seems implied, it was strange to them, their desire to hear it may stand as a pattern for us of that earnest wish to know God's will which is never cherished in vain. He who does not intend to obey does not wish to know the law. If we have no longing to know what the will of the Lord is, we may be very sure that we prefer our own to His. If we desire to know it, we shall desire to understand the Book which contains so much of it. Any true religion in the heart will make us eager to perceive, and willing to be guided by, the will of God, revealed mainly in Scripture, in the Person, works, and words of Jesus, and also in waiting hearts by the Spirit, and in those things which the world calls 'circumstances' and faith names 'providences.'

II. Verses 2-8 appear to tell the same incidents twice over—first, more generally in verses 2 and 3, and then more minutely. Such expanded repetition is characteristic of the Old Testament historical style. It is somewhat difficult to make sure of the real circumstances. Clearly enough there was a solemn assembly of men, women, and children in a great open space outside one of the gates, and there, from dawn till noon, the law was read and explained. But whether Ezra read it all, while the Levites named in verse 7 explained or paraphrased or translated it, or whether they all read in turns, or whether there were a number of groups, each of which had a teacher who both read and expounded, is hard to determine. At all events, Ezra was the principal figure, and began the reading.

It was a picturesque scene. The sun, rising over the slopes of Olivet, would fall on the gathered crowd, if the water-gate was, as is probable, on the east or south-east side of the city. Beneath the fresh fortifications probably, which would act as a sounding-board for the reader, was set up a scaffold high above the crowd, large enough to hold Ezra and thirteen supporters—principal men, no doubt—seven on one side of him and six on the other. Probably a name has dropped out, and the numbers were equal. There, in the morning light, with the new walls for a background, stood Ezra on his rostrum, and amid reverent silence, lifted high the sacred roll. A common impulse swayed the crowd, and brought them all to their feet —token at once of respect and obedient attention. Probably many of them had never seen a sacred roll. To them all it was comparatively unfamiliar. No wonder that, as Ezra's voice rose in prayer, the whole assembly fell on their faces in adoration, and every lip responded 'Amen! amen!'

Much superstition may have mingled with the reverence. No doubt, there was then what we are often solemnly warned against now, bibliolatry. But in this time of critical investigation it is not the divine element in Scripture which is likely to be exaggerated; and few are likely to go wrong in the direction of paying too much reverence to the Book in which, as is still believed, God has revealed His will and Himself. While welcoming all investigations which throw light on its origin or its meaning, and perfectly recognising the human element in it, we should learn the lesson taught by that waiting crowd prone on their faces, and blessing God for His word. Such attitude must ever precede reading it, if we are to read aright.

Hour after hour the recitation went on. We must let the question of the precise form of the events remain undetermined. It is somewhat singular that thirteen names are enumerated as of the men who stood by Ezra, and thirteen as those of the readers or expounders. It may be the case that the former number is complete, though uneven, and that there was some reason unknown for dividing the audience into just so many sections. The second set of thirteen was not composed of the same men as the first. They seem to have been Levites, whose office of assisting at the menial parts of the sacrifices was now elevated into that of setting forth the law. Probably the portions read were such as bore especially on ritual, though the tears of the listeners are sufficient proof that they had heard some things that went deeper than that.

The word rendered 'distinctly' in the Revised Version (margin, *with an interpretation*) is ambiguous, and may either mean that the Levites explained or that they translated the words. The former is the more probable, as there is no reason to suppose that the audience, most of whom had been born in the land, were ignorant of Hebrew. But if the ritual had been irregularly observed, and the circle of ideas in the law become unfamiliar, many explanations would be necessary. It strikes one as touching and strange that such an assembly should be needed after so many centuries of national existence. It sums up in one vivid picture the sin and suffering of the nation. To observe that law had been the condition of their prosperity. To bind it on their hearts should have been their delight and would have been their life; and here, after all these generations, the best of the nation are assembled, so ignorant of it that they cannot even understand it when they hear it. Absorption with worldly things has an awful power of dulling spiritual apprehension. Neglect of God's law weakens the power of understanding it.

This scene was in the truest sense a 'revival.' We may learn the true way of bringing men back to God;

namely, the faithful exposition and enforcement of God's will and word. We may learn, too, what should be the aim of public teachers of religion; namely, first and foremost, the clear setting forth of God's truth. Their first business is to 'give the sense, so that they understand the reading'; and that, not for merely intellectual purposes, but that, like the crowd outside the water-gate on that hot noonday, men may be moved to penitence, and then lifted to the joy of the Lord.

The first day of the seventh month was the Feast of trumpets; and when the reading was over, and its effects of tears and sorrow for disobedience were seen, the preachers changed their tone, to bring consolation and exhort to gladness. Nehemiah had taken no part in reading the law, as Ezra the priest and his Levites were more appropriately set to that. But he joins them in exhorting the people to dry their tears, and go joyfully to the feast. These exhortations contain many thoughts universally applicable. They teach that even those who are most conscious of sin and breaches of God's law should weep indeed, but should swiftly pass from tears to joy. They do not teach how that passage is to be effected; and in so far they are imperfect, and need to be supplemented by the New Testament teaching of forgiveness through the sacrifice of Jesus Christ. But in their clear discernment that sorrow is not meant to be a permanent characteristic of religion, and that gladness is a more acceptable offering than tears, they teach a valuable lesson, needed always by men who fancy that they must atone for their sins by their own sadness, and that religion is gloomy, harsh, and crabbed.

Further, these exhortations to festal gladness breathe the characteristic Old Testament tone of wholesome enjoyment of material good as a part of religion. The way of looking at eating and drinking and the like, as capable of being made acts of worship, has been too often forgotten by two kinds of men—saints who have sought sanctity in asceticism; and sensualists who have taken deep draughts of such pleasures without calling on the name of the Lord, and so have failed to find His gifts a cup of salvation. It is possible to 'eat and drink and see God,' as the elders of Israel did on Sinai.

Further, the plain duty of remembering the needy while we enjoy God's gifts is beautifully enjoined here. The principle underlying the commandment to 'send portions to them for whom nothing is provided'—that is, for whom no feast has been dressed—is that all gifts are held in trust, that nothing is bestowed on us for our own good only, but that we are in all things stewards. The law extends to the smallest and to the greatest possessions. We have no right to feast on anything unless we share it, whether it be festal dainties or the bread that came down from heaven. To divide our portion with others is the way to make our portion greater as well as sweeter.

Further, 'the joy of the Lord is your strength.' By *strength* here seems to be meant a *stronghold*. If we fix our desires on God, and have trained our hearts to find sweeter delights in communion with Him than in any earthly good, our religion will have lifted us above mists and clouds into clear air above, where sorrows and changes will have little power to affect us. If we are to rejoice in the Lord, it will be possible for us to 'rejoice always,' and that joy will be as a refuge from all the ills that flesh is heir to. Dwelling in God, we shall dwell safely, and be far from the fear of evil.

THE JOY OF THE LORD

'The joy of the Lord is your strength.'—NEH. viii. 10.

JUDAISM, in its formal and ceremonial aspect, was a religion of gladness. The feast was the great act of worship. It is not to be wondered at, that Christianity, the perfecting of that ancient system, has been less markedly felt to be a religion of joy; for it brings with it far deeper and more solemn views about man in his nature, condition, responsibilities, destinies, than ever prevailed before, under any system of worship. And yet all deep religion ought to be joyful, and all strong religion assuredly will be so.

Here, in the incident before us, there has come a time in Nehemiah's great enterprise, when the law, long forgotten, long broken by the captives, is now to be established again as the rule of the newly-founded commonwealth. Naturally enough there comes a remembrance of many sins in the past history of the people; and tears not unnaturally mingle with the thankfulness that again they are a nation, having a divine worship and a divine law in their midst. The leader of them, knowing for one thing that if the spirits of his people once began to flag, they could not face nor conquer the difficulties of their position, said to them, 'This day is holy unto the Lord: this feast that we are keeping is a day of devout worship; therefore mourn not, nor weep: go your way; eat the fat, and drink the sweet, and send portions unto them for whom nothing is prepared; neither be ye sorry, for the joy of the Lord is your strength.' You will make nothing of it by indulgence in lamentation and in mourning. You will have no more power for obedience, you will not be fit for your work, if you fall into a desponding state. Be thankful and glad; and remember that the purest worship is the worship of God-fixed joy, 'the joy of the Lord is your strength.' And that is as true, brethren! with regard to us, as it ever was in these old times; and we, I think, need the lesson contained in this saying of Nehemiah's, because of some prevalent tendencies amongst us, no less than these Jews did. Take some simple thoughts suggested by this text which are both important in themselves and needful to be made emphatic because so often forgotten in the ordinary type of Christian character. They are these. Religious Joy is the natural result of faith. It is a Christian duty. It is an important element in Christian strength.

I. Joy in the Lord is the natural result of Christian Faith.

There is a natural adaptation or provision in the Gospel, both by what it brings to us and by what it takes away from us, to make a calm, and settled, and deep gladness, the prevalent temper of the Christian spirit. In what it gives us, I say, and in what it takes away from us. It gives us what we call well a sense of acceptance with God, it gives us God for the rest of our spirits, it gives us the communion with Him which in proportion as it is real, will be still, and in proportion as it is still, will be all bright and joyful. It takes away from us the fear that lies before us, the strifes that lie within us, the desperate conflict that is waged between a man's conscience and his inclinations, between his will and his passions, which tears the heart asunder, and always makes sorrow and tumult wherever it comes. It takes away the sense of sin. It gives us, instead of the torpid conscience, or the angrily-stinging conscience—a conscience all calm from its accusations, with all the sting drawn out of it:—for quiet peace lies in the heart of the man that is trusting in the Lord. The Gospel works joy, because the soul is at rest in God; joy, because every function of the spiritual nature has found now its haven and its object; joy, because health has come, and the healthy working of the body or of the spirit is itself a gladness; joy, because the dim future is painted (where it is painted at all) with shapes of light and beauty, and because the very vagueness of these is an element in the greatness of its revelation. The joy that is in Christ is deep and abiding. Faith in Him naturally works gladness.

I do not forget that, on the other side, it is equally true that the Christian faith has as marked and almost as strong an adaptation to produce a solemn *sorrow*—solemn, manly, noble, and strong. 'As sorrowful, yet always rejoicing,' is the rule of the Christian life. If we think of what our faith does; of the light that it casts upon our condition, upon our nature, upon our responsibilities, upon our sins, and upon our destinies, we can easily see how, if gladness be one part of its operation, no less really and truly is sadness another. Brethren! all great thoughts have a solemn quiet in them, which not unfrequently merges into a still sorrow. There is nothing more contemptible in itself, and there is no more sure mark of a trivial nature and a trivial round of occupations, than unshaded gladness, that rests on no deep foundations of quiet, patient grief; grief, because I know what I am and what I ought to be; grief, because I have learnt the 'exceeding sinfulness of sin'; grief, because, looking out upon the world, I see, as other men do not see, hell-fire burning at the back of the mirth and the laughter, and know what it is that men are hurrying to! Do you remember who it was that stood by the side of the one poor dumb man, whose tongue He was going to loose, and looking up to heaven, *sighed* before He could say, 'Be opened'? Do you remember that of Him it is said, 'God hath anointed Thee with the oil of gladness above Thy fellows'; and also, 'a Man of sorrows, and acquainted with grief'? And do you not think that both these characteristics are to be repeated in the operations of His Gospel upon every heart that receives it? And if, by the hopes it breathes into us, by the fears that it takes away from us, by the union with God that it accomplishes for us, by the fellowship that it implants in us, it indeed anoints us all 'with the oil of gladness'; yet, on the other hand, by the sense of mine own sin that it teaches me; by the conflict with weakness which it makes to be the law of my life; by the clear vision which it gives me of 'the law of my members warring against the law of my mind, and bringing me into subjection'; by the intensity which it breathes into all my nature, and by the thoughts that it presents of what sin leads to, and what the world at present is, the Gospel, wheresoever it comes, will infuse a wise, valiant sadness as the very foundation of character. Yes, joy, but sorrow too! the joy of the Lord, but sorrow as we look on our own sin and the world's woe! the head anointed with the oil of gladness, but also crowned with thorns!

These two are not contradictory. These two states of mind, both of them the natural operations of any deep faith, may co-exist and blend into one another, so as that the gladness is sobered, and chastened, and made manly and noble; and that the sorrow is like some thundercloud, all streaked with bars of sunshine, that pierce into its deepest depths. The joy lives in the midst of the sorrow; the sorrow springs from the same root as the gladness. The two do not clash against each other, or reduce the emotion to a neutral indifference, but they blend into one another; just as, in the Arctic regions, deep down beneath the cold snow, with its white desolation and its barren death, you will find the budding of the early spring flowers and the fresh green grass; just as some kinds of fire burn below the water; just as, in the midst of the barren and undrinkable sea, there may be welling up some little fountain of fresh water that comes from a deeper depth than the great ocean around it, and pours its sweet streams along the surface of the salt waste. Gladness, because I love, for love *is* gladness; gladness, because I trust, for trust *is* gladness; gladness, because I obey, for obedience is a meat that others know not of, and light comes when we do His will! But sorrow, because still I am wrestling with sin; sorrow, because still I have not perfect fellowship; sorrow, because mine eye, purified by my living with God, sees earth, and sin, and life, and death, and the generations of men, and the darkness beyond, in some measure as God sees them! And yet, the sorrow is surface, and the joy is central; the sorrow springs from circumstance, and the gladness from the essence of the thing;—and therefore the sorrow is transitory, and the gladness is perennial. For the Christian life is all like one of those sweet spring showers in early April, when the rain-drops weave for us a mist that hides the sunshine; and yet the hidden sun is in every sparkling drop, and they are all saturated and steeped in its light. 'The joy of the

Lord' is the natural result and offspring of all Christian faith.

II. And now, secondly, the 'joy of the Lord' or rejoicing in God, is a matter of Christian duty.

It is a commandment here, and it is a command in the New Testament as well. 'Neither be ye sorry, for the joy of the Lord is your strength.' I need not quote to you the frequent repetitions of the same injunction which the Apostle Paul gives us, 'Rejoice in the Lord always, and again I say, Rejoice'; 'Rejoice evermore,' and the like. The fact that this joy is enjoined us suggests to us a thought or two, worth looking at.

You may say with truth, 'My emotions of joy and sorrow are not under my own control: I cannot help being glad and sad as circumstances dictate.' But yet here it lies, a commandment. It is a duty, a thing that the Apostle enjoins; in which, of course, is implied, that somehow or other it is to a large extent within one's own power, and that even the indulgence in this emotion, and the degree to which a Christian life shall be a cheerful life, is dependent in a large measure on our own volitions, and stands on the same footing as our obedience to God's other commandments.

We *can* to a very great extent control even our own emotions; but then, besides, we can do more than that. It may be quite true, that you cannot help feeling sorrowful in the presence of sorrowful thoughts, and glad in the presence of thoughts that naturally kindle gladness. But I will tell you what you can do or refrain from doing—you can either go and stand in the light, or you can go and stand in the shadow. You can either fix your attention upon, and make the predominant subject of your religious contemplations, a truth which shall make you glad and strong, or a half-truth, which shall make you sorrowful, and therefore weak. Your meditations may either centre mainly upon your own selves, your faults and failings, and the like; or they may centre mainly upon God and His love, Christ and His grace, the Holy Spirit and His communion. You may either fill your soul with joyful thoughts, or though a true Christian, a real, devout, God-accepted believer, you may be so misapprehending the nature of the Gospel, and your relation to it, its promises and precepts, its duties and predictions, as that the prevalent tinge and cast of your religion shall be solemn and almost gloomy, and not lighted up and irradiated with the felt sense of God's presence—with the strong, healthy consciousness that you are a forgiven and justified man, and that you are going to be a glorified one.

And thus far (and it is a long way) by the selection or the rejection of the appropriate and proper subjects which shall make the main portion of our religious contemplation, and shall be the food of our devout thoughts, we *can* determine the complexion of our religious life. Just as you inject colouring matter into the fibres of some anatomical preparation; so a Christian may, as it were, inject into all the veins of his religious character and life, either the bright tints of gladness or the dark ones of self-despondency; and the result will be according to the thing that he has put into them. If your thoughts are chiefly occupied with God, and what He has done and is for you, then you will have peaceful joy. If, on the other hand, they are bent ever on yourself and your own unbelief, then you will always be sad. You can make your choice.

Christian men, the joy of the Lord is a duty. It is so because, as we have seen, it is the natural effect of faith, because we can do much to regulate our emotions directly, and much more to determine them by determining what set of thoughts shall engage us. A wise and strong faith is our duty. To keep our emotional nature well under control of reason and will is our duty. To lose thoughts of ourselves in God's truth about Himself is our duty. If we do these things, we cannot fail to have Christ's joy remaining in us, and making ours full. If we have not that blessed possession abiding with us, which He lived and died to give us, there is something wrong in us somewhere.

It seems to me that this is a truth which we have great need, my friends, to lay to heart. It is of no great consequence that we should practically confute the impotent old sneer about religion as being a gloomy thing. One does not need to mind much what some people say on that matter. The world would call 'the joy of the Lord' gloom, just as much as it calls 'godly sorrow' gloom. But we are losing for ourselves a power and an energy of which we have no conception, unless we feel that joy is a duty, and unless we believe that not to be joyful in the Lord is, therefore, more than a misfortune, it is a fault.

I do not forget that the comparative absence of this happy, peaceful sense of acceptance, harmony, oneness with God, springs sometimes from temperament, and depends on our natural disposition. Of course the natural character determines to a large extent the perspective of our conceptions of Christian truth, and the colouring of our inner religious life. I do not mean to say, for a moment, that there is one uniform type to which all must be conformed, or they sin. There is indeed one type, the perfect manhood of Jesus, but it is all comprehensive, and each variety of our fragmentary manhood finds its own perfecting, and not its transmutation to another fashion of man, in being conformed to Him. Some of us are naturally fainthearted, timid, sceptical of any success, grave, melancholy, or hard to stir to any emotion. To such there will be an added difficulty in making quiet confident joy any very familiar guest in their home or in their place of prayer. But even such should remember that the 'powers of the world to come,' the energies of the Gospel, are given to us for the very express purpose of overcoming, as well as of hallowing, natural dispositions. If it be our duty to rejoice in the Lord, it is no sufficient excuse to urge for not responding to the reiterated call, 'I myself am disposed to sadness.'

Whilst making all allowances for the diversities of character, which will always operate to diversify the cast of the inner life in each individual, we think that, in the great majority of instances, there are two things, both faults, which have a great deal more to do with the absence of joy from much Christian experience, than any unfortunate natural tendency to the dark side of things. The one is, an actual deficiency in the depth and reality of our faith; and the other is, a misapprehension of the position which we have a right to take and are bound to take.

There is an actual deficiency in our faith. Oh, brethren! it is not to be wondered at that Christians do not find that the Lord with them is the Lord their strength and joy, as well as the Lord 'their righteousness'; when the amount of their fellowship with Him is so small, and the depth of it so shallow, as we usually find it. The first true vision that a sinful soul has of

God, the imperfect beginnings of religion, usually are accompanied with intense self-abhorrence, and sorrowing tears of penitence. A further closer vision of the love of God in Jesus Christ brings with it 'joy and peace in believing.' But the prolongation of these throughout life requires the steadfast continuousness of gaze towards Him. It is only where there is much faith and consequent love that there is much joy. Let us search our own hearts. If there is but little heat around the bulb of the thermometer, no wonder that the mercury marks a low degree. If there is but small faith, there will not be much gladness. The road into Giant Despair's castle is through doubt, which doubt comes from an absence, a sinful absence, in our own experience, of the felt presence of God, and the felt force of the verities of His Gospel.

But then, besides that, there is another fault: not a fault in the sense of crime or sin, but a fault (and a great one) in the sense of error and misapprehension. We as Christians do not take the position which we have a right to take and that we are bound to take. Men venture themselves upon God's word as they do on doubtful ice, timidly putting a light foot out, to feel if it will bear them, and always having the tacit fear, 'Now, it is going to crack!' You must cast yourselves on God's Gospel with all your weight, without any hanging back, without any doubt, without even the shadow of a suspicion that it will *give*—that the firm, pure floor will give, and let you through into the water! A Christian shrink from saying what the Apostle said, 'I *know* in whom I have believed, and am persuaded that He is able to keep that which I have committed to Him until that day'! A Christian fancy that salvation is a future thing, and forget that it is a present thing! A Christian tremble to profess 'assurance of hope,' forgetting that there is no hope strong enough to bear the stress of a life's sorrows, which is not a conviction certain as one's own existence! Brethren! understand that the Gospel is a Gospel which brings a present salvation; and try to feel that it is not presumption, but simply acting out the very fundamental principle of it, when you are not afraid to say, 'I *know* that my Redeemer is yonder, and I *know* that He loves me!' Try to feel, I say, that by faith you have a right to take that position, 'Now, we *know* that we are the sons of God'; that you have a right to claim for yourselves, and that you are falling beneath the loftiness of the gift that is given to you unless you do claim for yourselves, the place of sons, accepted, loved, sure to be glorified at God's right hand. Am I teaching presumption? am I teaching carelessness, or a dispensing with self-examination? No, but I am saying this: If a man have once felt, and feel, in however small and feeble a degree, and depressed by whatsoever sense of daily transgressions, if he feel, faint like the first movement of an imprisoned bird in its egg, the feeble pulse of an almost imperceptible and fluttering faith beat—then that man has a right to say, 'God is mine!'

As one of our great teachers, little remembered now said, 'Let me take my personal salvation for granted' —and what? and 'be idle?' No; 'and *work* from it.' Ay, brethren! a Christian is not to be for ever asking himself, 'Am I a Christian?' He is not to be for ever looking into himself for marks and signs that he is. He *is* to look into himself to discover sins, that he may by God's help cast them out, to discover sins that shall teach him to say with greater thankfulness,

'What a redemption this is which I possess!' but he is to base his convictions that he is God's child upon something other than his own characteristics and the feebleness of his own strength. He is to have 'joy in the Lord' whatever may be his sorrow from outward things. And I believe that if Christian people would lay that thought to heart, they would understand better how the natural operation of the Gospel is to make them glad, and how rejoicing in the Lord is a Christian duty.

III. And now with regard to the other thought that still remains to be considered, namely, that rejoicing in the Lord is a source of strength,—I have already anticipated, fragmentarily, nearly all that I could have said here in a more systematic form. All gladness has something to do with our efficiency; for it is the prerogative of man that his force comes from his mind, and not from his body. That old song about a sad heart tiring in a mile, is as true in regard to the Gospel, and the works of Christian people, as in any other case. If we have hearts full of light, and souls at rest in Christ, and the wealth and blessedness of a tranquil gladness lying there, and filling our being; work will be easy, endurance will be easy, sorrow will be bearable, trials will not be so very hard, and above all temptations we shall be lifted, and set upon a rock. If the soul is full, and full of joy, what side of it will be exposed to the assault of *any* temptation? If the appeal be to fear, the gladness that is there is an answer. If the appeal be to passion, desire, wish for pleasure of any sort, there is no need for any more—the heart is *full*. And so the gladness which rests in Christ will be a gladness which will fit us for all service and for all endurance, which will be unbroken by any sorrow, and, like the magic shield of the old legends, invisible, impenetrable, in its crystalline purity will stand before the tempted heart, and will repel all the 'fiery darts of the wicked.'

'The joy of the Lord is your strength,' my brother! Nothing else is. No vehement resolutions, no sense of his own sinfulness, nor even contrite remembrance of past failures, ever yet made a man strong. It made him weak that he might become strong, and when it had done that it had done its work. For strength there must be hope, for strength there must be joy. If the arm is to smite with vigour, it must smite at the bidding of a calm and light heart. Christian work is of such a sort as that the most dangerous opponent to it is simple despondency and simple sorrow. 'The joy of the Lord is your strength.'

Well, then! there are two questions: How comes it that so much of the world's joy is weakness? and how comes it that so much of the world's notion of religion is gloom and sadness? Answer them for yourselves, and remember: you are weak unless you are glad; you are not glad and strong unless your faith and hope are fixed in Christ, and unless you are working from and not towards the sense of pardon, from and not towards the conviction of acceptance with God!

SABBATH OBSERVANCE

'In those days saw I in Judah some treading wine presses on the sabbath, and bringing in sheaves, and lading asses; as also wine, grapes, and figs, and all manner of burdens, which they brought into Jerusalem on the sabbath day: and I testified against them in the day wherein they sold victuals. 16. There dwelt men of Tyre also therein, which brought fish, and all manner of ware, and sold on the sabbath unto the children of Judah, and in Jerusalem. 17. Then I contended with the nobles of Judah, and said unto them, What evil thing is this that ye do, and profane the sabbath day? 18. Did not your fathers thus, and did not our God bring all this evil upon us, and upon this city? yet ye bring more wrath upon Israel by profaning the sabbath. 19. And it came to pass, that when the gates of Jerusalem began to be dark before the sabbath, I commanded that the gates should be shut, and charged that they should not be opened till after the sabbath: and some of my servants set I at the gates, that there should no burden be brought in on the sabbath day. 20. So the merchants and sellers of all kind of ware lodged without Jerusalem once or twice. 21. Then I testified against them, and said unto them, Why lodge ye about the wall? if ye do so again, I will lay hands on you. From that time forth came they no more on the sabbath. 22. And I commanded the Levites that they should cleanse themselves, and that they should come and keep the gates, to sanctify the sabbath day. Remember me, O my God, concerning this also, and spare me according to the greatness of Thy mercy.'—NEH. xiii. 15-22.

MANY religious and moral reformations depend for their vitality on one man, and droop if his influence be withdrawn. It was so with Nehemiah's work. He toiled for twelve years in Jerusalem, and then returned for 'certain days' to the king at Babylon. The length of his absence is not given; but it was long enough to let much of his work be undone, and to give him much trouble to restore it to the condition in which he had left it. This last chapter of his book is but a sad close for a record which began with such high hope, and tells of such strenuous, self-sacrificing effort. The last page of many a reformer's history has been, like Nehemiah's, a sad account of efforts to stem the ebbing tide of enthusiasm and the flowing tide of worldliness. The heavy stone is rolled a little way up hill, and, as soon as one strong hand is withdrawn, down it tumbles again to its old place. The evanescence of great men's work makes much of the tragedy of history.

Our passage is particularly concerned with Nehemiah's efforts to enforce Sabbath observance. The rest of the chapter is occupied with similar efforts to set right other irregularities of a ceremonial character, such as the exclusion of Gentiles from the Temple, the exaction of the 'portions of the Levites,' and the like. The passage falls into three parts—the abuse (vs. 15, 16), the vigorous remedies (vs. 17-22), and the prayer (v. 22).

I. The abuse consisted in Sabbath work and trading. Nehemiah found, on his return, that the people 'in Judæa'—that is, in the country districts—carried on their farm labour and also brought their produce to market to Jerusalem on the Sabbath. So he 'testified against them in the day wherein they sold victuals'; that is, probably meaning that he warned them either in person or by messengers before taking further steps. Not only did Jews break the sacred day, but they let heathen do so too. The narrative tells, with a kind of horror, the many aggravations of this piece of wickedness. 'They'—Gentiles with whom contact defiled—'sold on the Sabbath'—the day of rest—'to the children of Judah'—God's people—'in Jerusalem'— the Holy City. It was a many-barrelled crime. Tyre was far from Jerusalem, and one does not see how fish could have been brought in good condition. Perhaps their perishableness was the excuse for allowing their sale on the Sabbath, as is sometimes the case in fishing-villages even in Sabbath-keeping Scotland. Such was the abuse with which Nehemiah struggled.

It is easy to pooh-pooh his crusade against Sabbath labour as mere scrupulousness about externals. But it is a blunder and an injustice to a noble character if we forget that the stage of revelation at which he stood necessarily made him more dependent on externals than Christians are or should be. But his vindication does not need such considerations. He had a truer insight into what active men needed for vigorous working days, and what devout men needed for healthy religion, than many moderns who smile at his eagerness about 'mere externalisms.'

It is easy to ridicule the Jewish Sabbath and 'the Puritan Sunday.' No doubt there have been and are well-meant but mistaken efforts to insist on too rigid observance. No doubt it has been often forgotten by good people that the Christian Lord's Day is not the Jewish Sabbath. Of course the religious observance of the day is not a fit subject for legislation. But the need for a seventh day of rest is impressed on our physical and intellectual nature; and devout hearts will joyfully find their best rest in Christian worship and service. The vigour of religious life demands special seasons set apart for worship. Unless there be such reservoirs along the road, there will be but a thin trickle of a brook by the way. It is all very well to talk about religion diffused through the life, but it will not be so diffused unless it is concentrated at certain times.

They are no benefactors to the community who seek to break down and relax the stringency of the prohibition of labour. If once the idea that Sunday is a day of amusement take root, the amusement of some will require the hard work of others, and the custom of work will tend to extend, till rest becomes the exception, and work the rule. There never was a time when men lived so furiously fast as now. The pace of modern life demands Sunday rest more than ever. If a railway car is run continually it will wear out sooner than if it were laid aside for a day or two occasionally; and if it is run at express speed it will need the rest more. We are all going at top speed; and there would be more breakdowns if it were not for that blessed institution which some people think they are promoting the public good by destroying—a seventh day of rest.

Our great trading centres in England have the same foreign element to complicate matters as

Nehemiah had to deal with. The Tyrian fishmongers knew and cared nothing for Israel's Jehovah or Sabbath, and their presence would increase the tendency to disregard the day. So with us, foreigners of many nationalities, but alike in their disregard of our religious observances, leaven the society, and help to mould the opinions and practices, of our great cities. That is a very real source of danger in regard to Sabbath observance and many other things; and Christian people should be on their guard against it.

II. The vigorous remedies applied by Nehemiah were administered first to the rulers. He sent for the nobles, and laid the blame at their doors. 'Ye profane the day,' said he. Men in authority are responsible for crimes which they could check, but prefer to wink at. Nehemiah seems to trace all the national calamities to the breach of the Sabbath; but of course he is simply laying stress on the sin about which he is speaking, as any man who sets himself earnestly to work to fight any form of evil is apt to do. Then the men who are not in earnest cry out about 'exaggeration.' Many other sins besides Sabbath-breaking had a share in sending Israel into captivity; and if Nehemiah had been fighting with idolatrous tendencies he would have isolated idolatry as the cause of its calamities, just as, when fighting against Sabbath-breaking, he emphasises that sin.

Nehemiah was governor for the Persian king, and so had a right to rate these nobles. In this day the people have the same right, and there are many social sins for which they should arraign civic and other authorities. Christian principles unflinchingly insisted on by Christian people, and brought to bear, by ballot-boxes and other persuasive ways, on what stands for conscience in some high places, would make a wonderful difference on many of the abominations of our cities. Go to the 'nobles' first, and lay the burden on the backs that ought to carry it.

Then Nehemiah took practical measures by shutting the city gates on the eve of the Sabbath, and putting some of his own servants as a watch. The thing seems to have been done without any notice; so when the country folk came in, as usual, on the Sabbath, they could not get into the city, and camped outside, making a visible temptation to the citizens, to slip out and do a little business, if they could manage to elude the guards. Once or twice this happened; and then Nehemiah himself seems to have taken them in hand, with a very plain and sufficiently emphatic warning: 'If ye do so again, I will lay hands on you.'

Of course, 'from that time they came no more on the Sabbath,' as was natural after such a volley. A man with a good strong will is apt to get his own way, even when he is not clothed with the authority of a governor. Then Nehemiah strengthened the guard, or perhaps withdrew his own servants and substituted for them Levites, whose official position would put them in full sympathy with his efforts. That priestly guard would be inflexible, and with its appointment the abuse appears to have been crushed.

The example of Nehemiah's enforcing Sabbath observance is not to be taken as a pattern for Christian communities, without many limitations. But it appears to the present writer that it is perfectly legitimate for the civil power to insist upon, and if necessary to enforce, the observance of Sunday as a day of rest; and that, since legitimate, it is for the well-being of the community that it should do so. Tyrians might believe anything they chose, and use the day of rest as they thought proper, so long as they did not sell fish on it. We do not interfere with religious convictions when we enjoin Sunday observance. Nehemiah's argument has sometimes to be used, even about such a matter: 'If ye do so again, I will lay hands on you.'

The methods adopted may yield suggestions for all who would aim at reforming abuses or public immoralities. One most necessary step is to cut off, as far as possible, opportunities for the sin. There will be no trade if you shut the gates the night before. There will be little drunkenness if there are no liquor shops. It is quite true that people cannot be made virtuous by legislation, but it is also true that they may be saved from temptations to become vicious by it.

Another hint comes from Nehemiah's vigorous word to the country folk outside the wall. There is need for very strong determination and much sanctified obstinacy in fighting popular abuses. They die hard. It is permissible to invoke the aid of the lawful authority. But a man with strong convictions and earnest purpose will be able to impress his convictions on a mass, even if he have no guards at his back. The one thing needful for Christian reformers is, not the power to appeal to force, but the force which they can carry within them. And it is better when the traders love the Sabbath too well to wish to drive bargains on it, than when they are hindered from doing as they wish by Nehemiah's strong will or formidable threats.

Once more, the guard of Levites may suggest that the execution of measures for the reformation of manners or morals is best entrusted to those who are in sympathy with them. Levites made faithful watchmen. Many a promising measure for reformation has come to nothing because committed to the hands of functionaries who did not care for its success. The instruments are almost as important as the measures which they carry out.

III. Nehemiah's prayer occurs thrice in this chapter, at the close of each section recounting his reforming acts. In the first instance (v. 14) it is most full, and puts very plainly the merit of good deeds as a plea with God. The same thing is implied in its form in verse 22. But while, no doubt, the tone of the prayer is startling to us, and is not such as should be offered now by Christians, it but echoes the principle of retribution which underlies the law. 'This do, and thou shalt live,' was the very foundation of Nehemiah's form of God's revelation. We do not plead our own merits, because we are not under the law, but under grace, and the principle underlying the gospel is life by impartation of unmerited mercy and divine life. But the law of retribution still remains valid for Christians in so far as that God will never forget any of their works, and will give them full recompense for their work of faith and labour of love. Eternal life here and hereafter is wholly the gift of God; but that fact does not exclude the notion of 'the recompense of reward' from the Christian conception of the future. It becomes not us to present our good deeds before the Judge, since they are stained and imperfect, and the goodness in them is His gift. But it becomes Him to crown them with His gracious approbation, and to proportion the cities ruled in that future world to the talents faithfully used here. We need not be afraid of obscuring the truth that we are saved 'not of works, lest any man should boast,' though we insist that a Christian man is rewarded according to his works.

Nehemiah had no false notion of his own goodness; for, while he asked for recompense for these good deeds of his, he could not but add, 'Spare me according to the greatness of Thy mercy.' He who asks to be 'spared' must know himself in peril of destruction; and he who invokes 'mercy' must think that, if he were dealt with according to justice, he would be in evil case. So the consciousness of weakness and sin is an integral part of this prayer, and that takes all the apparent self-righteousness out of the previous petition. However worthy of and sure of reward a Christian man's acts of love and efforts for the spread of God's honour **may be, the doer of them must still be 'looking for the mercy of our Lord Jesus Christ unto eternal life.'**

Lightning Source UK Ltd.
Milton Keynes UK
UKHW022150290119
336402UK00006B/199/P